DISCOVER ARCHAEOLOGY

DISCOVER ARCHAEOLOGY

*An Introduction
to the Tools and Techniques
of Archaeological Fieldwork*

GEORGE SULLIVAN

1980
DOUBLEDAY & COMPANY, INC.
GARDEN CITY, NEW YORK

ISBN: 0-385-14522-5
Library of Congress Catalog Card Number 79-7223

Contents

Introduction

When I first met George Sullivan, I was excavating in a field overlooking the Housatonic River in Connecticut. He said that he was doing a story on archaeology and archaeologists and just wanted to watch and ask a few questions. For the next few hours, he watched and asked questions while we shoveled, troweled, sifted, and mapped artifacts. It was hardly a formal interview.

Imagine my surprise when I received a call from George saying that he had finished his book and wanted me to read it. Of all the interviews I have had over the years, this was one of the few in which the author in his book actually kept statements in perspective without sensationalizing trivial points or omitting the truly important aspects. And so it goes throughout the entire book.

Discover Archaeology introduces archaeology to the general public. It is not meant to be a "cookbook" of techniques for the person who wants to dig his or her own site: take a good piece of ground, add trowel and personal sweat for two hours, and out comes a whole pot. It will not provide a complete summary of man's culture for the past three million years. *But,* it does provide a keen insight into why archaeology is important, what archaeologists hope to accomplish, and how artifacts, seeds, pollen, bones, and a myriad of other clues are interpreted to yield a history of the unwritten past.

As in all introductions, the author cannot provide a complete story, or the book would cease to be an introduction. Yet it is extremely frustrating to be introduced to something new and exciting only to be disappointed by not knowing where to go next. In this book you will not be let down, for the author tells you where to go. There is an up-to-date summary of archaeological societies and organizations, state archaeologists, sites open to the public, source materials, and fieldwork opportunities in each state. One need not travel to the pyramids of Egypt to do archaeology. Archaeology does begin at home.

I doubt that most readers will become professional or amateur archaeqlogists or even pursue its study beyond this book. But this is not to deny them a role in archaeology. One does not have to "do" archaeology to support it and participate. Archaeology is far more than the excavation of prehistoric arrowheads. It includes their analysis, interpretation, preservation, and display as well.

Aside from the technical site reports in professional books and journals, the results of excavations usually receive local newspaper coverage, giving everyone a better sense of what happened ten thousand years ago in the vacant lot next to the bank or in their own cornfield. The specimens from past excavations and collections may be displayed in museums for everyone to view, not just the archaeologists who found them. Since most museums have very active tour programs, the impact of seeing and touching actual specimens thousands of years old, coupled with a detailed explanation of how they were made and utilized, is so much better than seeing mere pictures in books.

Having taught all age groups from young children to senior citizens, I know that they are more interested when they can relate their own interests to archaeology. Everyone has something to contribute once they see the connection between their previous knowledge and the "unknown" field of archaeology. A certain garden-club group was only mildly interested in what archaeologists did until we did an exhibit showing how carbonized seeds are separated from the rest of the dirt in a pit using flotation, and how they were then identified by genus and species. Once the genus and species are known, then the season of the year the Indians collected the seeds could be determined. Since different plants only grow in certain areas, the surrounding environment can be reconstructed. The association of the seeds with artifacts provides the necessary clues for determining how the seeds were used and processed for possible food, medicinal, dyeing, beverage, smoking, or other functions.

Suppose that you wish to assist archaeologists, but you don't want to dig. What else is there to do? Since most professional archaeologists are associated with museums or universities, give them a call and volunteer. You will be amazed at the number of tasks that require no previous experience or training. If you have specialized training or experience, so much the better, but this is not necessary for you to be of assistance.

Once the artifacts come into the laboratory, the real work begins: washing, cleaning, sorting, weighing, counting, measuring, cataloguing, putting on the catalogue numbers, storing, typing, and filing, which are a few of the necessary tasks. Recent programs in museums accept volunteers with an aptitude for explaining exhibits and presenting programs to all age groups. If all of these suggestions do not quite suit you, remember that pure research is almost impossible to fund. If it were not for admissions, store sales, and donations, museums could not support archaeological excavations. "Salvage" or contract archaeology, which is an assessment of the impact of proposed construction on archaeological resources, cannot support all of the other excavations necessary for the archaeologist to learn of the lifeways and history of the people who once occupied this land.

But, for now, read, enjoy, and learn about archaeology.

Dr. Roger W. Moeller
American Indian Archaeological Institute
Washington, Connecticut

DISCOVER ARCHAEOLOGY

CHAPTER 1

Archaeology for Beginners

Before there were kings in Egypt, before the birth of Christ, people lived in what is now Theodore Koster's cornfield and hog farm near Kampsville, Illinois. They fished, hunted waterfowl and, occasionally, deer and wild turkey. They cooked their food, they made their tools, they buried their dead, and then moved on.

Every time they moved, a layer of soil washed down from the bluffs above the farms and covered the village. But the low hills and a nearby stream made for such an amiable site, that soon other people arrived. The cycle continued for ten thousand years and involved fourteen successive communities.

Koster's farm, or at least that portion of it that is being excavated, is a neatly packaged slice of American prehistory. Located about fifty miles north of St. Louis, it is one of the most significant archaeological sites on the North American continent. Digging, troweling, sifting, sorting, and interpreting have been going on there for more than a decade.

In the summer of 1968, Stuart Struever (rhymes with fever), now an associate professor of archaeology at Northwestern University, was digging at a Hopewell Indian site on a farm near Kampsville, when a farmer named Harlin Helton started pestering him to visit a local cornfield to look at something he had found. Eventually, Struever went. "We waded through growing corn," Struever once recalled, "and, my God, it was fantastic! There was pottery all over. The biggest Hopewell village I'd ever seen was maybe five acres, but this covered twenty-five to thirty acres. . . . I thought, This place has *got* to be dug."

The following summer, Struever and several colleagues dug test pits and did some probing. Probing involves sinking five-foot-long steel rods into the ground. Each rod is tipped with a hollow metal ball that traps dirt that can be brought to the surface for examination. Soil in the area is brown or buff-colored. But the rods came up with black soil, an indication of organic material, and organic material meant that the site was once inhabited by humans.

Within three weeks, Struever and his associates had found five different layers—or horizons—of human habitation. And each horizon was separated from the one next to it by a layer of sterile soil that had accumulated when no one lived on the site.

Struever's probings triggered a period of change for tiny Kampsville (population: four hundred), as Northwestern University began turning the town into a unique archaeological laboratory. Over thirty buildings—about a quarter of the community—have been purchased and partially renovated and now serve as dormitory houses, laboratories, a library, and a dining hall. During the summer, the town bulges with students, faculty members, and staff workers. About thirty thousand visitors come just to watch and sight-see. There are now about eight hundred known archaeological sites within thirty minutes' driving time of Kampsville, which someone has dubbed "the archaeological capital of the universe."

What's been going on at Kampsville is not without significance. Discoveries at the Koster site have radically changed many ideas about early man. He was not primarily a big-game hunter, but depended more on plants than animals for food. Hickory nuts were one of the staples of his diet. His life was not one of hardship; actually, he had a great amount of leisure time.

Archaeologists have been able to reach such conclusions through a painstaking analysis of seeds, bones, tools, and other artifacts that have been recovered. Ten specialized laboratories operate at Kampsville during the summer months. Experts in zoology, botany, osteology, malacology (the study of mollusks), and palynology (the study of spores and pollen) perform on-the-scene analyses of recovered materials.

There are also novice archaeologists at Kampsville, individuals without a bit of previous training and experience. They've signed up for one of the week-long Adult Field-School programs. It begins on Sunday night when students assemble in an old bank building in Kampsville that has been converted to the Audrey Lab. Audrey is the name of the site that adult students dig. It is of Mississippian Indian culture, covering the years from A.D. 900 to A.D. 1400. One recent class, five men and twenty-one women, ranged in age from eighteen to seventy-seven. It included a teacher from Wilmette, Illinois, a salesman from Chicago, two retired dentists from Lansing, Michigan, and a university student from St. Louis.

On Monday morning after breakfast, students gather up pens, clipboards, mosquito repellent, and suntan lotion and head out into the field. The Audrey site is on "disturbed land," that is, it is planted every season. But the farmer who owns it has left space for the archaeologists to dig. Students are paired up and given the option of working a two-by-two-meter square that was started by a previous class or starting a square of their own. Either way, they shovel carefully in shallow strokes and also keep shaving the sides of the square with a mason's trowel to keep them rod-straight. Every ten centimeters, digging stops and the students fill in a report form detailing what's been found and plot their finds on a grid.

"It's not merely the archaeological aspects of what's going on that you enjoy," says Carol Goland, a senior at Beloit (Wisconsin) College, who has participated several summers at Kampsville. "There's a spirit of cooperation among the students that you don't ordinarily find anywhere else. People seem transformed. They react to one another's needs. It's marvelous to see, to be a part of it."

Students dig three days each week. There are also laboratory briefings, ecological field trips, and artifact-making demonstrations. One of these involves flint-knapping, the manufacture of tools of flint or chert. Working with a pointed tool made from moose antlers, a knapper can turn out a Clovis projectile point (like those made by Paleo-Indians ten thousand years ago) in about two hours. When the knapper strikes the chert on one side, a chip flies off the other. "You've got to know what you're doing to make these points," says one knapper. "Paleo man was no dummy."

What's going on at Theodore Koster's farm is somewhat typical of what's happening in other parts of the country. There's a burgeoning interest in archaeology, with tens of thousands of individuals—from students to lawyers, from stenographers to retired schoolteachers—discovering the joys of digging, scraping, measuring, sifting, and sorting as members of archaeological research teams.

"Amateurs," they're frequently called. But the word is a poor one. As someone has noted, no one ever hears of amateur psychologists or amateur physicists. Why, then, amateur archaeologists? Maybe paraprofessional would be a better term.

Professional response to this army of neophytes was mixed at first. Some professionals reacted the way a surgeon would react if you asked to be present at a relative's appendectomy. But their attitude has been changing, and most professionals now regard the influx of the untrained as a blessing and have recognized that they can develop a productive relationship with these apprentices. One result is that exciting programs for volunteers and those who seek training and experience have been established in almost every part of the country.

In central Iowa, John and Barbara Feeley, working closely with the office of the state archaeologist, have surveyed thousands of acres of Hardin County in search of potential archaeological sites. They look for surface clues, for flakes of chert, shards of pottery, bits of charcoal, or shells. They've been trained to interpret their finds and file detailed site reports.

"When we do a survey, we're very systematic about it," says thirty-two-year-old John Feeley, a foreman with a metal-fabricating company. "If we're working along the Iowa River, for example, we stay on one side of the river and work one section at a time. We don't leave a section until we've carefully measured it and recorded all that's been found. Then we do the next section. I don't like the 'shotgun method.' When we leave a section, I want to feel we've done the best job possible.

"Archaeology is more than just a hobby to us. We work at it, maybe thirty to forty hours a week in the spring and summer. Not only is there our work in the field, but there's laboratory sorting and classifying, and we give lectures on local archaeology to schools, and Rotary clubs and Kiwanis clubs, organizations like that.

"We get a tremendous satisfaction out of what we do. We feel we're making a contribution toward a better understanding of mankind, that we're helping in the preservation of what we have. We've stirred up interest in an awful lot of young people."

There are also opportunities to work and contribute overseas. Every summer hundreds of American volunteer archaeologists join excavations in foreign countries, principally Israel and Great Britain. Jan Smith, a thirty-seven-year-old San Diego bookkeeper, took part in a two-week expedition recently that was investigating the megalithic stone structures found on Machrie Moor on the Isle of Arran off the northeast coast of Scotland.

Working with a group of British archaeologists under the direction of Dr. Aubrey Burl, professor of evolution and prehistory at Hull College of Higher Education, she helped unearth a complete and previously unknown Bronze Age circle of stones along with evidence of stake holes, postholes, and burial pits.

She lived in a pleasant cottage a few miles from the site. Food was hearty fare prepared by the staff cook. There were lectures almost every night. She remembers the island for its moors and rolling hills and the lush, purple heather that covered the countryside.

Whether it involves a Scottish moor or a strip of Iowa farmland, there is one characteristic that applies to all of these excavations, and that is professional supervision. You can't go out and dig a site on your own. Professionals dig, of course, but a professional can, in theory, at least, put a site back together exactly as he found it from his notes, reports, plans, drawings, and pictures.

"Beginners should stay the hell away from *all* sites" is the way one professional puts it. "They have about as much business doing independent site work as a paramedic has in opening a medical office and doing surgery."

If you go off on your own and dig, you're not an archaeologist, amateur or otherwise; you're a pothunter. Nothing could be worse.

In what they do, pothunters cover a wide range. At one end of the scale are the curiosity seekers and souvenir hunters. They're looking for a few arrowheads or some Civil War bullets to display on the mantel above the fireplace. Using a garden trowel or perhaps a trenching shovel, they dig a few holes and probe through the soil for the artifacts. They fail to see anything wrong with what they're doing. The fact that they're vandals doesn't seem to occur to them.

At the other end of the scale are those pothunters who are organized and equipped in the manner of heavy-construction crews. They operate mostly in the Southwest. They have jeeps, dumptrucks, backhoes, and bulldozers. They can ravage a site in a matter of hours. One observer came across a gang that was "armed to the teeth" and posted lookouts as they worked, just as hold-up men might do when robbing a bank.

Homolovi II near Winslow, Arizona, serves as evidence of what these destroyers can do. A Proto-Hopi camp that was abandoned around A.D. 1425, it ranks as the largest known Indian site along the Little Colorado River. Never professionally excavated, it is looked upon by some archaeologists as a critical site in the understanding of Hopi prehistory. "Today," according to a recent article in *Art News*, "it looks like a prairie-dog village, pitted and gashed by the shovels and backhoes of pothunters. The research potential of the site," said the magazine, "is a fraction of what it might have been."

In Southern California, concerned volunteers have banded together in an effort to halt this wanton destruction, specifically to protect one of the world's largest concentrations of petroglyphs—carvings on rocks made by ancient people. The very existence of these petroglyphs was—and is—threatened by thoughtless vandalism. The rock art figures are shot at for target practice. People take chunks home for their rock gardens.

Ike Eastvold, a professor of art history at the University of California, Riverside, has organized "Petroglyph Watch," in which volunteers take turns spending weekends camping near petroglyph sites in heavily used desert areas. When anyone approaches a site, a volunteer explains the importance of the art and cites the state and federal laws protecting it.

At six important sites—two in the eastern Mojave Desert, four in the northern Mojave—volunteers erected barriers, enclosing more than ten thousand petroglyphs. Private companies donated the fence posts and cables. The fencing permitted access on foot but shut off the areas to vehicles, and thus forestalled the temptation of hauling away the rock art.

Another major cause of destruction is what is called "societally approved" activities—the clearance of land for agriculture, the construction of roads, dams, and reservoirs, and, simply, the ongoing urbanization of the nation. In his book *Public Archeology*,

Dr. Charles McGimsey III, director of the Arkansas Archaeological Survey, declares that 25 per cent of Arkansas' known archaeological sites was destroyed in the period of 1963–72. In one five-year period, 703,000 acres in Arkansas were newly cleared. "Not only are sites destroyed during clearing," according to Dr. McGimsey, "but also, once cleared, these sites are subject to modern but archaeologically destructive practices such as chisel plowing, subsoiling, and land leveling." Once land is leveled, as much as 90 per cent of the archaeologically related information can be destroyed.

The next twenty-five to fifty years are going to be critical, says Dr. McGimsey. "What is recovered, what is preserved, and how these goals are accomplished during this period will largely determine *for all time* the knowledge available to subsequent generations . . . concerning their heritage."

The situation is just as grim in other areas. In California in one recent year, fourteen hundred prehistoric sites were lost before they could be surveyed or excavated. In Los Angeles, a contractor, who knew months in advance that his housing project would destroy an important archaeological site, waited until his model homes were ready for public inspection before he notified authorities. Once he had capitalized on the publicity value of the archaeological discoveries, he ejected researchers and ordered the sites bulldozed. Another California developer, upon hearing the tract of land upon which he was building contained archaeological remains, invited Mom and Dad to look over his model homes while the kids looked for "Indian relics" nearby.

In New York State, dozens of sites that were rich in artifacts and information have been bulldozed. In Oregon and Florida, the Army Corps of Engineers, working with state agencies, calmly destroyed unexamined sites to accomplish "beach improvement." In Mississippi, prehistoric mounds have routinely been removed for landfill.

In the area surrounding the northern Great Lakes, resort developers have been responsible for the destruction of countless sites. One Michigan developer advertised: "140 acres, historical Indian grounds, stone carvings, artifacts. Adjoins—Michigan's only petroglyph site. Top-notch land development."

Archaeologists grieve over such tales. And it's not simply the lost artifacts that cause their grief. Of course, the arrowheads and stone implements are important. But to the archaeologist, *everything* within a site is important—seeds and pollen, stones and stone chips, human and animal remains, the tiniest piece of debris.

The location of each of these in relation to every other one is also critical. An archaeologist may fix the date of an arrowhead by the potsherds found nearby. A few inches below, another arrowhead may be datable to an earlier time period because it can be associated with a fragment of charred wood. And several inches below that, a third arrowhead may be dated to still an earlier period because it is embedded in a particular kind of sandy soil. Thus, the archaeologist has established three different stages of human occupation, but only because he was able to remove each of the artifacts in its proper archaeological context. The arrowheads by themselves would have been fairly meaningless.

In addition, the data gathered in connection with the excavation must be recorded in such a way that it can be interpreted, not only by one's self, but by any professional archaeologist. This means that standardized recording techniques must be followed, including making diarylike accounts of the work performed, photographing the various stages of excavation, and setting down detailed descriptions of the artifacts and the circumstances surrounding the recovery of each.

Almost all states now have at least one organization that brings together professional and nonprofessional archaeologists. These organizations (listed in Chapter 9) schedule a variety of archaeological activities. Anyone can become a member. Besides these organizations, many states have established an Office of Archaeology, presided over by a state archaeologist who supervises and coordinates archaeological activity (state archaeologists are also listed in Chapter 9).

If you know of any archaeological site that is endangered, you should notify your state archaeologist or the state archaeological society. Maybe it's your own land that is involved. Plowing, clearing, or leveling may be planned that are going to disturb archaeological resources. Notify the representative as far in advance as you can. Perhaps a site that is threatened can be saved. The first professional investigation of a Caddo Indian mound in west central Arkansas was made possible because the landowner notified the appropriate state authority almost a full year before he planned to level the mound. Because there was plenty of advance notice, the University of Arkansas Museum was able to schedule an excavation at the site.

If you are uninformed about archaeological activities in your state, and want to find out what's going on, start by contacting your state archaeologist or a representative of one of the archaeological organizations. There may be a program you can join wherein you'll be trained in archaeological techniques—site surveying, excavating, classification, and analysis.

Not everyone is capable of doing archaeological work. "You have to have sufficient stamina to stay outside, maybe in the hot sun in open fields, for an eight-hour day," says Dr. Roger Moeller, director of research for the American Indian Archaeological Institute in Washington, Connecticut. "Some people can't do this, even though they may be physically active in one sport or another. But it's a basic requirement."

There are some motor skills required, too, but these can be easily learned. They involve wielding a shovel or shaking a sifter. "Once in a while we get a volunteer who doesn't know how to use a shovel," says Dr. Moeller. "One woman didn't know whether she was supposed to straddle it—or what. But it takes only a day or so to become skilled."

One other quality is vital, and that's curiosity. "I'm suspicious of anyone who doesn't show any desire to know, to learn," says Dr. Moeller. "If someone joins an excavation team and says to me, 'I just want to sift. I don't want to do anything else,' it's like a warning signal to me. A person should not be satisfied in performing one job. A volunteer should be inquisitive about everything."

CHAPTER 2

Prehistory in America

All archaeologists, no matter where they happen to be at work, have the same goal: They are trying to reconstruct man's life and culture in past ages through the systematic study of what they find.

It's the term "past ages" that is the concern of this chapter and the two that follow it. It refers to such a vast field of activity that it has to be divided and subdivided.

The first distinction to make is between prehistoric archaeology and historic archaeology, each of which can involve either the Old World (the Eastern Hemisphere, with special reference to Europe) or the New World (the Western Hemisphere, North and South America). Then within each of these four basic classifications, there are many subdivisions.

No one could possibly study in depth more than one of the subdivisions. The truth is not many people want to. An archaeologist who may have helped to unearth the cathedral of Pachoras, found beneath an Arab fortress on the present borders of Egypt and Sudan, could never envision himself trekking along the Erie Canal in upstate New York seeking a nineteenth-century millsite. And what the historical New World archaeologist knows about classical archaeology may only be based on the reading he has done.

The various subdivisions that archaeologists recognize are of quite recent origin. During the eighteenth century, educated people of Europe became interested in the classical worlds of Greek and Rome. The ruins of those civilizations were all about them, and they were able to identify various structures and objects because they had an imposing body of literature from classical times. Out of this interest, they began to probe amid what remained of classical sites. But these were largely treasure-hunting expeditions. The diggers kept no records and threw away what they deemed to be ordinary objects. Excavations were conducted for the purpose of enriching the private collections of the great nobles who commissioned them. Wealthy men thus acquired such masterpieces of sculpture as the Venus de' Medici and the Farnese Bull. In 1816, Lord Elgin shipped off to England most of the sculptured friezes from the Parthenon in Greece, one of the most revered monuments of the ancient world.

Classical antiquity wasn't the only field that interested scholars of the nineteenth century. Expeditions were also launched to biblical cities, and eventually biblical archaeology began a specialty in itself. But, generally, the Bible worked to restrain scientific investigation. Even educated men of the Western world were reluctant to admit that there was a time, in the human chain of development, before the events recounted in the Bible.

These beliefs began to change when geologists were able to show that geological features of the earth were the result of slow evolution and had not been caused almost overnight, as biblical scholars claimed. Then, in 1832, a Danish professor, C. J. Thomsen, discerned three distinct "past ages" by means of very ancient tools found in various stratigraphical layers he studied. Thomsen concluded that people of antiquity made objects first of stone (the Stone Age), then bronze (the Bronze Age), and finally of iron (the Iron Age). During the 1830s, Boucher de Perthes, a French archaeologist, wrote several books that theorized that man had existed during the Ice Age, which had probably begun 1.5 million years before. But what really enabled scientists to throw off the Bible's yoke of chronological interpretation was *The Origin of the Species*, published by Charles Darwin in 1859. Thereafter, the study of prehistoric archaeology grew by leaps and bounds.

While classicists and historians were in the forefront of the development of archaeology in Europe, in the United States and throughout the New World it was different. There were no written records to guide researchists who wanted to study ancient people and their cultures. So it was not historians who took up the study of Western civilization; it was left to a new discipline, to anthropology.

These distinctions exist to this day. European archaeologists who specialize in one aspect or another of the story of man from the earliest times are sometimes called "prehistorians." In this country, they are archaeologists, too, but they have been trained as anthropologists. They may be called "paleoanthropologists."

In the century or so that has passed between the beginning of archaeology and our time, the study of recovered objects from excavations all over the world has enabled us to learn far more about our origins and ancient ancestors than did the generations that preceded us. Out of this explosion of information and knowledge, different categories in archaeology were established.

As mentioned earlier, prehistoric archaeology and historic archaeology are the two basic divisions, and each of these can refer to either the Old World or New World.

Old World prehistoric archaeology is often divided into these categories:

Paleolithic—The period beginning with the earliest chipped or stone tools, about 750,000 years ago.

Mesolithic—The period following the Paleolithic Age, characterized by the appearance of the bow and cutting tools.

Neolithic—The period beginning around 10,000 B.C. in the Middle East, and later elsewhere, and characterized by the invention of farming and the making of technically advanced stone implements.

Bronze Age—The period that developed following the use of stone implements, characterized by the use of bronze weapons and implements.

Iron Age—The period succeeding the Bronze Age, characterized by the introduction of iron metallurgy; in Europe, beginning around the eighth century B.C.

New World prehistoric archaeology has these classifications: Paleolithic, Archaic, and Woodland, explained later in this chapter.

Historical archaeology begins with the introduction of writing in an area. If you're concerned with New England or the Middle

Atlantic states, historical archaeology begins with the early seventeenth century. If you're studying Florida, it's the sixteenth century, when the Spanish arrived. In Europe, historical archaeology can begin as early as 10,000 B.C.

In recent times, other subdivisions of historical archaeology have been introduced. These include industrial archaeology and salvage archaeology. Industrial archaeology has to do with the investigation of the early manufacturing processes of the Western world, with investigators seeking to learn the chain of development of each. Salvage archaeology is hurry-up archaeology. It can be prehistoric as well as historic. Its definition refers more to when it is done than to what it is. It is the type of rescue work that is performed just before a road or a dam, a pipeline or a power line is built. Land development projects and urban renewal programs often trigger salvage archaeology expeditions.

Which specialty you pursue will depend to some extent on where you happen to live, that is, on what sites happen to be convenient. This doesn't mean you're not going to have a choice. Suppose you happen to live in western Massachusetts. The Connecticut River Valley has a long history of prehistoric occupation. There are also countless Colonial sites. The cities of Springfield and Hartford, Connecticut, have been engulfed in vast urban renewal projects in the past decade, and there have been scores of opportunities for those interested in salvage archaeology.

There are archaeologists who are technical specialists, too. There are ceramic technologists, for example. There are individuals who concentrate on lithics. There are paleobotanists. There are palynologists (specialists in spores and pollen) and dendrochronologists (specialists in the growth rings of trees). But technical specialization is another book.

The Paleo-Indian Age

Who were the first inhabitants of America north of Mexico? Archaeologists have been seeking the answer to that question for more than a century.

It is now generally accepted that the American Indian immigrated to North America from Asia to discover this continent at a time when vast ice sheets covered the northern stretches of

North America and Eurasia. (Indian, the term applied to the aboriginal peoples of North America, is a misnomer. It was first used by Columbus, who was searching for, and believed that he had found, the East Indies. But no other term has evolved to replace it, although several have been suggested. Amerind is one. While some academicians persist in its use, it has never attained common usage.) The point of entry was what is now the Bering Strait, that strip of water about sixty miles wide that separates western Alaska and northeastern Siberia. The first settlers could have come by boat, or by foot, traveling at a time when the strait was frozen over or across a land bridge that may have existed at the time. It is believed that the Alaska interior was free of ice during this period, providing easy access to the mid-continent area.

These people did not come in great waves; there was no sustained migration. They arrived in a slow trickle.

These early stages of human habitation are known as the Paleo-Indian period, commonly described as a time of big-game hunting, with hunters stalking bison, mammoth, and other animals, not only for food, but for hide and bone.

But recent excavations near the Delaware Water Gap have revealed carbonized seeds (chenopodium, grape, blackberry, amaranth, smartweed, ragweed, sedge, plum, and pokeweed) and fishbone, in association with Paleo man, and no evidence of the larger animals usually associated with the period. Paleo-Indian research, conducted by Roger Moeller of the American Indian Archaeological Institute at a site in Washington Depot, Connecticut, has brought to light the residue of red oak and either juniper or white cedar, "reinforcing the idea of a deciduous environment," Dr. Moeller says.

As these paragraphs suggest, the Paleo classification and also the Archaic and Woodland labels (described on the pages that follow) should be regarded as somewhat artificial classifications, forms which need constant redefining in the light of new excavations and techniques that provide new data.

Countless sites have been excavated in an effort to determine when these migrations took place and to establish how long the New World has been inhabited. Most of these have been concentrated in the Great Plains area and the Southwest. One of the best-known sites is near Folsom, New Mexico; another is not far from Clovis, New Mexico; and a third is the Lindenmeier site, north of Fort Collins, Colorado. From evidence gathered at these and other sites, it now seems likely that the first immigrants arrived in North America anywhere from ten thousand to twenty thousand years ago.

Several Paleo excavations have been designated National Historic Sites, but visitors usually see nothing more than a commemorative plaque. One exception is Sandia Man Cave in the Sandia mountains just north and east of Albuquerque. Some archaeologists believe that the Sandia site yielded artifacts even older than those recovered at Folsom, Clovis, or Lindenmeier.

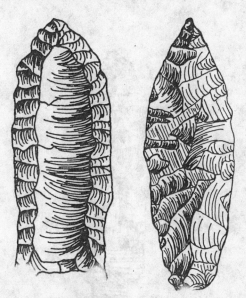

A Clovis spearpoint showing fluting (left). (State of Iowa; Office of the State Archaeologist)

Paleo hunters often used weapons with distinctively shaped points. One kind of point has been named the Clovis point because it was first found at the Clovis site. A typical example is from three to six inches in length, thin, finely chipped, and shaped more or less like a laurel leaf. But what makes a Clovis point really distinctive is its fluting. A groove runs perpendicular to the base up each side. The end of a shaft would be split down the middle, and then each of the two halves would be inserted in one of the grooves. This enabled the spearpoint to be fixed securely to the shaft.

Usually these points are recovered along with the remains of large extinct animals—the mammoth, camel, early forms of bison, and the American horse. Near Naco, Arizona, in 1952, archaeologists excavated an ancient stream bed that contained the skeleton of a mammoth. The animal had once weighed about five tons and had been killed in the open (not mired in a swamp as was the usual practice) by a total of eight Clovis points, all of which were clustered on the creature's most vulnerable area, the back of the neck.

A Clovis spearpoint hafted to its shaft. (State of Iowa; Office of the State Archaeologist)

Herd hunting led Paleo man from the Rocky Mountain areas of the west, across the Great Plains, far to the east. Wherever these early hunters went, they left Clovis points behind. They have been found on a 34,000-foot-high mountaintop in West Virginia; they have been found in the San Joaquin Valley of California.

Thousands have been found in Kentucky, Tennessee, and Alabama. In 1965, on the east side of Hare Run, a tributary of the Cedar River in Cedar County, Iowa, a cache of some eleven whole and fragmentary Clovis points was discovered.

The Folsom site has also given its name to a distinctive type of spearpoint. The Folsom point is somewhat smaller, but it has the same lengthwise fluting, with the grooves extending all the way to the top. There are earlike projections at the base of the point. Other stone artifacts found at Folsom sites include scrapers of various kinds and a variety of knives, choppers, drills, and hand hammers. Bone tools, including punches, awls, and fine bone needles, have also been recovered.

The oldest evidence of human presence in the New York City area comes from a spot near Florida, New York, in Orange County, where a fluted projectile point—believed to be a spearhead—was found in Dutchess Quarry Cave. It was found in association with a caribou bone, which, after testing, was found to be 12,530 years old.

The largest Paleo-Indian site in New York State—West Athens Hill—is likely to have been a prehistoric quarry, where people camped and manufactured stone tools. Over a thousand artifacts, including fluted points and stone knives, were recovered there in 1966. Other Paleo-Indian sites in the New York area are Zierdt in the northwest corner of New Jersey; Plenge, near Washington, New Jersey; Twin Fields, near Dwaar Kill, New York; and Port Mobil on Staten Island.

In Paleo-Indian times, sea level in what is the metropolitan New York area was a hundred feet lower than it is today, and the coastline was twenty to thirty miles to the east and south of where it now is. Most of Long Island was a dry valley. Since it was usual for people to live near the water for fish and shellfish, it is likely that most of the sites of Paleo-Indian habitation are under water.

Archaic Period

At some point about ten thousand years ago, big game began to
die out, and when it disappeared, the age of the Paleo-Indian
ended. The Archaic period was next. People of the Archaic period
have been described, not as herd hunters, but as hunter-gatherers.
They fished from the banks of streams; they gathered nuts and
acorns. They hunted for deer and smaller game. Nomadic, they
moved with the seasons.

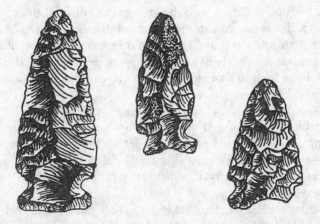

*Side-notched points from the Archaic period. (State of Iowa; Office of
the State Archaeologist)*

Arrowheads of the Archaic period are as distinctive as Clovis
points. Triangular in shape, they were stemmed at the base so as
to provide a shank which aided in attaching the point to the
shaft. Often the edges of the base and shank were blunted so the
material used to bind the head to the shaft would not be frayed or
severed by a sharp edge.

Indians of the Archaic period also produced wood-working
tools, such as axes and adzes, and various types of grinding stones
for reducing seeds and nuts to meal. Their fishing tools included
nets, sinkers, and fishhooks.

A mano and metate were used during Archaic period for grinding nuts and seeds. (State of Iowa; Office of the State Archaeologist)

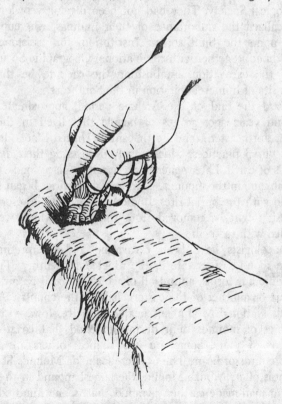

Animal hides were first scraped in making clothing. (State of Iowa; Office of the State Archaeologist)

They manufactured bone artifacts, too, including bone awls; and punches and scraping tools, the last named used for dressing hides, have been found. Tubular bones, each drilled with several holes, have also been unearthed. These probably served as flute-like musical instruments, or perhaps they were merely whistles used for signaling.

Like Paleo sites, those dating to the Archaic period are quite rare. One, open to the public, is Russell Cave National Monument near Bridgeport, Alabama. It is interesting not only because it serves as a detailed record of eight thousand years of human life, but also because the exhibit shows exactly how archaeologists conducted the excavation. The Russell cavesite was discovered by amateur archaeologists in 1953, members of the Tennessee Archaeological Society. They had not been digging very long when they realized the importance of their findings, whereupon they called upon the Smithsonian Institution for assistance. The Smithsonian, together with the National Geographic Society, concluded the excavation, establishing the cave to be the oldest known site of human habitation in the Southeast.

Toward the end of the Archaic period, approximately three thousand years ago, groups of people that lived in the southeastern, northeastern, and north central United States developed special burial practices, which involved covering their dead with mounds of earth. Later generations began to place food, weapons, or ornaments in the mounds. Ceremonial activities began to be associated with the burial rites. Bodies were sometimes cremated or the flesh might be removed from the bones, which were then sprinkled with red ochre.

Archaeologists have been excavating and interpreting these earthen mounds since late in the nineteenth century. They take many different forms, almost all of which can still be observed in one part or another of the eastern half of the country. At Effigy Mounds National Monument near Marquette, Iowa, visitors can see scores of mounds built during a period that covered many hundreds of years. Some are cone-shaped; others are built to resemble birds or bears. The 650-acre Cahokia Mounds State Park in Illinois offers Monks Mound, the largest mound in the United States, a man-made earthen pyramid that is one hundred feet in height. The Crystal River State Archaeological Site near Crystal

River, Florida, has mounds of three different types—refuse mounds, burial mounds, and a temple mound.

In the West, the Archaic-period lifestyle was much different. Land areas had grown arid because of a lack of rainfall. Men who had once hunted big game came to depend on small animals. Plant food took on increasing importance. People made baskets for holding seeds and tools for grinding them down.

Perhaps around the year 2000 B.C., western Archaic people known as the Cochise began to cultivate corn. They later added squash and beans to their diet. Once they began to farm, they gave up their nomadic existence and built permanent dwellings.

The changes triggered by agriculture were not the same in every part of the Southwest. Several different cultures developed. The Anasazi, Hohokam, and Mogollon were the most important of them.

The Anasazi civilization, which has been traced to approximately A.D. 200, inhabited what is termed the "four corners" region of the Southwest, the area surrounding the meeting points of the states of Utah, Arizona, Colorado, and New Mexico.

The Anasazi are called "basket makers," an art they pursued with great skill until pottery making was introduced. They stored food and water in baskets. They cooked in baskets. They lived in elevated regions, at levels from four thousand to seven thousand feet, building shelters in the open or in caves. While they were hunters and gatherers, they also did some farming.

Superb cliff dwellings of what is known as the Kayenta branch of the Anasazi can be seen today at Navajo National Monument in north central Arizona, a short distance from Yuba City. An eight-mile trail winds down a canyon and along a stream to a remarkable cliff village with 160 rooms, abandoned in the 1200s for reasons that are not fully understood. Colorado's Mesa Verde National Park and New Mexico's Chaco Canyon National Monument offer other opportunities to see evidence of the Anasazi culture.

The Hohokam Indians occupied central and southern Arizona, beginning from about 300 B.C. The present-day Pimo and Papajo Indians of southern Arizona are descendants of the Hohokam.

Whereas the Anasazi occupied the plateau regions, the Hohokam was more a desert culture. They built their villages on terraced land above the Gila River, where they grew their crops. Corn was their staple food. They hunted with bows and arrows, and small game was their usual quarry. They were pottery makers, creating ceramic material of several different types. Their early pottery was buff-colored, with red geometric designs. Later, they decorated what they made with bird, animal, or human forms.

The Mogollon culture is believed to date to about 100 B.C. The Mogollon people lived in structures called pithouses, circular in shape, built partly below the ground, partly above it. They lived mostly on seeds, berries, nuts, and insects. Hunting was probably not important to them, since few arrowheads or spearheads have been found at Mogollon sites. They were pottery makers, and at least three different types of ceramics are associated with them. It is plain and undecorated, and brown or red in color.

Those members of the Mogollon culture that lived along the Mimbres River developed a more sophisticated style of pottery making, decorating their bowls with striking geometric patterns or brushstroke drawings of animals, birds, insects, reptiles, and humans. Fine collections of Mimbres pottery are displayed at the Palace of Governors in Santa Fe, New Mexico, the Philbrook Art Center in Oklahoma City, and the Peabody Museum in Cambridge, Massachusetts.

Woodland Period

Two important developments marked the end of the Archaic period and the onset of what is called the Woodland period—the beginning of pottery making and the first successful attempts at farming. These had a tremendous impact on the Indians' way of life. Farming increased and stabilized the supply of food. Villages and towns began to develop, and a richer, fuller social life was possible.

But the change from one stage to another did not occur at the same time in every part of the country. The practice of farming began several hundred years earlier in the Southwest than in the East, and pottery making occurred earlier in the Southwest than anywhere else in North America.

Since potsherds are virtually imperishable, they furnish solid ev-

idence as to the presence of pottery and pottery makers. In the
case of farming, however, reliable evidence as to when it began in
an area is often scarce. Farming implements were made of wood,
which is subject to decay, and evidence of the crops themselves
has rotted away. Often the archaeologist has to assume the existence of agriculture because of certain cultural patterns. Evidence
of a permanent village, combined with a lack of evidence pertaining to hunting or food gathering, might be taken to mean that
farming was prevalent.

The first potters of the Early Woodland period are likely to
have copied the shapes and designs of their woven or leather con-
tainers in making their ceramic vessels. Often these were thick-
walled, and straight-walled, with flat bottoms.

Paddling and coiling were early methods of pottery making. In
paddling, a lump of clay would be held firmly against an anvil
stone and molded into shape with a small, flat board—a paddle.
Often the board would be covered with fabric, and thus fabric
markings would appear on the clay as it was worked.

*Techniques of pottery manufacture. (State of Iowa; Office of the
State Archaeologist)*

In coiling, the potter rolled a lump of clay into a long, thin
strand, then coiled it. Additional coils were then placed one atop
the other. The junctures of each layer were then smoothed out
with a wooden paddle.

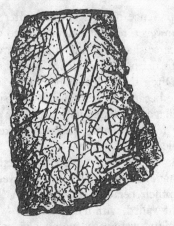

*A potsherd dating from the Early Woodland period. (State of Iowa;
Office of the State Archaeologist)*

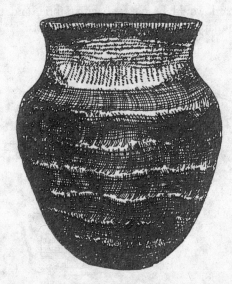

*Cord-marked pottery of the Middle Woodland period. (State of Iowa;
Office of the State Archaeologist)*

In the eastern United States, Woodland sites have either disappeared or are fast disappearing. Some of the better-known sites in New York State included Old Place, which is just north of the Goethals Bridge abutment of Staten Island; Bowman's Brook on the northwestern shore of Staten Island; Clason's Point in the Bronx; Clearview in Queens; Garview Point in Nassau County; and Stony Brook in Suffolk County. These sites, most of which were excavated for the first time in the early part of the present century (and which have been obliterated by housing developments, industrial plants, and warehouses, and the like), also contained, at deeper levels, remains of the Archaic period.

The Bowman's Brook site is particularly interesting. Last excavated in 1950, it yielded evidence of a settled village about nine hundred years old, where people appear to have lived chiefly on shellfish.

One of the most significant archaeological investigations in the past fifteen or so years concerns an alliance of Woodland Indian tribes who lived near Lake Ontario in New York State and spoke the Iroquoian language. This research brought to light new evidence concerning the origins and social development of these people, and demonstrated the profound effect they had upon colonial America and Canada.

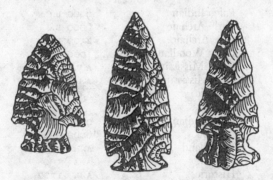

Woodland period projectile points. (State of Iowa; Office of the State Archaeologist)

Once the federated Iroquois tribes acquired firearms in the seventeenth century, they ranged east into the maritime provinces of Canada and surged across what is now the northwestern corner of Pennsylvania, into Ohio and Indiana, and as far west as northeastern Illinois. They defeated Iroquoian-speaking tribes that did not belong to their confederacy and crushed their traditional enemies, the Algonquian-speaking tribes that lived nearby. Since the Algonquians were allied with the French, the Iroquois helped shift the balance of power to England in the struggle for the control of Canada during the century. Historian Francis Parkman called the Iroquois the "Romans of the New World." Yet archaeologists have been able to establish that the five tribes of the confederacy had no more than twelve thousand members, and the number of fighting men never exceeded twenty-five hundred.

Approximate dates of Indian culture in different geographic areas of the United States.

Northeast

Paleo-Indian	7000 B.C.
Early Archaic	6000 B.C.
Late Archaic	2500 B.C.
Early Woodland	1000 B.C.
Middle Woodland	A.D. 1
Late Woodland	A.D. 500
Historic	A.D. 1500

Southeast

Paleo-Indian	9000 B.C.
Early Archaic	6000 B.C.
Late Archaic	2500 B.C.
Early Woodland	1000 B.C.
Early Mississippian	A.D. 1
Late Mississippian	A.D. 500
Historic	A.D. 1500

Plains

Paleo-Indian	9000 B.C.
Archaic	6000 B.C.
Woodland	A.D. 1
Farmers	A.D. 500
Historic	A.D. 1700

Southwest

Paleo-Indian	12,000–6000 B.C.
Hohokam	300 B.C.
Mogollon, Anasazi	A.D. 1
Historic	A.D. 1500

Pacific Coast

Early Archaic	2100 B.C.
Middle Archaic	1000 B.C.
Historic	A.D. 1500

As representatives of the Late Woodland period, the Iroquois were farmers and hunters. They lived in villages in forest clearings with a stockade built of saplings—a palisade—encircling the village for protection from raiding parties. In open fields just outside the palisade, women of the village raised corn, beans, squash, and tobacco. The men hunted, fished, and collected berries, bark, and other wild plant foods. They called themselves Ongwehoweh—the True People.

Inside the stockade, the Iroquois people erected several longhouses. Each consisted of a framework of saplings covered with sheets of bark. They were "long," indeed. The remains of one longhouse, excavated at a site known as Furnace Brook on a hilltop near Syracuse, yielded the dark humus of rotted saplings that once constituted the house walls. They indicated a structure that was 22 feet wide and 210 feet long. Like other longhouses, it was divided into a series of living spaces, each occupied, archaeologists surmise, by closely related families. A corridor divided the house down the middle, and along the corridor were placed the hearths that the families shared.

The archaeological investigations embrace a period from the end of the twelfth century through the eighteenth century. The earliest site was excavated in 1959 and 1960 by William A. Ritchie of the New York State Museum in Albany. Known as the Maxon-Derby site, it was located near Owasco Lake in the center of the state and covered approximately two acres. The remains of seven houses were recovered. By carbon-14 dating (see Chapter 8), Ritchie was able to establish that the site was occupied around A.D. 1100.

Excavations at the Maxon-Derby site yielded the remains of the bones of birds, fish, and mammals, and charred kernels of corn. Archaeologists also unearthed triangular-shaped stone arrowheads and clay tobacco pipes. Many pottery fragments were also found. The rims of vessels had been decorated with imprints made by a paddle that was wrapped in cord.

During the 1960s, additional sites were excavated, both by Ritchie and by archaeologists and students of Syracuse University under the direction of James A. Tuck. These investigations revealed a developmental sequence that covered seven hundred years, a sequence out of which the Onondaga tribe was founded. The Onondagas were the central group in the Iroquois confederacy, which also included the Senecas, Cayugas, Oneidas, and Mohawks.

The first suggestion of the eventual forming of the confederacy

was traced to the early decades of the fifteenth century, when
tribes began occupying villages in pairs, one village no more than
a few miles from the other. This practice was followed for the
next three centuries, with tribal members changing sites many
times. The largest number of sites was concentrated in an area
just east of Syracuse. Such villages could not have existed so close
together, James A. Tuck points out, without some understanding
regarding mutual defense. "At the very least," Tuck stated in an
article in *Scientific American*, "some kind of a nonaggression pact
would have been needed to prevent clashes that would have been
disastrous for one village, if not both." These "nonaggression
pacts," Tuck believes, served as basis for more comprehensive
agreements that gave rise to the Iroquois confederacy. There is
also physical evidence to support a melding of tribal cultures. Ceramic remnants reveal that the Onondagas, Oneidas, and Mohawks adopted pottery styles that eventually were all about the
same.

The confederacy's greatest influence came during the mid-
seventeenth century when its members controlled vast stretches of
land from the Kennebec River in the east to the Illinois River in
the west, and from the Ottawa River in the north to the Tennessee River in the south. The confederation allied itself with Britain
in the frontier campaigns of the French and Indian wars.

Before the Revolutionary War, the Iroquois were friendly with
British colonial authorities under Sir William Johnson, and, thus,
when the war erupted, the tribes chose to be British allies. The
Oneidas were an exception; they fought with the colonists.

The war was more of a disaster for the Iroquois than it was for
the British. The British lost only a colony. The Iroquois saw their
fighting forces decimated and their homelands destroyed. Some
tribal members resettled in the Grand River Valley in Canada,
while others took refuge on reservations in New York.

The Woodland period of prehistory lasted until the arrival of
European traders and colonists in the fifteenth and sixteenth centuries. Kaolin pipes, iron knives, gun flints, metal buttons, beads,
and brass and iron kettles, all of European manufacture, were
items that the Indians wanted and for which they bartered. They
now appear when Indian sites are being excavated. As this
implies, and as historians now realize, Indians abandoned their
own crafts to embrace a dependent culture.

This is often designated as the contact period. As early as 1500,

French, English, Spanish, and Portuguese fishing vessels began to visit the Grand Banks during the cod season, and there is evidence that they made contact with the inhabitants along the Newfoundland and New England coasts, putting ashore probably to obtain food and water. Ponce de Leon "discovered" Florida in 1513; the first permanent settlement in Florida was established in 1565.

Hernando De Soto explored the region between Florida and Arkansas beginning in 1539, penetrating as far as Mississippi by 1541. In the region that now embraces the Middle Atlantic states, the period of contact was earlier. In 1526, the Spanish attempted to found a colonial outpost somewhere between the James River and Cape Fear.

Jacques Cartier sailed up the St. Lawrence in 1534, the first of an army of French and English traders. Henry Hudson sailed into New York harbor in 1609, making the first substantial contact in that area. It has been estimated that there were between sixty and seventy thousand people living in the Hudson basin at the time, the largest population that had ever inhabited the area.

There is an enormous amount of reading material available concerning the American Indian. "The amateur [archaeologist] must keep abreast of technical and scholarly developments in the field," says Dr. J. O. Brew of Southern Methodist University. "He or she must read and read and read."

Joe Thompson of American Indian Books (533 Summit Street, Webster, MO 63119) has compiled a list of thirty very practical books he sells, most with reference to Indian archaeology, including such titles as *The Art of Flint Knapping*, *Prehistoric Relics*, *The Midwest Indian Relic Manual*, and *Indian Trade Goods*. Write and request a list; it's free.

The Museum of the American Indian (Broadway and 155th Street, New York, NY 10032) offers a more comprehensive list, describing over a thousand volumes. It costs $1.00.

Ancient Rock Art

Amateur archaeologists of the Southwest and Pacific Coast have the opportunity of studying cultural remains that are much different, much grander than those of the East. The Indians of the West left behind an enormous legacy of rock art. There are probably fifteen thousand sites where rock art panels of one type or another can be found. While age, subject matter, technique, and style vary widely from site to site, almost all examples fall within one of three categories. There are petroglyphs, pictographs, and intaglios. Petroglyphs are drawings incised in stone. Pictographs are rock paintings. Sometimes they are somber monotones; other times, brilliant polychrome.

Intaglios are decorative designs created by scraping away a layer of dark pebbles from the surface of hard-packed terrain, so as to expose the lighter material underneath.

It's believed that this art was created some time before A.D. 1300; but aside from that fact, we know little about the people who were responsible for it. We do know they were the same people who built towering cliff dwellings along most of the drainage systems of the Colorado River.

The oldest of the rock art panels are thought to be those that show hunters using the atlatl, a primitive spear-throwing device. Later examples depict the bow and arrow, which replaced the atlatl in the Southwest around A.D. 300.

As the centuries passed, more profound changes were recorded. Rock art of the Navahos and Utes reflects the Spanish invasion and the introduction of the wheel, horse, cattle, and other domesticated animals; there are symbols of Christianity and representations of swords and firearms.

For every twelve experts you ask to interpret a rock art panel, you get a dozen different opinions as to what the designs and figures mean. In recent years, they have even been taken as evidence of extraterrestrial visitation. A more mundane interpretation says that they are no more than random scribblings, a kind of ancient graffiti. Another common point of view is that the major figure designs are magical or occult symbols of some type, meant to ward off evil spirits, promote fertility, or provide for a successful hunt. Some panels, it's thought, may depict actual events or record important ceremonial occasions.

Some of the designs and symbols occur and reoccur. The human hand is one such figure. Some panels are composed entirely of handprints. Sometimes they are solidly painted, and other times a stencil-like design has been formed by placing the hand against the rock and blowing pigment into the open spaces. Many of the handprints are those of small children. There are many explanations for the handprints. According to one, each is simply a primitive signature. Another interpretation has it that they may be an early census device.

Circular designs also occur with great frequency. Sometimes circles appear within circles, giving the design a bull's-eye effect. Other times close lines radiate out from a central point, like spokes of a wheel. Sometimes the design is more a spiral than a circle, or the line will undulate in a manner that resembles the course of a meandering river, which it may represent.

It is believed that hunters of early times frequently sought sheep, and thus drawings of sheep are often seen. Perhaps, it has been said, the sheep figures are symbols of some hunting magic. The atlatl or a bow is often drawn in relation to the sheep, and some rock artists drew in the sheep's heart, the hunter's surest target.

The Indian groups that inhabited the Pacific Northwest looked out toward the sea, and these rock drawings are replete with serpentlike creatures. They also include a fairly accurate image of the sperm whale, beluga, and the porpoise.

Some of the most elaborate rock art is to be found within the Horseshoe Canyon Unit of Canyonlands National Park, a short drive from Moab, Utah, in the Maze District of the park and the Needles District south of the Squaw Springs Campground. These areas can be reached only by a four-wheel-drive vehicle, on horseback, or by means of an extended backpack trip.

At El Morro National Monument, just west of El Morro, New Mexico, there are hundreds of petroglyphs on display. And at a site called Three Rivers Petroglyphs, not far from Carrizozo, New Mexico, more than five hundred rock carvings can be seen.

One of the world's biggest concentrations of prehistoric art is to be found in the California desert, an enormous expanse of land that stretches north beyond Death Valley to Eureka Valley and south to the Mexican border, a distance of more than two hundred and fifty miles. The desert is bordered on the east by the Nevada state line and on the west by the Sierra Nevada and coastal mountain range. About one half of its 25 million acres is managed by the Bureau of Land Management of the Department of the Interior.

Often this art takes the form of intaglios. Some are human or animal figures, while others are in the form of geometric designs. Some of the designs are as much as two miles in diameter.

Sadly, these treasures are being destroyed at a rapid clip. The desert begins only twenty-five miles north or eighty-five miles east of downtown Los Angeles and just fifty-five miles east of downtown San Diego, which puts it in easy access of the several million Californians. On winter weekends, thousands upon thousands of them climb into or onto their off-road vehicles (ORVs)—their motorcycles, dune buggies, and four-wheel-drive vehicles—and pour out into the desert to camp, fish, take photographs, hike, collect fossils, or "ride and play." What they have done to archaeological treasures and resources of the desert is not less than tragic. Petroglyphs and pictographs are carried away as souvenirs. Almost all of the desert's known intaglio sites are now crisscrossed by ORV tracks.

It's not just archaeological sites that are being ravaged. In prehistoric times, the California desert was a great grassland pocked with broad lakes, and now it contains the fossilized remains of that era. The ORVs are destroying the fossil beds just as they are the archaeological remains.

On May 24, 1977, President Carter signed an executive order which required land-management agencies to close trails or areas to ORVs whenever it was determined that "the use of off-road vehicles will cause or is causing considerable adverse effects on the soils, vegetation, wildlife habitat or cultural or historic resources." *Smithsonian* magazine reported in 1978 that 4 per cent of the land under the control of the Bureau of Land Management was "closed" to ORVs; 8 per cent was open to cross-country ORV use; and the remainder was "restricted," meaning the ORV users were to keep to existing roads and trails. The loophole in the government's program is the lack of Land Management personnel to enforce the regulations. With about 12 million acres under its control, the agency has about a dozen rangers to call upon. "A person can drive all day on a motorcycle," said *Smithsonian*, "and never see a BLM sign or an enforcement officer."

All prehistoric rock art, cliff dwellings, and other ancient artifacts on public land are protected under the Federal Antiquities Act of 1906. And most of the land in the Southwest *is* public land, owned by the federal government and Indian tribes. The Forest Service and the Bureau of Land Management each administer about 12 million acres, and the Defense Department, the Bureau of Indian Affairs (with the various tribes), and the National Park Service are also each responsible for enormous preserves. Considering the amount of land involved, the number of law enforcement personnel available is ridiculously small. Up until very recently, the Forest Service had only two criminal investigators covering its 12 million acres. The Bureau of Land Management is even worse off. It has no enforcement authority at all and must call upon other federal personnel or local enforcement officials. It's sad but true that a majority of rock panels survive only by reason of their inaccessibility.

Pothunters, even when they do happen to be apprehended and convicted, are scarcely inconvenienced by the sentences they receive. Federal law provides that violators may be fined up to $500 or imprisoned for up to ninety days, or both, but the usual "punishment" is a small fine. Considering that a Hopi pot can sell for anywhere from $1,000 to $2,000, and some vessels bring several thousand dollars, it's obvious that pothunting is an avocation that is well worth the risk. Sellers have become bold enough to advertise in newspapers of the Southwest. When queried as to where they obtained an artifact, the pothunter simply says it belonged to his grandparents.

The theft of the pot itself and the destruction of an archaeological site are not the worst of it. Pothunters are often guilty of desecrating sacred Indian land or shrines. After one sortie by pothunters into an ancient and traditional site within the Hopi reservation near Tucson, Arizona, the Hopis closed all sites to non-Hopis. The tribe has protested that violators of their sacred lands are allowed to plea bargain for lenient fines that amount to no more than "a slap on the wrist."

CHAPTER 3

Pre-Columbian Myth and Mystery

Take Interstate 93 heading north out of Boston, drive north for about twenty-five miles, and you cross into New Hampshire. Not far beyond the state border, north of Salem, turn right onto Route 11. You then begin seeing highway signs that announce you're approaching Mystery Hill—"America's Stonehenge," as it bills itself.

Stonehenge itself, of course, is that prehistoric ceremonial ruin on the Salisbury Plain in Wiltshire, England, made up of huge upright stone slabs and lintels arranged in circular formations. It dates to at least 1800 B.C.

Are the stone structures at Mystery Hill at all comparable to those in England?

Was the New Hampshire site, as its supporters claim, once occupied by people who crossed the Atlantic from what is now Spain and Portugal two thousand years before Columbus arrived?

Take the walking tour through the thirty-acre Mystery Hill complex. See the "Sacrificial Table," a 4½-ton grooved, bell-shaped granite slab that rests on short stone legs. "Its use," according to a brochure you're given, "is believed to have been for an oracle sacrifice during a ceremony. . . ."

The table tilts slightly so that a shallow groove that runs just inside the outer perimeter acts as a drain. Any liquid collected is channeled into a gutter at the table's right-hand corner.

Did human blood once flow from the stone onto the hollowed-out bedrock below? Was the table used for only sacrifices or did it, as skeptics say, serve simply as an apple press in making cider?

See "Sun Dial Rock," a crudely carved stone with a hole in the center that, according to the brochure, "could have been an ancient sun symbol."

Walk along what has been dubbed the "Astronomical Alignment Trail" or ascend the "Astronomical Viewing Platform" and observe the many astronomical alignment monoliths, each said to stand in a perfect line with one or another of important celestial bodies. These monoliths, it is claimed, were used in determining annual solstices and equinoxes.

Who were these ancient inhabitants? The brochure explains: "Stones have been located containing carved inscriptions in Iberian-Punic and Ogham—both utilized by the ancient Celts. As a result, we now know that Mystery Hill was occupied by the Celto-Iberians tentatively between 800 and 45 B.C."

Amazing—if true.

Mystery Hill isn't the only site in the United States where pre-Columbian contact is said to have been made. In the state of Oklahoma, seven different stones have been identified as bearing runic or at least runiclike symbols. (The runic alphabet is one that was used by ancient Germanic peoples, especially by Scandinavians and Anglo-Saxons.) One such stone is located in a state park in Poteau Mountain near Heavener, Oklahoma. "The Vikings were *here*," is Heavener's claim.

There is the Kensington stone in Minnesota and the Newport Tower in Rhode Island, both of which have been offered as evidence of Viking visits. Popham Beach, Maine, has claims to have a runestone, too. Norse artifacts have been reportedly found in Wisconsin, Michigan, North Dakota, and Tennessee.

All of these sites have one thing in common: None of the claims made for them has been validated by individuals trained and experienced in archaeological research.

Nevertheless, the public never stops hearing about these sites and the theorizing concerning them. They have served as a basis for books, magazine articles, and television productions. Mystery

Hill is probably as well established in the public's mind as all but a handful of "real" archaeological sites.

In some cases, the finds involved have been branded as plants—misleading pieces of evidence placed so as to be discovered. In other cases, the finders have simply been guilty of mistaken identification. Instances of scientific methodology are rare.

"It's a terrible problem," says David Orr, head archaeologist for the National Park Service's Mid-Atlantic Region. "A project of ours may bring to light an appealing story, a very human story, but our findings aren't likely to be spectacular. So it's hard for us to get equal attention."

What's eerie, what's bizarre attract much more attention than what is usual. But you should be wary about becoming associated with any project whose claims have not been, or cannot be, authenticated. Check with your state archaeologist if you have doubts. He or she should, at the very least, recommend sources you can consult to help you establish which claims are valid. In this regard, be wary of articles in most of the archaeological publications (*Archaeology* is an exception). They are just as guilty of perpetuating myths as the general press.

North America *was* visited by pre-Columbian explorers, by Viking explorers. It has been long established that sometime between A.D. 1000 and 1400, Norse settlers occupied two areas of western and southern Greenland. At one time, the colonies there consisted of some three thousand people. Scholars further established that the efforts to colonize Vinland—as the land west of Greenland was sometimes called—were undertaken in the eleventh century along the coast of Labrador and Newfoundland.

This theory was confirmed in the early 1960s through archaeological investigations led by Dr. Helge Ingstad. In five expeditions between 1960 and 1964, Dr. Ingstad found important Norse ruins and relics in L'Anse aux Meadows in Newfoundland. What he found included pieces of worked iron and slag, a stone anvil, and layers of sod that indicated the outlines of houses. The biggest structure measured sixty by forty-five feet and had a great hall in the Viking manner, with a hearth in the center. Some of the house sites contained stone fireplaces and "ember pits"—small squarish stone holes where coals were kept alive overnight. These ember pits were similar to those found at Norse settlements in Greenland.

Dr. Ingstad's discoveries were not made by accident. He spent years accumulating and studying ancient Norse prose narratives. Then he applied his knowledge by exploring by boat and airplane the coasts of Rhode Island, Nova Scotia, Quebec, Labrador, and Newfoundland. The setting and location of L'Anse aux Meadows corresponded with descriptions in the accounts of Leif Ericson's settlement.

In the smithy on the site, Dr. Ingstad's expedition uncovered the stone anvil, several hundred pieces of slag, and small bits of iron. Extensive deposits of bog iron, or iron nodules, lay under the turf nearby. At the time these discoveries were made, Dr. Henry B. Collins, a Smithsonian Institution anthropologist, pointed out that the Eskimos and Indians, both prehistoric and modern, "had no knowledge of extracting iron from bog deposits." The Vikings did.

Enough material was found to get a series of radiocarbon measurements. The readings were clustered about the year 1000, with the latest reading dating from 1080, plus or minus seventy years.

At a press conference at the National Geographic Society in Washington, in 1963, archaeological experts from the Smithsonian Institution and the American Museum of Natural History unequivocally supported Dr. Ingstad's findings, that what he had discovered was Norse and pre-Columbian. "There is no evidence to the contrary," said Dr. Henry Collins.

The following year, 1964, Dr. Ingstad returned to L'Anse aux Meadows to make the most significant find of all, a tiny soapstone wheel, measuring only 1¼ inches across, the first household article of the Norse explorers ever found in North America. The stone was a spinning ball. It was placed on a round shaft to help in rotating it when spinning thread around the shaft. The tiny wheel was technically called a spinning whorl. Many similar whorls had been found in Scandinavia and Greenland.

Dr. Ingstad described his explorations and findings in two books, Land Under the Polar Star (1963) and Westward to Vinland (1969), both published by St. Martin's Press. The sites he excavated, protected by seven big, barnlike structures, are now open to the public during the summer months. They're found at the northern terminus of Newfoundland's Route 81 on the northern tip of the Great Northern Peninsula.

There are qualities of excitement and intrigue in any claim of Viking contact, which is one reason that spurious claims find so many supporters. Local pride is a factor, too. And sometimes state authorities, unwittingly or not, lend credence to such claims.

All of these factors are present in the case of Oklahoma's runestones, which achieved prominence largely through the efforts of Gloria Stewart. As a young girl growing up in Oklahoma, she became familiar with a massive chunk of sandstone, bearing strange-looking inscriptions, that was found on Poteau Mountain, not far from her home. It was called Indian Rock. The inscriptions were believed to be of Indian origin. Years later, as a student, she came upon a photograph of an ancient Scandinavian alphabet and immediately saw the similarity between the pictured letters and those inscribed on Indian Rock. She began to theorize that Norsemen had visited Oklahoma.

How did Norse visitors get to Oklahoma? They are said to have sailed down the east coast of the United States, around the southern tip of Florida, and through the Gulf of Mexico to the mouth of the Mississippi River. Then it was up the Mississippi to one or another of the many tributaries that brought them west and into the continental interior.

In 1950, after her marriage to J. Ray Farley, she moved to Heavener, Oklahoma, where Indian Rock was located. After interviewing residents of the area, Gloria Stewart Farley learned the location of two other runestones similar to the one on Poteau Mountain. When she informed scholars of her discoveries and told them of her belief that Norsemen had reached Oklahoma, they all but laughed at her. No one with professional training would substantiate her findings.

Something of a turning point came in 1967, the year in which Dr. Ole G. Landsverk, an engineer, and Alf Monge, a cryptographer, after studying the stones, published a book titled, *Norse Medieval Cryptography in Runic Carvings*, in which they declared the Farley inscriptions to be cryptological puzzles. The authors claimed, however, that they were able to "crack" the code and, by so doing, were able to establish a date for each of the stones. The dates were: November 11, 1012; December 25, 1015; and December 30, 1022.

Today, persons touring eastern Oklahoma are invited to visit Clem Hamilton State Park where the first of the runestones discovered by Mrs. Farley is now enshrined. Literature available at the visitors' center at the park declares: "It is now conceivable that some daring Norse traveler could have ventured up the Mississippi River, then up the Arkansas River and, finally, up the Poteau River. The Poteau leads to within a mile of the Heavener Runestone. . . ."

During the late 1960s, the findings of Landsverk and Monge were scrutinized by cryptologists, runic specialists, and scholars of Scandinavian history, and many significant errors were found. These involved misrepresentations concerning the data on runic usage and the translations of runic alphabets. Mistakes were also pinpointed in the authors' cryptological approach.

But by the time the refutations were published, the runestones were already esteemed by many Oklahomans. Some residents of Heavener had convinced themselves the stones were genuine. There was to be no turning back.

A story that is similar has been evolving at New Hampshire's Mystery Hill. But this site has gained much wider recognition and even acclaim.

Some old-timers in the town of North Salem refer to the structures at Mystery Hill as "Pattee's Caves." The Pattee family once owned the land that now comprises the Mystery Hill site and built a wood-frame house there in 1826. The house was destroyed by fire in 1855. Whether the family also built the Mystery Hill's wells, walls, drains, root-cellar-type caverns, and other stone structures is a controverted topic. Probably they did not. The size of the project and the nature of the construction tend to rule out the Pattees as builders.

During the period of the Pattee habitation, countless tons of stone slabs were carted away to be used in the construction of curbstones, sidewalks, and dams in neighboring towns. Mark Feldman, in his book *The Mystery Hill Story*, quotes a contemporary (unnamed) source as saying, "Day after day, all through spring, summer, and fall, cartload after cartload of rocks and stones from the site was carried off." Feldman estimates that "at least 40 per cent" of the site was destroyed in this manner.

The first real research involving the Mystery Hill stone structures dates to 1933, the year that William B. Goodwin, a retired insurance executive from Hartford, Connecticut, vacationing in New Hampshire, was shown the site by a friend. Goodwin was fascinated by what he saw and made arrangements to purchase the site. He had always been interested in history, particularly the early history of Ireland, Greenland, and Iceland. He became convinced that the Mystery Hill structures had been built by Irish Culdee monks, who had come to America many centuries before Columbus.

Lacking archaeological training and experience, Goodwin was less than meticulous in the treatment of the land and its features. He hired workers to clean up the site, for there was much debris scattered about. He moved stones around. He did some reconstruction work. But he kept no records of what he did. For instance, when he cleared away the dirt from the legs of the Sacrificial Table, he failed to measure or record the depth at which it was buried. That might have been valuable information in establishing the period to which the table dates.

To his credit, Goodwin did photograph much of the site as it was at the time he found it, and then had photographs taken again once he had completed his work. But the fact that what he did was so lacking in scientific methodology, and because he lacked credentials in archaeology or any other science, his findings were never taken seriously. What he did do, unfortunately, was endow the site with a reputation for amateurism in the worst sense of the word.

Goodwin died in 1950, and Malcolm Pearson was named heir to the site. Pearson was associated with a research organization known as the Early Sites Foundation, and he leased the site to the Foundation in 1954. Not long after, the Foundation hired Gary Vescelius, a Yale University graduate student in archaeology, to undertake some excavations.

Vescelius and four associates worked for six weeks, then prepared a report concerning what they had found. Their chief conclusion was that the structures they encountered had been built during Pattee's period of ownership, that is, during the late eighteenth and nineteenth centuries. Vescelius based his conclusions on the many hundreds of artifacts he excavated, which he said were Indian or Colonial in nature.

Vescelius' specialty was Peru, and, in fact, the weeks he devoted to his research at Mystery Hill were but a brief interlude before beginning important and extended research in that country. Mark Feldman quotes individuals who were with Vescelius at Mystery Hill as saying that he "was anxious to get to Peru" and "hoped to be out of New Hampshire as soon as possible." Whatever the quality of Vescelius' research, his findings have been the subject of claims and counterclaims for more than twenty years, and those who smirk, whenever the name Mystery Hill is mentioned, brandish the Vescelius study as proof that the site is about as pre-Columbian as Fenway Park.

Mystery Hill changed hands again in 1957 when the land was purchased by Robert E. Stone, a resident of nearby Derry, New Hampshire, an electronics engineer and also a student of American history and an amateur archaeologist. Stone felt that nobody was giving the site the attention it deserved, and he felt he could change that. At the time he acquired the property, the site was still known as Pattee's Caves. Stone rechristened it Mystery Hill Caves and, later, dropped the word Caves. Stone also opened the site to the public, charging each visitor a small admission fee.

Stone knew of other sites in New England where stone structures, every bit as puzzling as those he now owned, could be found. Since those at Mystery Hill were bigger and more impressive than the others, he reasoned that perhaps his stone structures were a focal point, a headquarters site, for the entire area. In 1964, Stone, along with several associates, formed the New England Antiquities Research Association (NEARA), one of the purposes of which has been to investigate other man-made stone formations. At the time, twenty to thirty such sites were known. By 1978, NEARA members had located and recorded detailed information for approximately three hundred such sites. Not only did these include structures similar to those at Mystery Hill, but also unusual cairns, menhirs, stone huts, and grooved stones and carved stones, as well as earthworks of various types. NEARA publishes a quarterly journal and is working to establish an information center and library containing books and articles relating to the organization's research.

Since the time Stone assumed ownership of Mystery Hill, the most highly regarded evidence concerning its antiquity comes from a series of radiocarbon determinations made by the Geochron Laboratories of Cambridge, Massachusetts, the first of which dates to 1967. (Radiocarbon dating is explained in Chapter

8.) In one report, the laboratory declared that the remains of a pine root had been tested and was found to contain wood that had a calendar date of A.D. 1690. This supported the belief that the Mystery Hill structures were Colonial or pre-Colonial.

In July 1971, charcoal fragments mixed with soil were obtained from between wall stones and, when tested, provided startling results. Their radioactive age was determined to be 1525 B.C. Through a correction factor, the date was later amended to 2025 B.C.

Stone had long suspected that a number of monoliths at Mystery Hill were so positioned that they had astronomical significance. One stone in particular, he believed, was aligned in such a way that it indicated the setting sun at the winter solstice. He was not able to confirm this belief in his own mind until December 20, 1970, when Stone and several colleagues took up a position at a viewing area they had determined to watch the sun as it slipped toward the horizon. As they watched its descent, the stone that they had chosen as the solstice stone stood out in a silhouette in the center of a wide swath they had cleared through the woods.

Working with his cousin, Osborn Stone, an engineer, Bob Stone later established many other correlations between Mystery Hill monoliths and celestial bodies. There is the "Summer Solstice Sunset Monolith," which lines up with the setting sun on June 21. There is the "North Stone," which is positioned on a true north line when observed from the viewing area.

Other stones have been assigned significance insofar as the ancient Celtic calendar is concerned. There is, for example, the "May Day Monolith," which is said to be aligned with the position of the sun on May 1, the Celtic festival of Beltane. "The whole place is a calendar site," says Osborn Stone. "People in ancient times couldn't run down to the First National Bank and get a calendar once a year, so they put in a permanent version. They could have used it for the planting of crops. They could have used it in determining when their holidays were to occur."

Research at Mystery Hill took another tack beginning in June 1975, when Barry Fell first visited the site. The genial Fell, a New Zealander by birth, in his late fifties when he first became interested in Mystery Hill, regards himself as an epigrapher—a specialist in the study and interpretation of ancient inscriptions—

although he is a marine biologist by profession. He first studied ancient languages during his undergraduate days at the University of Edinburgh. Later, in a study of the marine biology of Polynesia, he came upon hundreds of unreadable inscriptions on rocks and cavern walls.

From 1964 through 1972, Fell spent much of his time studying at Harvard's Widener Library, known for its collection of books on obscure languages and writing systems. He became knowledgeable about half a dozen ancient alphabets, including Egyptian hicroglyphics; Punic, a Carthaginian script uscd by several ancient people; and Ogam, an all but forgotten script used by pre-Christian Celts.

In *America B.C.*, published in 1976, Fell described Mystery Hill as "a complex of stone-slab chambers and associated henge stones oriented so that the sun sets behind particular standing stones. . . ." He said that some of the slab chambers reminded him of *dunans*—"little fortresses"—of the ancient Goidelic Celts that he had studied in Scotland.

A triangular-shaped inscribed stone that he studied on his first visit to Mystery Hill, Fell identified as being Punic. He said that the stone was a dedication tablet, and that the chamber from which it had been recovered had been dedicated to the Phoenician god *Baal*. Fell went on to say that the other stone chambers at Mystery Hill were dedicated to other deities, and that the entire complex once served as a religious center and astronomical observatory.

Fell returned to Mystery Hill later that summer to make more discoveries. A stone unearthed during his visit he interpreted as furnishing clear-cut evidence of "a Celtic-Carthaginian partnership in exploration and settlement on a scale hitherto never imagined."

It kept getting better and better. "Within ten days, we were seeing dozens of Ogam inscriptions on other less-damaged but more remote sites in central Vermont," Fell states in *America B.C.* "It became clear that the ancient Celts have built the New England megalithic chambers, and that Phoenician mariners were their welcome visitors. . . ."

Fell has set the antiquity of Mystery Hill as ranging from 800 to 600 B.C., a conclusion he bases on the writing style of the Phoenician inscriptions he's observed. He has also concluded, again from inscribed stones, that the Celts were still inhabiting the site as recently as 45 B.C.

Mystery Hill is only one of several sites that have caught Fell's attention. He says that Egyptians, Libyans, and Celtic Iberians were living together in Iowa in 900 B.C. He has perceived an Iberian presence in Arkansas that dates to about the same period.

Fell's theorizing has received widespread acclaim. An article in *The Reader's Digest* declared that American history is about to undergo vast change ". . . thanks to the genius of a single man." Said the magazine: "For the first time, we must include in our American heritage fighting Celts from Spain, and daring Semitic seafarers from Carthage, Libya, and Egypt. Who knows how many others will be added before the end of Barry Fell's epic voyage into the past?"

No one has yet started to rewrite the history books, not on the basis of any of Barry Fell's findings. Even those most closely associated with Mystery Hill merely shrug when Fell and his theories are mentioned. "What Fell did was make us better known than we ever had been," says Andrew Rothovius, a founder of the New England Antiquities Research Association, and now the secretary of the organization. "As far as the lay person is concerned, our carbon-dating determinations are a bit too technical, too abstract. The same is true of the astronomical alignments. But the inscriptions brought to light by Fell are different; they're something a lay person can readily understand.

"But," continues Rothovius, "Fell revealed too much too quickly. He would have found greater acceptance if he had been more judicious. He should have had one set of findings substantiated before disclosing others."

Others are less gentle in their criticism. More and more, Fell is being taken to task for his epigraphic interpretations. Epigraphy has played an important role in unraveling archaeological mysteries of the past. The Rosetta stone is the best example. The Rosetta stone is a basalt tablet inscribed with a decree of Ptolemy V in Greek and Egyptian hieroglyphic and demotic, dating to 196 B.C. It was discovered in 1799 near the town of Rosetta, Egypt, and provided a key in the deciphering of hieroglyphics. In other instances involving the study and interpretation of esoteric inscriptions, epigraphers have had similar keys, or they have had alphabets or long monographs as their starting point. But Fell is faulted because he had no such body of knowledge. In most cases he had only individual stones with incidental markings, and these he managed to interpret without reference to the letters of a given language system.

I recall standing with an archaeologist on a piece of freshly tilled Connecticut farmland and asking him about Fell and his methodology. The archaeologist reached down and picked up a flat rock that happened to be at his feet. "Look at this," he said. "It's inscribed with lines that look as if they form the letter A. Now, you can say they're the letter A, or you can interpret them in a hundred other different ways. And because the rock was once split, you can say that this is only a portion of the message, and you can start looking for related rocks."

Then he walked several steps to his left, and he picked up a second rock that seemed to be in the same mineral family, and it, too, bore distinctive lines. And for these he reeled off another interpretation.

"Anyone can do this," he said, grinning. "The point is that you don't begin with random stones that happen to have markings on them. You begin with a system of characters and symbols arranged in order and fixed by custom."

"Well, how did the marks get there?" I asked him.

"Any number of ways," he said. "They could be frost cracks, or root marks. They can result when a rock is struck by a plowshare or a pick."

Two British archaeologists, Anne Ross of Southampton University and Peter Reynolds of the Butser Ancient Farm Project in Hampshire, are among Fell's most recent critics. They take exception to Fell's claim that the marked stones he encountered in New England were inscribed in Ogam (which they spell Ogham), an alphabet used for writing Irish beginning in the fourth or fifth century. Ogam was unknown at the time claimed by Fell, the two British archaeologists say. An American Celt would have written in the Iberian, Punic, Libyan, or Egyptian dialect.

"It may be," says Anne Ross, "that once the necessary preliminary fieldwork in this absorbing and vitally important subject has been carried out, it will really be possible to turn the 'fanciful' America B.C. into a perfect valid reality; but this must wait the conclusions of an objective, competent scientific program of valid research."

Fell's severest critics accuse him of giving incorrect or misleading interpretations to inscriptions he encounters. He bends the evidence to fit. "His reproductions of inscriptions as they appear in his articles or books," says Robert Stone, "are sometimes different from the related inscriptions as they appear on the stones themselves."

Edward S. Meltzer, an Egyptologist in the Department of Near Eastern Studies at the University of Toronto, in a letter that appeared in the July 1978 issue of the *Central States Archaeological Journal*, stated that Fell, in his attempt to read his "hieroglyphs" as connected passages in Egyptian, "comes out with a hodgepodge that disregards even the most elementary rules of Egyptian grammar and syntax." He accuses Fell of "errors in word-order as well as wrong or strained meanings of words."

A specific example of a gross distortion concerns page 96 of *America B.C.*, wherein Fell reproduces a page of drawings of a number of metal objects from *The Mound Builders*, a book by Rev. S. D. Peet, published in 1892. Fell's caption reads: "Bronze weapons found in Mound Builder sites and at other localities . . . from Ohio and Wisconsin that conform to well-known European and North African patterns of the later Bronze Age and early Iron Age."

But in the Reverend Peet's book, the drawings have this caption: "Copper implements from Wisconsin and Ohio." This error was brought to light by A. G. Fredrickson, who teaches chemical engineering at the University of Minnesota and has read widely in archaeology and prehistory. Professor Fredrickson points out that Rev. Peet tells his readers that there was no Bronze Age in North America. The University of Minnesota professor also tracked down the source of ten of the objects in Rev. Peet's drawings as being derived from illustrations that appeared in *Ancient Monuments of the Mississippi Valley*, by E. G. Squier and E. H. Davis, published by the Smithsonian Institution in 1848. He notes that these authors say that while the prehistoric people of North America could work native copper, they did not know how to reduce it from ores or alloy it with other metals.

"Fell surely recognizes the difference between copper and bronze," Fredrickson said in a letter to the *Central States Archaeological Journal*, "and he must also know what a revision of current ideas on North American prehistory would be, forced by the finding of bronze artifacts in undisputed prehistoric contexts from eastern North America." Fredrickson concludes that Fell's erroneous labeling is something more than a simple mistake. He calls it ". . . another example of fabrication of evidence to support his theories. . . ."

The dubious nature of Fell's evidence isn't the only problem at Mystery Hill. There are other reasons why professional archaeologists are unready to accept the site as pre-Columbian, other reasons why the archaeological community is, to quote Osborn Stone, "cold" toward the proffered evidence.

Professional archaeologists want to know why the Mystery Hill residents left nothing behind. Not a single remnant of the early civilizations has been found. "These must have been the neatest, cleanest people of all time," says one archaeologist. "They didn't create a single piece of refuse."

Nor is there any evidence that these people had the slightest bit of influence on Indians of the day, or that the Indians influenced them. When the Celtic people returned to Europe, it would have been logical for them to manifest one characteristic or another of the Indian civilization, with which they had coexisted. Maybe they would have smoked pipes. Maybe they would have grown corn. But there were no sociological crosscurrents.

There are important lessons to be learned from Mystery Hill. Much of what has happened there demonstrates the importance of the role the professional archaeologist must play. The professional, for the most part, was written out of the script at Mystery Hill. The result is that the evidence gathered there over the past fifty years or so is questionable evidence. What may, indeed, be one of the country's most important archaeological sites, if not *the* most important site, may never rise above the status of a roadside tourist attraction.

CHAPTER 4

Historical Archaeology

We know, from the few historical documents that do exist, when the *Mayflower* arrived and where it dropped anchor. We know how the British and Dutch assigned land grants and to whom. We know the names of the first governing officials.

But historical documents don't tell us anything about the colonists' chief sources of food, what kinds of animals they raised, or how they built their houses and what materials they used. It's the archaeologist—the historical archaeologist—who has provided the answer to these and many other questions.

When it comes to the work that is performed in the field, there is little difference between historical and prehistorical archaeology. Both follow the same methods. But for the historical archaeologist, there is a different starting point. It involves digging among the archives that concern the site or the historical period. It may mean investigating old land records or deeds, or reading contemporary source books, or letters, or diaries, if they exist (Chapter 6 discusses this subject).

Historical archaeology is usually described as a field that concerns the historic sites of the Colonial and post-Colonial ages. But it sometimes is more broadly defined as the study of all foreign contact on the American continent. If you use that definition, you can trace the beginnings of historical archaeology (as has John L. Cotter, associate curator of North American Archaeology of the

University Museum in Philadelphia) to 1620 and to Corn Hill on Cape Cod. Pilgrims there, who were looting Indian storage pits, came upon the body of a light-haired young man of obvious European heritage who was dressed as a sailor. This was near to Provincetown, where the Pilgrims stopped briefly before making their more revered landing at Plymouth. The Founding Fathers left a written record of their discovery. "Their find was, to be sure, an unplanned discovery," says Dr. Cotter, writing in *Archaeology* magazine. "But then," he notes, "quite a few archaeological discoveries are unplanned."

One of the most important dates in historical archaeology, again according to Dr. Cotter, is 1797. That was the year that interested parties conducted an investigation of St. Croix Island on the St. Croix River between Maine and Canada. Artifacts recovered there and foundations that were discovered were associated with DeMonts-Champlain, a French settlement that had been founded in 1604–5. Because of this evidence, the border between Canada and the United States was established farther south than American representatives wanted.

Actually, historical archaeology predates the U.S.-Canada border discussions, and it goes back to before the Pilgrims, too. It starts with the year 1541 and Hernando De Soto's expedition from Florida to the Mississippi River. It embraces the founding of Fort Raleigh in North Carolina by the English, in 1585, and the French settlement at Fort Caroline, Florida, established in 1564.

There was little interest in historical archaeology until late in the nineteenth century when William Louis Calver and Reginald Pelham Boland began excavating at Colonial and Revolutionary War sites in and around New York City. They continued their work for more than thirty years, ranging as far as West Point, Fort George, and Fort Ticonderoga. Many of the artifacts they unearthed are now part of the collections of the New-York Historical Society.

Other early excavations in the field of historical archaeology were undertaken by the Works Projects Administration and the Civilian Conservation Corps in the years just before World War II. Their chief concern was the excavation of Revolutionary War sites, particularly the earthworks at Yorktown and Morristown. The National Park Service began to uncover the Jamestown settlement in 1934.

In those days, according to Dr. Cotter, work was performed by architects and archaeologists who were trained in prehistory, plus students who learned as they went along. Not until 1960 was the first course in historical archaeology offered. It was taught at the University of Pennsylvania. The Society for Historical Archaeology (see Appendix) was founded in 1967.

During the early 1970s, in anticipation of the celebration of the nation's Bicentennial, many historical sites pertaining to the Revolution were investigated. These included Benjamin Franklin's home in Philadelphia, or at least what was left of it, soldiers' huts at Valley Forge and Morristown, where Washington's armies spent several winters between 1776 and 1780, and the historic road between Lexington and Concord in Massachusetts. At Yorktown, the National Service located and restored the French and American trenches and their earthworks.

What can be accomplished by historical archaeology is probably best exemplified by the Colonial Williamsburg Restoration, where excavations and investigations involving approximately four hundred different structures have been going on for three decades under the direction of Ivor Noël Hume, one of the most respected figures in the field. He is the author of *Historical Archaeology*, the definitive book on the subject.

Archaeologists are still making discoveries at Williamsburg, incidentally. In mid-1978, Noël Hume found what he believed to be the remains of a ruined fort on what is now Carter's Grove Plantation in Williamsburg. At the fort site, archaeologists found a crushed skull and parts of a skeleton, thought to represent the victim of an Indian raid. This was deduced from a pathologist's report that determined the body had sustained a blow to the back of the head. According to Noël Hume, the type of blow corresponded to a method of attack favored by the Indians. Also found at the site were bits of charcoal, pieces of seventeenth-century armor, early pottery shards, and a coin minted in 1613, a mere six years after the arrival of the first American colonists at Jamestown.

Jamestown is another site where extensive archaeological excavations have been undertaken. While, as mentioned above, work began there in the 1930s, it continued sporadically for twenty years, with the most significant accomplishments being recorded in the mid-1950s. Fort Raleigh, North Carolina, the sixteenth-century English settlement on the upper end of Roanoke Island, is another example of large-scale archaeological research.

One of the most interesting examples of historical archaeology in recent years involves an obscure battle in the French and Indian War, and the site of the battle, Fort Necessity. Extending from 1754 to 1763, the French and Indian War was the final struggle between the French Government and its colonies in America and the English Government and *its* colonies for control of the North American continent.

In the years just preceding the outbreak of hostilities, both the French and English colonists attempted to project their control into a disputed area of what is now western Pennsylvania, with the French, in 1753, beginning the construction of a chain of forts from Presque Isle, along the Allegheny River, to the forks of the Ohio, thus invading territory claimed by the colony of Virginia. Alarmed by the French aggressiveness, Governor Robert Dinwiddie of Virginia sent a twenty-one-year-old, inexperienced colonial officer by the name of George Washington on an expedition into the disputed territory, with instructions to warn the French they were encroaching on English soil and to scout a suitable location for a fort.

The following year, 1754, commanding a force of about one hundred fifty men, Washington returned to the area and encamped at Great Meadows, approximately ten miles east of the present site of Uniontown, Pennsylvania. On May 27 that year, Washington learned that a small French force was hidden a few miles to the north. Leaving a small contingent at the Great Meadows camp, he made a night march and in a surprise attack just after sunrise routed the French, killing several of them, including their commanding officer, Sieur de Jumonville, the brother of the commanding officer at Fort Duquesne. Washington's forces also took twenty-one prisoners, whom he sent to Williamsburg. Washington then returned to Great Meadows, and there he hastily erected a small fortification which he called Fort Necessity.

A few weeks later, on July 3, a force of nine hundred French and Indians attacked the fort, firing from a heavily wooded area that encircled the clearing where the fort stood. Washington's contingent held off the attack through a long, drizzly day. At nightfall, after both sides had nearly exhausted their ammunition, the French commander requested a parley. It ended with Washington consenting to capitulate. After turning over hostages to the French to assure the return of the French prisoners, Washington abandoned the fort and led his troops back to Virginia, carrying their wounded. So ended Washington's first test as a military commander.

Excavations that were to lead to the restoration of Fort Necessity began as early as 1901. More serious digging was undertaken in 1932, as historians sought to complete the reconstruction by 1932 to coincide with the two-hundredth anniversary of Washington's birth. There were several firsthand reports of what the fort had looked like, and although not terribly detailed they did give definite clues as to the structure's appearance. Five years after the battle, Colonel James Burd, a British officer, wrote that he had seen Fort Necessity. "It is a small circular stockade," he wrote, "with a small house in the center; on the outside . . . a small ditch goes around it about eight yards from the Stockade."

Unfortunately, this and other accounts of the fort's appearance were ignored by both the 1901 and 1931 excavators. Instead, they allowed themselves to be influenced by maps and surveys prepared in the early 1800s, which were entirely erroneous. Some of these stated that Fort Necessity had been triangular in shape; others said it was a four-sided structure. The 1932 restoration consisted of a stockade that was generally rectangular in shape, with a small log cabin inside the enclosure.

In 1952, the National Park Service, which had assumed authority over the site in 1933, began planning for the bicentennial anniversary of the Fort Necessity battle. By this time, the restored stockade had fallen into disrepair and had to be rebuilt. A minor excavation was undertaken to settle some disputed points concerning the stockade's placement. Excavators came upon some of the pieces of rotted wood that had, both in 1901 and 1931, been identified as the remnants of the original structure. But the 1952 archaeologists recognized the wood to be tree roots, the remains of the wooded area from which the French and Indians had launched their attack.

This caused investigators to go back to original sources, such as the Burd document cited above, for a description of the fort. It wasn't long before they came to the realization that it had been circular in design. New excavations were dug. In the very first trench, at a point about three feet below the surface, archaeologists came upon the decayed top of a stockade post, still in its original position. Additional excavations unearthed a perfect circle of post stumps, complete except for one area that had been intruded upon by the 1932 restoration.

The lower portions of the posts, which happened to be below ground-water level, were well preserved. The tops were charred, evidence of the fire set by the French and Indians. Musket balls, all of them misshapen from impact, were found along the exterior side of the post line. Aside from these, there were few other artifacts. This was not surprising to archaeologists, since records indicated that following the battle, the French allowed the Indians to forage in the ruins, taking whatever they wanted.

Not only did the archaeological investigations at Fort Necessity serve to embellish a critical chapter in the career of George Washington, but they demonstrated how historical archaeology can correct interpretive errors. But the archaeological evidence has to be compared to documentary records, whenever they are available. Doing so assures there's much less of a chance of misinterpretation.

Today, excavations in the field of historical archaeology are being conducted in every section of the country. Despite this, and despite the work that has gone before and the importance of that work, historical archaeology has not flowered as its suppporters once hoped it might. Archaeology is more firmly grounded in anthropology than in history, and there are countless academicians who want to keep things that way. This conflict is not likely to affect you in the slightest. It rages, or at least endures, on the upper levels. If your interest is history, or, more specifically, applying archaeological skills toward the study of history, then you are likely to find the field of historical archaeology an exciting one.

The Pompeii of the Caribbean

While most of the evidence of the Dutch and English colonization along the eastern seaboard of what is now the United States exists either in remnants or is represented by means of restorations, the still-standing seventeenth- and eighteenth-century structures of a tiny West Indian island permit one to actually see and savor something of what life was like centuries ago. The island is St. Eustasius, one of the Dutch Windwards.

About one half the size of Manhattan Island, St. Eustasius is one hundred fifty miles east of Puerto Rico and just north of St. Kitts and the British Leewards. It is linked to St. Maarten—thirty-five miles directly north—by daily flights of Windward Island Airways. Most people refer to the island by its nickname of Statia.

Someone once dubbed St. Eustasius the "Pompeii of the Caribbean." To compare the island with the ancient city of Campania is quite an exaggeration, but the implication is clear. From the standpoint of historical archaeology, at least as it refers to Dutch and English efforts to migrate and settle, St. Eustasius has to be considered one of the richest sites in the world, offering enormous potential for serious research.

"It's amazing that any place in the world can continue to remain that untouched," says a former resident. "What's saved the island is that it doesn't have an airfield that can accommodate jets. And the island's black sand beaches are a factor, too. The American tourist wants *white* sand."

St. Eustasius is fascinating from a historical standpoint, as the life and development of the country is closely linked to the history of the United States. Let's go back to 1775, to the period just following the strife at Lexington and Concord. Early in July that year, George Washington was chosen as commander of the Colonial forces by the Continental Congress. Not long after, he called for a report on the amount of available gunpowder his men had. He was told there were only ninety barrels, good for not more than nine rounds by each soldier. "In moments of great shock," says Washington's biographer James Flexner, "Washington was inclined to recede into a deep silence. On hearing the truth about the powder, he did not utter a word for half an hour."

But after he regained his equanimity—and his power of speech—Washington moved smartly. He leaked word to the British that his storehouses were crammed with powder and he issued a warning to his troops not to be careless around the huge munitions stores. He also ordered all random firing to cease, because, he said, it drew "the ridicule of the enemy." Washington then dispatched messages to Congress and every colony asking for powder because he was expecting an enemy bombardment and "wanted to reply to it."

An elderly gentleman by the name of Benjamin Franklin solved the great powder problem. As early as 1773, Franklin realized that the friction between the colonies and Britain might become deadly serious. If that happened, he knew that his homeland would be at a severe disadvantage from lack of powder and arms. Franklin had a remarkable number of influential acquaintances in France, Spain, and Holland. Not only did they include individuals at the diplomatic level, but also many of Europe's great merchants and shippers. Using these contacts, Franklin set up an extensive gunrunning network. Of course, European merchants could not deal directly with the colonies. The British blockade prevented that. The Caribbean island of St. Eustasius, a tiny speck of rock in the Netherlands Antilles not far from St. Maarten, was designated as the transshipment point.

The Dutch had already made St. Eustasius a swashbuckling port. There were days when as many as two hundred ships filled its harbor. The island's warehouses bulged with merchandise, and its streets were thronged with merchants. It was nicknamed the "Golden Rock."

Dutch, French, and Spanish vessels carrying powder for the American rebels were probably on their way to St. Eustasius even before the first shots were fired at Lexington and Concord. Britain had to let the ships pass; to molest them on the high seas while they were bound for a neutral port was to risk war. So even as Washington ached for gunpowder in the fall of 1775, huge stores of it were already piling up in the warehouses of St. Eustasius.

Some of the powder was sold to smugglers who were willing to attempt to run the British blockade. But most was sold in St. Eustasius to agents of the Continental Congress or to other merchants who, in turn, would sell to these agents. Then the powder was sent north in sleek Bermuda sloops. Or some arrived by way of "powder cruises" sponsored by the various states. The Massachusetts Board of War, for instance, had thirty-two "trading vessels," most carrying French names, that were assigned to collecting gunpowder in the Caribbean (and European ports, too). South Carolina, Maryland, Connecticut, Virginia, and Pennsylvania also sponsored fleets of gunrunners.

On September 18, 1775, Congress appointed Franklin Silas Deane, Robert Morris, and others to a Secret Committee of Correspondence, and assigned them the task of munitions procurement. Granted considerable money and power, the committee quickly expanded the gunrunning network founded by Franklin, and managed to provide Washington's forces with a steady stream of munitions and supply.

While St. Eustasius' importance ebbed as a result, merchants there continued to trade with the American rebels. The British complained to the Dutch but it did no good. The crowning blow, as far as the British were concerned, came on November 16, 1776, when Johannes de Graaff, who commanded the island for the Dutch, ordered the guns of Fort Oranje to fire a salute to the *Andrew Doria*, an armed North American brigantine flying the rebel flag. The act was interpreted as the first official recognition of the rebellious colonies. (An earlier salute by St. Croix was rendered a merchant ship, not a warship, and thus has not been accorded the significance of the St. Eustasius salute.)

The act, understandably, served to increase British wrath. On December 20, 1780, England declared war on the Netherlands. Early the following February, a British squadron under the command of Admiral George Bridges Rodney, consisting of fourteen ships of the line, three frigates, and three galleons, sailed into the harbor of St. Eustasius and quickly overcame the meager Dutch defenses. "This rock of only six miles in length and three in breadth," said Rodney, "has done England more harm than all of the arms of her most potent enemies and alone [has] supported the infamous American rebellion." Rodney retaliated by cannonading St. Eustasius, damaging some buildings, destroying others. He then proceeded to plunder the island. Just before taking his leave in August 1781, Rodney leveled every building that remained standing. He also ordered his ships to destroy the harbor's protecting sea wall. St. Eustasius' prosperity ended with Rodney's visit—and it never returned.

Some tourist guidebooks say that Columbus sighted and named St. Eustasius in 1493, but historians are not certain of this. It is an established fact the first Dutch settlers began arriving in 1636 ". . . to plant good tobacco and make substantial profits."

During the next fifty years, the island became the center of mercantile activity in the Caribbean, thriving mostly as a result of pirating and contraband trade. The main settlement during the seventeenth century was located on the high bluff overlooking the bay and was called Upper Town. Below, at the base of the bluff, was Lower Town. In 1684, a visitor to St. Eustasius reported that there were one thousand buildings in Upper Town and Lower Town, and more than ten million pounds of sterling passed through the island each year.

Disaster struck in 1687—some sources say it was 1690—when violent earthquakes shook the island intermittently for two full days. Hundreds of buildings in Lower Town crumbled and fell into the churning sea, and about half of the structures in Upper Town tumbled or slid from the bluff down to where Lower Town once stood. Hundreds of lives were lost.

St. Eustasius quickly recovered from the earthquake. Within a decade or so it was thriving again as a trading center, and also as a haven for merchants from nearby islands who were seeking to dodge British taxes. By the beginning of the eighteenth century, St. Eustasius was well on its way toward becoming the most important port in the Caribbean, its harbor jammed with masts of ships of a dozen nations, and ready to play its role in the American Revolution.

Robert Marx, a free-lance writer, recalls visiting Statia in 1960, not long after a hurricane had struck the area, uncovering a large portion of the sunken city. Using only snorkeling equipment (a swim mask, breathing tube, and swim fins), Marx explored the ruins of more than fifty old brick buildings. "The governor of the island at the time was a historically minded chap who joined me," Marx recalled, "and together we recovered hundreds of artifacts such as pewter and silver tankards, plates, bowls, mugs, spoons, and forks; bottles, crockery, clay smoking pipes, tools, weapons, and even a few silver coins."

St. Eustasius has a population of thirteen hundred today. Viewed from an approaching boat, it looks like two truncated cones connected by an open plain. Oranjestad, the capital, perched on the bluff, was built after Rodney destroyed the harbor town below and is probably best described as unpretentious. Lack of rain, poor soil, and a general languidness on the part of most residents have combined to keep affluence away.

In the Museum of the City of New York, nine yellow Dutch bricks, used in the construction of townhouses during the seventeenth and eighteenth centuries, are on display. Bricks of the same type are also exhibited in the Smithsonian Institution and other historical institutions of the Northeast and Middle Atlantic states. In St. Eustasius, such bricks are not esteemed at all. Random samples are strewn along the island's beaches and alongside its blacktopped roadways.

Historic artifacts are everywhere. There's no need to dig. "At a place called Mary's Point," says a recent visitor, "we discovered artifacts right on the surface of the ground among the ruins of old stone and brick buildings. I doubt if anyone had been there for years. Less than a five-minute walk from the airstrip, we found other relics, some predating the first settlement in 1640. The site may have been a base for pirates that frequented these waters."

Potsherds and pieces of clay smoking pipes litter every open lot. When paving material is made on the island, small pieces of eighteenth- and nineteenth-century chinaware often go into the mixture. Thus, it can be said that the roadways of St. Eustasius are literally paved with potsherds.

There are dozens of roofless, crumbling buildings constructed of yellow bricks, including one of the most venerable synagogues in the Western Hemisphere. In 1973, a group of volunteers from the Caribbean Mitsvah Corps, under the supervision of Rabbi Leo Abrami of Berkeley, California, sought to spruce up the synagogue ruins and a nearby cemetery. During the course of their work, they discovered a *mikvah*, or ceremonial bath, used by Jewish women as part of a prenuptial ritual.

Not far away from the synagogue are the deteriorating ruins of the Dutch Reformed Church, constructed in 1775 largely of round natural stones that are called "face stones" by the Statians. Yellow bricks were used to frame the windows and doors. The church was severely damaged by a hurricane in 1792 and never repaired.

One of the oldest and best maintained of the eighteenth-century structures is the "Huis de Graaff," once the home of St. Eustasius' most famous govenor, Johannes de Graaff. Ironically, the house later served as the headquarters of the infamous Rodney.

In recent years, the government of the Netherlands Antilles has restored what is perhaps the most important structure on the island, Fort Oranje, built in 1636 on the site of earlier fortication. Unfortunately, it is the kind of restoration that has given restorations a bad name. "Maybe the sun and rain will soften all those bright colors they've used," says one local resident. "Right now, it has a Disneyland quality."

Forts once ringed St. Eustasius. Only Fort Oranje has been tampered with. The others are largely rubble. At some, rusting cannons lie about.

Lining the island's western shore are the ruins of seventeenth- and eighteenth-century warehouses, merchants' shops, and taverns. A tumbling-down cotton gin has been restored so as to serve as a comfortable inn, the Mooshay Bay Public House. A nearby warehouse of Dutch red and yellow bricks now houses a power plant.

At one time, the slave trade flourished on St. Eustasius, and in 1726 a slave house was built on the island within a structure known as the Waterfort. The walls of the structure are still standing on the western shore.

Glass beads, called "slave beads," are sometimes found on local beaches. Most are blue or deep green. Some are cylinder-shaped; others have straight sides. Some are tiny, only ⅛ inch long; others are a full inch in length. Laboratory tests at the University of California indicated the beads were made during the seventeenth and eighteenth centuries. But how the beads came to St. Eustasius is something of a mystery. It is not known whether they were sold on the island or brought from Africa by slaves.

In 1923, Professor J. P. B. de Josselin de Jong of the Netherlands, conducting the first archaeological research program in the history of St. Eustasius, unearthed evidence of several Indian settlements, which later were found to date to A.D. 300. Beneath a ten-inch layer of topsoil, de Jong and his associates found earthenware shards, and artifacts made of stone, coral, shell, and even pumice. More recent research, conducted by an archaeological team from the Virgin Islands, has been devoted to the Arawak and Caribe Indians who once inhabited the island.

For more information on the historical background of St. Eustasius, two books are recommended:

The History of St. Eustasius, Dr. J. Hartog, 1976, The Central U. S. A. Bicentennial Committee of the Netherlands Antilles. The book is distributed by DeWith Stores, Aruba, N.A.

St. Eustasius, A Short History of the Land and Its Monuments, Ypie Attema, 1976, De Walburg Pers Zutphen, Holland.

It's also helpful to contact the St. Eustasius Historical Foundation (P.O. Box 171, St. Eustasius, N.A.). The Historical Foundation maintains a small museum on the island.

Anyone can undertake excavation on the island, providing the local chief of police is first contacted, according to Oswald G. Bell, Administrator of St. Eustasius. "Activities [must] take place in the presence of a member of the St. Eustasius Historical Foundation," says Mr. Bell, "and all artifacts of value found have to be turned over to the Foundation."

Urban Archaeology

After the news of Henry Hudson's voyage of exploration to the New World in 1609 reached Holland, plans were immediately laid for additional expeditions to "the great river" to capitalize on the fur trade. In 1610 and again in 1611, successful trading expeditions were made from Dutch ports.

In June 1613, two vessels left Amsterdam together, the *Tiger* and the *Fortune*. When they arrived in the harbor of New Amsterdam, the *Tiger* anchored off Manhattan, while the *Fortune* sailed up the Hudson River to the present site of Albany.

Adriaen Block, an Amsterdam lawyer who commanded the *Tiger*, spent the summer bartering with the Indians, and by fall his vessel was heavily laden with furs. In November, disaster struck. While riding at anchor offshore what is now Dey Street in Manhattan, the *Tiger* was destroyed by fire. Block eventually returned to the Netherlands aboard the *Fortune*.

Three hundred years pass. Workmen are excavating at the corner of Dey and Greenwich streets to build a subway, when their pickaxes strike charred timbers. After testing to date the wood and the metal bolts, it is concluded that the timbers are from the *Tiger*.

James A. Kelly, the foreman of the subway construction crew, wanted to dig out the ship, but was prevented from doing so by the impatient contractor and apathetic bureaucrats. His only alternative was to shear off the exposed section of the vessel.

That is not the end of the story. In the years that followed, Kelly campaigned to remove the rest of the *Tiger*, but he was thwarted at every turn. He got one more chance in the late 1960s.

The Koster site at the
Kampsville Archaeological Center.
(Northwestern University;
D. Baston)

Drawing stone profiles at
Machrie Moor, Isle of Arran,
Scotland.
(Earthwatch;
Anthony Van Riper)

Above, American volunteers at
the Temple Mount excavation,
Jerusalem. (Consulate General of
Israel in New York)

Left, a man-made earthen mound
at the Crystal River
Archaeological Site,
Crystal River, Florida.
(Crystal River State
Archaeological Site)

One of the more than two hundred mounds at Effigy Mounds National Monument near Marquette, Iowa. (National Park Service)

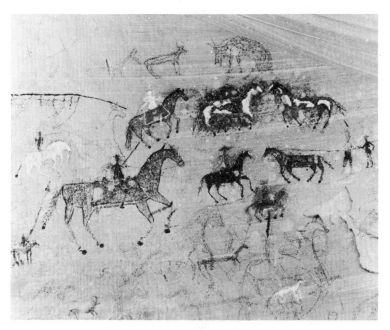

Navaho pictographs at the Canyon del Muerto, Canyon de Chelly National Monument, Arizona. (National Park Service)

Petroglyphs at
Bishop, California.
(Bishop Chamber of Commerce)

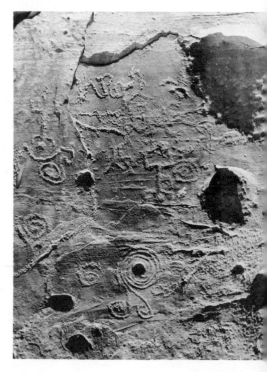

Pictographs at Chaco
Canyon National Monument,
New Mexico.
(National Park Service)

Excavation had begun for the World Trade Center, and a portion of the construction site involved the very same site that Kelly's men had excavated years before. The Port Authority of New York and New Jersey, in charge of the construction, cooperated by allotting $20,000 for hand digging at the spot where it was believed what remained of the *Tiger* would be found. The wood sections the hand shovelers finally unearthed were charred, twisted, and broken, and to the workmen they looked like pieces of an old wharf. Without bothering to consult anyone, they loaded the debris into a dump truck and it was hauled away, never to be recovered.

The New York *Times* has called the *Tiger* a ghost ship that haunts the city's archaeologists, both professional and amateur. All that is left of it is the sheared-off section that Kelly managed to salvage. It is now on display at the Museum of the City of New York, billed as one of the earliest artifacts made by Europeans to have been found in the New York area.

A similar story unfolded in San Francisco in 1978. When construction crews began excavating for a downtown office building, they unearthed the remains of the seventy-five-foot hull of the *Niantic*, one of the first ships used to bring gold-seekers to California in 1849. Like many of the hundreds of other ships that sailed into San Francisco that year, the *Niantic* was abandoned by its crew, the majority of whom became inflicted with gold fever.

For ten days, Karl Kortum, director of the San Francisco Maritime Museum, managed to hold back the bulldozers while he sought to raise the money necessary—$630,000—to remove the hull intact and store it properly. "It was all very intense," he recalls. When Kortum's efforts failed, the bulldozers moved in. As in the case of the *Tiger*, Kortum had to be satisfied with a section of the ship's hull.

These two sagas are somewhat typical cases in that branch of historical archaeology known as urban archaeology. Frustration is one of the chief characteristics of the field. It is often hurry-up archaeology, an attempt to gather as much information as possible before the backhoes and bulldozers are set loose. It often becomes salvage archaeology.

If you are going to be working in an urban setting, don't fail to read the real estate section of your local newspaper on a regular basis. It will help to keep you informed of construction projects that are scheduled and the excavation work that is sure to result.

Twenty-nine-year-old William Asadorian, an assistant curator of manuscripts at the New-York Historical Society, follows this practice. As an urban archaeologist, he's fought off dog packs and been mired in quicksand in quest of artifacts. He admits he frequently works with a bulldozer hovering in the background. With workers' permission, he'll jump down into a construction trench during lunch hour for a quick inspection.

Despite the frantic nature of his avocation, Asadorian has made some significant finds. During the summer of 1976, when the city of New York was relandscaping Bowling Green Park in Lower Manhattan, Asadorian found a Spanish copper coin of the early 1600s, green from its long burial. No other coin of its type had ever been found in New York, according to the American Numismatic Society. Asadorian believes the coin was brought to New York, a Dutch colony at the time, by one of the Jews who came to New York from Brazil in the 1650s. Brazil and Spain were trading partners.

Asadorian has also found the white clay bowl of a Dutch pipe in Bowling Green Park. "Dutch pipes from New York are very rare," he says. "Of all the clay pipes that have been found in New York, less than 1 per cent have been Dutch."

As Asadorian's experiences may suggest, professionally conducted excavations in New York City are about as rare as big lawns. The last one of any note occurred in 1971. Lehman Brothers, an investment banking concern, was about to begin construction of a new company headquarters in Lower Manhattan, when archaeologists pointed out that part of the site included the foundation walls of New York's first city hall. The Lehman firm not only granted permission for the archaeologists to excavate, but arranged for several workmen employed by the construction firm to assist them.

The site, on Pearl Street, not far from historic Fraunce's Tavern (or at least the Tavern in its somewhat restored form), was pinpointed through years of research both in this country and the Netherlands by Regina Kellerman, a historian who represented the Landmarks Preservation Committee. Working in an excavation that never got much deeper than ten feet, Mrs. Kellerman and her associates found not only a section of wall, but a staircase, fragments of pottery, Dutch and English clay pipes, nails, and sections of Dutch roofing tiles. The wall, the staircase, and the roofing tile were determined to be the remains of a three-story Dutch structure built in 1641 as a tavern. "We know the building was standing in 1641," an archaeologist explained, "because our records show a man named John Hobson was arrested for stealing a bedsheet from the inn on November 19, 1641."

The top of the bricks in the building's wall were found at a depth of about three feet. Slightly deeper, and at right angles to the walls, excavators unearthed the staircase. Joseph Shelly, an archaeologist and professor at the City College School of Architecture, said that the composition and color of the mortar between the stones indicated that it was the wall of the city hall, the *Stadhuis*, as it was called. In addition, wall measurements perfectly matched measurements in old records. The roof tiles served as additional evidence that the building was a Dutch structure. The English did not use such tiles for their roofs.

At the time the building was constructed, it was only a half block from the waterfront. Landfill operations through the years extended the shoreline by several hundred feet.

Beginning in 1653, the building not only served as the Stadhuis, but it also housed the police and fire departments, courts, and a jail. The building was sold at auction in 1699, and two houses were constructed on the site in 1701. These were demolished in 1825. Another building went up in 1826, and this remained standing until 1970.

Lehman Brothers later tabled its plan to build a company headquarters. The Stadhuis site was covered over with sand to protect it from water and freezing temperatures which could have crumbled the foundation's clamshell-limestone mortar. Then the entire parcel of land was blacktopped. It served as a parking lot throughout the rest of the 1970s.

In recent years, archaeologists excavating in New York City have concentrated on what is known as the Schermerhorn Row Block, which consists of twenty buildings erected between 1810 and 1812, the only group of slant-roofed warehouses still standing in the city. The block faces Fulton Street between South and Front streets at the East River.

In the seventeenth and eighteenth centuries, the river served as a garbage dump for Manhattan's residents. They generated so much garbage that they extended the island several blocks into the river.

Digging through the basements of some of the Schermerhorn Row buildings, archaeologists have probed into the fill, retrieving trinkets from the West Indies, Delft pottery shards, pieces of Chinese import porcelain, and thousands of shards of clay pipes. They also found many deer and rabbit bones, indicating that early settlers consumed more game meat than previously supposed.

Anyone digging through the concrete or asphalt of Lower Manhattan below Wall Street, and who manages to reach a depth of fifteen or twenty feet, may encounter pine logs which have been bored lengthwise and are fitted end to end. Salt-water seepage has kept them well preserved. Such logs were part of New York's first water system. During the 1790s, the city's fifty-six thousand inhabitants were confronted by a fierce yellow fever epidemic. Hundreds died. Medical authorities said that the epidemic was caused by polluted water and urged construction of a central water system.

The city itself had tried and failed to establish a municipal waterworks in the 1770s, but the later efforts were spearheaded by a citizens' committee headed by Alexander Hamilton, and which included Aaron Burr as a prominent member. The committee recommended the founding of a private company, to be known as the Manhattan Company, to furnish the city with pure water. A bill creating the company was passed by the state legislature in Albany on April 2, 1799.

The group moved rapidly, negotiating to build a reservoir and tap sources of water just north of where City Hall now stands. Arrangements were also made to manufacture wooden pipes from pine logs.

By the end of the first year, six miles of pipe had been laid, stretching from the reservoir on Chambers Street down Broadway, to supply four hundred homes and shops. Later, additional pipe was put down that extended at right angles to the Broadway mains, that is down the side streets leading to the Hudson and East rivers. Several fountains were located at convenient points along the waterfront to provide water for ships in the harbor. A horse-powered pump was put into operation. The horses were replaced in 1803 by a steam engine.

The company's original plan was to charge individual customers on the basis of the number of fireplaces contained in the building being supplied. An advertisement outlining this policy appeared in Greenleaf's New York *Journal* of June 20, 1799. It read:

> For every house or building containing not more than four fireplaces, there will be paid the sum of $5.00 per annum, and for every fireplace exceeding four in any house or building there shall be paid an additional $1.25, provided, however, not more than $20.00 shall be paid for any private house or dwelling.

Customers abused this policy by giving away vast quantities of water to friends and neighbors. Grocers all over the city subscribed to the service and supplied customers with free water to secure their patronage. There were instances of single pipes supplying entire neighborhoods.

The Manhattan Company sought to overcome such misusage by establishing a fee system. It included these charges:

For lead pipe	$ .50 per foot
For a draw cock	$ 1.00
For providing homes of only one family	$10.00 per year
For each additional family in the house	$ 3.00 per year
For grocery stores	$15.00 per year
For counter fountains	$10.00 per year
For stores and offices without family	$10.00 per year
For factories, steam engines, boarding houses, hotels, taverns, sugar refineries, distilleries, breweries, dye houses, bathing establishments, etc.	(According to private agreement)
For supplying water to lay 100,000 bricks in mortar with interior plastering	$25.00
Without interior plastering	$15.00

The water system rendered a valuable service in the case of fire, by never charging for water that was used to extinguish a blaze, even though vast quantities were frequently squandered after the fire was out. Occasionally it was necessary to drill a hole directly into the wooden pipe to secure water for fire-fighting purposes. Large wooden plugs were used to close these taps. Some sources say that the term fireplug has been derived from this practice.

The Manhattan Company's system eventually consisted of twenty-five miles of water main, serving more than two thousand homes. It stayed in operation for forty-three years.

There's an interesting footnote to the story of the Manhattan Company and its founding. When the bill providing for the company's creation was before the legislative committee, Aaron Burr, without Hamilton's knowledge, had it amended so as to enable the company to use any of its capital stock not required in the water business "in the purchase of public stock or in other monied transactions or operations not inconsistent with the Constitution and laws of the United States." Thus, Burr, an anti-Federalist, was able to establish a bank—the Bank of the Manhattan Company—to rival the two powerful Federalist banks in operation in New York City at the time. Hamilton, a Federalist leader, had remained in New York while Burr worked on the legislation in Albany, and so was unaware of Burr's anti-Federalist machinations.

When he did learn of Burr's maneuvering, Hamilton became infuriated. The antagonism between the two men culminated in the duel they fought in Weehauken, New Jersey, on July 11, 1804, when a bullet from Burr's pistol tore into Hamilton's abdomen. He died the next morning.

The Bank of the Manhattan Company grew steadily during the 1800s. The state legislature permitted the company to sell its waterworks to the city of New York, in 1808, and to employ all of its capital in banking. The company played a leading role in the construction financing of the Erie Canal. Through mergers and the opening of branch offices, the company became one of New York's leading commercial banks. In 1955, the Bank of the Manhattan Company merged with the Chase National Bank, the nation's third largest bank at the time. Out of the merger came the Chase Manhattan Bank.

The huge bank's beginnings as a supplier of water have not been forgotten entirely. In many of the branch offices of the Chase Manhattan Bank, there are displayed disks of wood, carefully stained and polished, most having about the same diameter as a dinner plate. They were sliced from wooden water pipes that have been recovered through the years. An embossed metal plate explains their provenience.

Industrial Archaeology

While America's industrial revolution is scarcely two hundred years old, great gaps exist in the history of how it occurred. The economy of the nation is dependent upon industrial processes; the development of some of these is almost entirely unrecorded. The forges and foundaries that put the industrial revolution in motion have been buried over by new factories or, worse, by parking lots and housing developments.

In recent years, however, archaeologists have begun to piece together the story of American industry. In perhaps as many as a dozen different sites in the northeastern United States, "industrial monuments"—buildings, earthworks, and machinery, or the remains of these—are being surveyed, measured, recorded, and placed in their proper historical setting.

The beginnings of industrial archaeology have been traced to a site near Birmingham, England, where, during the 1950s, bulldozers uncovered what was revealed to be one of the first furnaces to smelt iron with coked coal instead of charcoal, a technique that triggered the first stages of England's industrial revolution. The discovery of the furnace resulted in a successful effort to set aside the land it occupied as a historical site, and it also caused archaeologists to undertake similar excavations in other parts of England.

During the late 1960s, the field came into its own in this country when Rensselaer Polytechnic Institute of Troy, New York, one of the nation's oldest engineering and technological institutions, established an Institute of Industrial Archaeology. One of the institute's first important discoveries occurred in Troy. In the dank, dark basement of a huge, five-story building, which extended for almost a fifth of a mile along the Mohawk River, three giant water turbines, dating to the early 1800s, were found. They demonstrated how millwrights diverted water from the rivers into vertical pipes which, when fed through large turbines, provided sufficient horsepower to operate heavy machinery. This, and other instances in the use of big water-driven turbines in the Troy vicinity, showed clearly how thoroughly early industry in the United States depended on waterpower. England, by contrast, utilized steam to power its industrial activity.

Other significant findings concerning the rise of American industry have emerged from excavations along the grassy banks of the Mill River in Whitneyville, Connecticut. Financed by grants from the National Park Service and the New Haven Historical Society, archaeologists and students from nearby Yale University have dug into the ruins of the old Whitney Arms Company, founded by Eli Whitney. It was at this site that Whitney mass-produced ten thousand muskets for the United States Army from 1798 through 1802. The important phrase in that sentence is "mass-produced." Before Whitney, everything—from candleholders to spinning wheels—had to be made by hand. It was slow; it was tedious.

Thanks to his invention of the cotton gin, which had revolutionized southern agriculture, Whitney was already a well-known figure as he prepared to launch his gunmaking venture. In 1798, he was awarded a $134,000 contract to produce the aforementioned muskets in twenty-eight months. With that type of production quota, he could not allow his workers to make one part at a time, fit it to the preceding part, make another part, fit it, and so forth, until the musket was complete. Instead, Whitney made plans to produce each musket part in quantity by machine. When the full supply of parts had been turned out, they would be assembled to produce the required number of muskets.

The identical parts were to be manufactured by means of a jig —a device for guiding a tool. Once in operation, the factory was considered a marvel of its day, and countless dignitaries and government officials toured the site in the early 1800s to witness the machines and their tenders performing their mass-production tasks. Written records of the operation are meager, to say the least. One fragment of evidence as to what went on within the factory walls is contained in a note written by Whitney's ten-year-old nephew Philos Blake to his sister Abigail in 1801. "There is a drilling machine and a bouring machine for bouring berels," the young man wrote, "and a screw machine and two large buildings."

About the only other evidence of what Whitney was doing has

come from the excavations. The first artifacts unearthed were triggers, barrels, cartridges, and bayonets that dated to the 1880s, a period when Oliver Winchester, who had bought the factory, was manufacturing rifles there. But, later, at what was dubbed "the Whitney level," workers turned up flints, lead musket balls, and big grindstones.

One conclusion that archaeologists reached is that the parts of Whitney's muskets were really not interchangeable or truly standardized. Each had to be touched up, filed a little here, drilled a little there, so they'd fit together. "It is now recognized that Whitney got pretty close to his goal," says Dr. David R. Starbuck of Yale University, who directed the excavation, "but he was never able to mill metal to close enough tolerances."

Despite such conclusions, it is generally agreed that mass production did get started at the Whitneyville factory. The technique was later perfected by Simeon North, Samuel Colt, and others, and applied not only to the manufacture of arms, but to the making of sewing machines and farm machinery. In time, Whitney's inventiveness led to the end of the artisan era.

While Whitneyville, Connecticut, and Troy, New York, have yielded significant findings in the growth and development of American industry, to observe what is perhaps the biggest and busiest program in industrial archaeology, one must visit Paterson, New Jersey, a city of 153,000 in the northeastern corner of the state.

Paterson likes to call itself "the Cradle of American Industry." There is a solid base for such a claim. In 1778, Alexander Hamilton visited Paterson and watched the Passaic River careen over the cataract which even then was known as the Great Fall, and he recognized that the surging water could be an important source of power for a developing nation. As Secretary of the Treasury in 1791, Hamilton reported to Congress that industrial strength was vital to the continued independence of the country and advocated that one city be devoted solely to industry, and he designated Paterson as that city. A year later, Hamilton and other directors of what had been designated as the Society for Establishing Useful Manufactures (S.U.M.) met at the falls to ratify their choice of Paterson as the site for a "national manufactory."

A system of millraces—fast-moving streams of water to drive mill wheels (and, later, turbines)—was constructed. The first factory in the nation's first industrial city was a cotton mill that went into operation in 1793. A paper mill, more textile mills, machine shops, and other factories soon followed. In 1827, John Colt erected a plant to make cotton duck for sails. In 1836, another Colt, Samuel, built a factory for manufacturing revolvers.

By the mid-nineteenth century, Paterson was on its way to fulfilling Hamilton's vision. Not only was the city a major textile center, but the nation's locomotive industry was based there, with four great locomotive works operating. One, the Rogers Locomotive Works, built many of the locomotives that helped to conquer the West, supply the arms of the Civil War, and even served the Trans-Siberian railroad.

The textile business kept getting bigger and bigger. By the early 1900s, three hundred factories in the silk industry alone were in operation in Paterson, ranging from weaving mills to yarn-twisting and dyeing plants.

A turning point in the city's fortunes came in 1913 when the silk industry was ravaged by a six-month strike that cast twenty thousand workers into the streets. It was a body blow from which the city never recovered. After World War II, the period of decline accelerated, with businesses continuing to close and companies moving away.

Not much attention was paid to the abandoned mills and factories that made up the old S.U.M. industrial district until the 1960s when scores of buildings were threatened with demolition because of a proposed six-lane elevated highway that was to cut through its heart. Suddenly support began to crystallize for the preservation of historic Paterson. The highway was never built. The industrial center of the city became the Great Falls S.U.M. Historic District. In 1976, the entire 119-acre, 49-building district became the first industrial area in the country to be named a National Historic District.

Even before that, archaeological teams had moved in. At the Rogers Erecting Shop, a part of what was once the largest locomotive manufacturing complex in the world, one archaeological team unearthed massive foundations for drop-forge hammers, huge pits filled with iron scalings (thought to be a possible source of air for the furnace), and, at one spot, more than three hundred metal files, believed to be hand tools supplied to workers by the factory management. When restoration work is completed, the building will house an industrial museum, a cultural center, and the book-processing division of the Paterson Public Library.

The famous falls that triggered more than a century of growth and development for Paterson are a scenic attraction now, and nothing more. Almost 80 feet in height and 280 feet wide, they are the second largest falls in the eastern United States. To the left of the falls, at their base, is the S.U.M. hydroelectric plant, closed since 1969. But the city believes the plant has a future, and there are plans to repair the dam that diverts the water to the millrace and hydroelectric plant. One hope is to combine the restoration of the power plant with a sewage plant project that will provide methane gas to run other generating equipment. By combining the electricity from the S.U.M. hydroelectric plant with that produced by the methane-fueled plant, the city would be in a position to sell power at a profit to the local utility company.

Much of the archaeological work involves Paterson's complex system of raceways, headraces, tailraces, and flumes that carried the water that powered the mills and factories. During the summer of 1978, an archaeological team under thirty-one-year-old Jim Lally, one of six teams at work in the city that summer, excavated a series of test trenches in an old raceway, designated the Upper Raceway. The object of the investigation was to get an idea of the raceway's original form and structure. The information derived by Lally and his crew was turned over to an engineering firm charged with restoring the raceway, which eventually is to be an integral part of a park that is planned for the area.

The raceway proved to be a treasure trove for industrial artifacts—broken tools, old pieces of machinery, and other items discarded by factory workers. During the winter of 1978–79, these items, along with thousands upon thousands of artifacts recovered from other excavations, were sorted and evaluated.

"Everything we're doing has two objects," archaeologist Marjorie Ingle points out. "One has to do with providing scholarly information, the cataloguing, the interpreting of what we find. The other is more immediate, to provide information to the construction crews."

In the future, archaeological work in Paterson will become more involved with the documentation of the city's various industrial technologies. "That's down the road some, however," says Barry Brady, supervisor of the archaeological program in 1979.

Brady has his heart set on excavating a site where he believes he will discover a turbine. "All the other turbines have been carted away," he says. "But if there's one still here some place, we'll find it."

Aboveground Archaeology

The term archaeology refers to the systematic recovery by scientific methods of material evidence remaining from man's life and culture in past ages, and the detailed study of that evidence. There is nothing in that definition about "digging." The word "buried" does not appear there.

The point is that there are many clues to man's historic past in many other places. One's attic or cellar may contain valuable evidence of what life was like years ago, before automobiles and automatic dishwashers, before television and air conditioning. A buggy whip, fire kindler, saltbox, or water dipper—all of these are artifacts.

A Columbus, Ohio, homeowner found in his attic a small cardboard box containing a harness made of leather straps, which promotion literature, also in the box, hailed as, "The Gamble Brace for Men; The Perfect Cure for Round Shoulders." It had cost $1.50 a century or so ago and was described in these terms: "It is the most comfortable brace made, and will brace a man up so he will grow fat and healthy." Something of that nature contributes to our understanding of the past every bit as much as a spearpoint or a ceramic storage vessel.

Dr. John L. Cotter, associate curator of the American Historical Archaeology at the University of Pennsylvania Museum, is one of the principal champions of aboveground archaeology. In a booklet he wrote on the subject, Cotter points out that important clues to the past can be found in old letters, diaries, notebooks, magazines, newspapers, and in books of many kinds. "For instance," Cotter says, "an old textbook of fifty to a hundred years ago or more is excellent evidence concerning what people in school were learning at that time, and how it compares with classwork today. An old children's book or a game or a toy may tell about familiar, everyday experiences of our ancestors."

Cotter suggests a simple card file to record physical evidence of the past. You can use a three-by-five-inch card, or larger ones. You can set up several such files, one for artifacts or objects, another for documents, et cetera.

	ARTIFACT
Number	Date
Identity	Location
Description	

Suppose you establish an "A" file for artifacts. The first artifact recorded would be identified as A-1-1980 (the year). The card would name the object and tell where it was found. Also include a sentence or two of descriptive information, perhaps telling where and when the object was obtained, giving the names of previous owners, the cost, and so on.

Then label the artifact with its identification number. Naturally, you don't want to deface or damage it. If the object is metal, wood, or ceramic material, the best method may be to apply a small rectangle of liquid paper with a fine brush, allow it to dry, and then add the identifying number with a fine-pointed pen and India ink. You can also use Hyplar, an acrylic polymer plastic that can be washed from the bristles (or the object) with water when it is in a liquid state, or removed with denatured alcohol when dry.

In the case of letters or documents, put the item in a polyethylene sleeve or envelope first, and then put the identifying symbol

on the envelope. For storing anything that's rare or delicate, seek
the advice of a professional curator or conservator, or consult one
or more of the publications of such organizations as the American
Association for State and Local History or the International Institute for the Conservation of Historic and Artistic Works (see
Appendix).

Photographs are another area in which to specialize. Cotter suggests that a person collect, inventory, and catalogue photographic
prints that tell family and community history. Photographic negatives, he says, are even more important than prints, and he la-
ments the fact that they are commonly lost through carelessness,
neglect, or by improper storage. "Watch for rare glass negatives,"
Cotter says, "that may record persons, places, and events of a hundred years ago."

If you're skilled in the use of a camera, Cotter suggests making
a photographic record of houses and buildings in your community
—those that represent the community's various stages of development and those associated with notable people and/or events.
"Many times," Cotter says, "such buildings are destroyed by
'progress' or by accident, and the photographs are all that remain."

The techniques and attitudes implicit in this type of research
can also be applied by groups of concerned individuals on a community basis. Take for example an organization called the Friends
of Cast Iron Architecture, which is devoted to the identification
and preservation of the unique iron buildings, most of them over
a century old, that are found in the older commercial sections of
many American cities and towns.

· These iron buildings are among the earliest prefabricated structures. Their many modular parts were cast in iron foundries, then
transported to the sites for assembly. When bolted together, the
castings formed the building's exterior walls. In cases where entire
iron fronts were used, it was possible to have long expanses of
glass on every floor. Such structures were the lineal ancestors of today's curtain-wall skyscrapers.

Buildings of this type could be put up quickly and economi-
cally. At the same time, they could be made to meet the aesthetic
standards of the time and were ornamented with arches and
brackets, balconies and balustrades, and castings of fancy capitals,
fluted columns, and elegant cornices. Most buildings of this type

have been painted so as to resemble stone, and passers-by usually
have no idea the structures are made of iron.

Philadelphia, Boston, San Francisco, Seattle, Charlestown, and
Savannah have examples of iron-front buildings, but the greatest
concentration is in New York City. St. Louis and Cincinnati leveled groups of such structures in riverfront urban renewal projects,
and Baltimore, with some exceptions, has done the same.

The Friends of Cast Iron Architecture, with headquarters in
New York, seeks to draw attention to these buildings and spur appreciation of them. The organization tries to get, maintain their
buildings properly, paint them, and protect them against rust. It
decries wanton remodeling of handsome, period ground floors.

One example of what the organization tries to accomplish
requires some background. The idea of building commercial structures of prefabricated iron and glass was first popularized by London's Great Exhibition of 1851, which was housed entirely in the
Crystal Palace, an astonishing structure that consisted of a network of columns, girders, and trusses which were bolted together
and then sheathed with eighteen thousand panes of glass. Soon
after, train stations and produce markets utilizing the new technology began to spring up.

The first cast-iron structures in this country were of modest proportions, the work of James Bogardus, a watchmaker, inventor,
and self-proclaimed "architect in iron." One of these structures
was Bogardus' own factory, the Eccentric Mill Works, built of
prefabricated iron piers and wall paneling in a matter of weeks in
1849.

In 1851, New York's Board of Aldermen contracted with
Bogardus to build the city's first iron fire tower, and it was erected
at Ninth Avenue and Thirty-third Street. Street-corner fire
alarms did not begin to appear until 1871. Before that, the city
was dependent on a system of tall towers manned by sharp-eyed
lookouts, sitting in enclosures at the top, scanning the rooftops
through a telescope for signs of smoke and flame. The earliest
towers were built of wood, but Bogardus was able to convince the
city of the practicality of building them of prefabricated iron
parts. The first one proved so sturdy, and at the same time so eco-
nomical, that the city ordered two more. One of these was erected
on top of a hill in what was then called Mount Morris Park in

Harlem, later named Marcus Garvey Park. It is the only tower remaining to this day.

The tower consists of three tiers of fluted iron columns, each tier thirteen feet in height and arranged to form an octagonal iron frame. A spiral staircase sweeps through the framework to the enclosure at the top where the lookout was posted. If clad with plate glass, the tower would be a mini skyscraper. Engineers and architects consider it historically significant.

During the past few years, the members of the Friends of Cast Iron Architecture have worked diligently in an effort to preserve the tower. It requires painting desperately. Hollow columns, open at the top, permit rainwater to run down inside, causing rusting which eventually could prove fatal to the structure. Neighborhood youngsters use the tower as a playground gymnasium.

"We've aroused interest in the tower," says a spokesman for the organization, "and we're pleased with the response we've gotten, not only from the city as a whole, but from the Harlem community, in particular. But the tower stands in the city park, and the Park Department has no money. So we haven't been able to get it painted—yet. Nor has any repair work been done.

"It's a continuing battle. But we're hopeful."

A tale with a happier ending can be told by architectural historian Carolyn Pitts and her associates who struggled for almost a decade to restore and preserve the richly ornamented homes and hotels of Cape May, New Jersey, one of America's most noted strongholds of Victorian architecture.

Cape May, located at New Jersey's southernmost tip, where the waters of Delaware Bay meet the Atlantic Ocean, began earning its reputation as a resort community almost two hundred years ago. In 1801, Ellis Hughes advertised to Philadelphians the availability of his beachfront hotel—no more than a converted barn—for overnight guests. In 1832, the Mansion House, Cape May's first plaster-and-lath hotel, opened for business. Tourists began flooding in during the summer, and on July and August weekends during the 1850s, they arrived at the rate of three thousand a day. Many of the visitors were southern plantation owners who made the journey north by railroad or steamboat. The resort's most splendid hotel opened in 1853. Named the Mount Vernon, the four-story structure provided accommodations for thirty-five hundred guests. But before the last wing was completed, the Mount

Vernon was destroyed by fire. "Not surprising," noted a recent article in *Smithsonian* magazine, "since the place was lighted with gas manufactured on the premises."

During the latter half of the nineteenth century, a succession of American Presidents visited Cape May. President Franklin Pierce was the first. President U. S. Grant was a frequent visitor; President Chester Alan Arthur stopped by. In 1890, President Benjamin Harrison made the Congress Hotel, the resort's most famous hotel at the time, his summer White House. The structure is still standing.

When well-to-do Philadelphians sought to vacation at Cape May, and found transportation facilities jammed and the leading hotels booked to capacity, they began building their own "cottages," relying upon Philadelphia's most noted architects and carpenter-builders of the day. The result was an impressive collection of spacious frame homes painted in muted tones, and featuring huge porches, shaded high windows, and an array of ornamental framework that must have had every jigsaw in New Jersey humming. *Smithsonian* called it ". . . an unparalleled ensemble of Victorian architecture."

Terribles fires swept Cape May in the late 1800s, and one of them, in 1878, destroyed some thirty acres of hotels and related buildings. By 1900, Cape May had an even worse problem. The resort was falling out of fashion, as vacationers switched their allegiance to Atlantic City and other resorts. Year after year of decline followed. In the spring of 1962, Cape May was the victim of one of the worst storms in years. It came raging out of the Atlantic to pound the city with wind, rain, and surf, tearing roofs from frame cottages, flooding them, filling many with debris.

A government-sponsored Urban Renewal program, financed by millions of federal dollars, seemed to be the solution to Cape May's problems, even though it meant demolishing many of the old buildings. But some citizens resisted. Carolyn Pitts was one of the first. In 1963, she began to catalogue the town's architectural riches on a house-by-house basis. Her careful and detailed research pointed up the historic value of Cape May and proved discomforting to anyone who happened to be recommending the replacement of old structures with new ones. Dr. Irving Tennenbaum joined the fight. He began installing gaslights along the streets of the "historic district," which one day would consist of six hundred inhabited wooden structures, and to organize a "historical renewal conference" sponsored by the National Trust for Historic Preservation. Arthur "Mickey" Blomkvest ran for a city council post on the "historic values" issue—and won. Later he became Cape May's mayor. Architectural historians and students from the University of Pennsylvania were enlisted in support of the cause.

The results achieved are of historic proportions. During October 1977, the *entire city* of Cape May was designated a National Historic Landmark.

CHAPTER 5

Getting Training and Experience

Archaeology is one of the few scientific fields that gives the non-professional an opportunity to make a contribution. The opportunity to learn and work can be available in your hometown, certainly in your state, or even in some out-of-the-ordinary overseas setting. There are projects to suit every taste and level of experience.

How do you get involved? Here are some of the ways:

• Contact your local state archaeological society (listed in the Appendix). These organizations meet regularly for discussions and lectures, and they publish bulletins and papers concerning local archaeology. Frequently they undertake excavations under professional supervision or with professional assistance.

• Sign up for a course in field archaeology. Scores of colleges and universities offer field-school opportunities during the summer months. There are also field schools operated by private, nonprofit organizations.

• Earn a certificate of proficiency from a state-sponsored archaeological training program. States that offer these programs present seminars in such topics as mapping and surveying and laboratory techniques, in addition to providing training in excavation. Such programs have won high praise. Your local archaeological society will know whether such a program is being offered in your state.

• You can sign up as a volunteer worker at a site overseas. Those who direct overseas excavations prefer workers who have field-school training, but sometimes it is not a requisite. If you're accepted, be prepared to work hard. Also be prepared for hot weather and things that bite.

Field Schools

There is no better introduction to the techniques of archaeological investigation than a field school. These are open to interested amateurs, and you do not need to be involved in a full-time degree program. Supervised by trained professionals, you learn how to wield a pick, shovel, and trowel; how to handle a wheelbarrow and use a sifter. You learn how to record data recovered in the process of digging, and how to deal with perishable artifacts. You learn how to catalogue artifacts. Surveying and photography are other topics studied. You may even get some practical experience in first aid and auto mechanics.

More and more American colleges and universities are offering field-school training each year. A list of these institutions is published each spring by the Society for American Archaeology, in cooperation with the American Anthropological Association. The list can be obtained from the American Anthropological Association, 1703 New Hampshire Avenue, N.W., Washington, D.C. 20009. It's free.

Another list containing the names and addresses of colleges and universities with field-school programs is published each January by Archaeological Institute of America, 53 Park Place, New York, New York 10007. Ask for the *Fieldwork Opportunities Bulletin.* It costs $3.50.

Perhaps the best known of all the field-school programs is that offered by Northwestern University, beginning each spring and continuing through the summer and into the fall, at its Kampsville Archaeological Center in Kampsville, Illinois, about fifty miles north of St. Louis. There are more than eight hundred known archaeological sites in the Kampsville area, including the famous Koster site which is still being excavated and is the chief reason why a fully developed teaching and research center was established at Kampsville. The facility includes a dormitory house, a dining hall, laboratories, a library, and a museum—thirty buildings in all.

Each field-school participant is asked to make a contribution to the Foundation for Illinois Archaeology in the amount of $135 for each one-week session attended. For those participating in field schools for two weeks, a fee of $260 is requested. It costs $375 for three weeks and $480 for four weeks.

The fee covers the cost of instruction, housing, meals, and the use of excavation equipment. A clipboard and a ballpoint pen are about the only things a participant is expected to provide. The fee also includes a one-year membership in the Northwestern archaeological program and this, in turn, includes a subscription to *Early Man*, a newsletter that chronicles activities at the Koster site.

Each week begins with an orientation lecture on Sunday evening at 8 P.M., a session meant to provide background information on the archaeological history of the Illinois Valley. Besides one's participation in archaeological excavations, there are laboratory briefings, artifact-making demonstrations, and ecological field trips. The final event of the week is a lecture-discussion to review what's been achieved.

The Kampsville Center offers training programs for junior and senior high school students, as well as for college undergraduate and graduate students. The junior high school program involves a prehistoric village in the lower Illinois Valley. Students receive training in excavation and preparing field notes, and there's also a special laboratory for those with field experience. Any student eleven to fourteen years of age is eligible to join the program. There are two, two-week sessions each summer. For additional information, including an application form, contact Mrs. Genevieve MacDougall, Carleton-Washburne School, 515 Hibbard Road, Winnetka, IL 60093.

The senior high field school also involves students in the excavation of a prehistoric village site, but in addition, there are seminars, laboratory sessions, and artifact-making demonstrations. Students also participate in experimental projects in which they manufacture objects by using prehistoric technology, including pottery, stone tools, and wooden utensils. Two five-week sessions

Chicago ●

Mississippi River

Illinois River

KAMPSVILLE
ARCHEOLOGICAL
CENTER

● St. Louis

Kampsville Archaeological Center is about a fifty-mile drive from St. Louis.

are offered each summer. Sophomores and juniors from any high school in the country are eligible.

The archaeological field school for college undergraduates, graduate students, plus high school seniors, is a ten-week program. It begins in mid-June and extends until mid-August and is a regular part of Northwestern University's curriculum. It is open to all interested students, regardless of prior training or experience in archaeology.

In recent summers at the Koster site, the fieldwork has involved Horizons eleven and twelve which, respectively, date to 6500 B.C. and 6800 B.C. Along with excavating, students participate in a course titled "Archaeology and the Natural Sciences." This combines lectures, seminars, workshops, and field trips in an effort to explain the relationship that archaeology bears to such fields as botany, geology, biology, zoology, and pollen studies. There are laboratory sessions in which students are instructed in the analysis of artifacts and plant and animal remains. For more information concerning these field schools, write: Ms. Virginia Gilman, Northwestern Archaeological Program, 2000 Sheridan Road, Evanston, IL 60201.

Another exciting program in terms of the site involved and the material being recovered is what is known as the Orendorf Project, a joint project of the Upper Mississippi Valley Archaeological Research Foundation in cooperation with Western Illinois University.

The Orendorf site represents one of the largest of a series of seven political and ceremonial centers called temple towns that flourished in the central Illinois River Valley at different times between A.D. 1050 and 1550. During the two hundred years of its existence, the location Orendorf town was moved several times, resulting in a series of separate settlements, the most fully occupied of which contained large public buildings and many private structures surrounding a public square. It served as the administrative center for a series of smaller villages and single-family farmsteads, one indication of the high level of social organization attained. Located on a bluff overlooking the Illinois River Valley, Orendorf town was ringed by a series of stockade lines that served to provide defensive strength.

Through 1978, more than eleven acres of habitation area had been excavated, bringing to light some two hundred different structures, twenty-two hundred nonstructural features, such as hearths, storage pits, and stockade lines, plus an enormous array of artifacts, including more than one million pieces of pottery, tools, pipes, weapons, ornaments, corncobs, bones, shells, et cetera. Those supervising the project believe that work has already provided sufficient data to make possible the most thorough reconstruction of a Middle Mississippian temple yet undertaken.

As all of this may imply, participants in the Orendorf field-school program are not simply involved in a classroom exercise, but serious research as well. Instruction is provided in excavation, recording, mapping, and laboratory techniques.

Don't look upon it as an organized vacation; hard work is involved. The normal work week consists of five ten-hour days, plus an additional work day every other Saturday. In addition, there are lectures to attend at least one evening a week. "When you first get into the field," one information bulletin advises, "you may find you are bothered by heat, dust, sore muscles, and a short temper.

"But these will pass," the bulletin advises.

The base of operations is a modern school building in Canton, Illinois, a town of fifteen thousand about thirty miles southwest of Peoria. Sleeping accommodations are "barracks" style. Breakfast usually consists of cold cereal, toast, milk, and coffee; lunch, a peanut butter and jelly sandwich, plus a piece of fruit. A large meal is served in the evening. Students perform all the maintenance chores in the living areas and take turns helping to cook.

To take part in the Orendorf field school, good health and a good attitude are the chief requirements. Minimum age is sixteen. For a nine-week stay, the cost is $200. A shorter stay is possible, but project officials don't recommend it. Student fees go toward helping to underwrite project expenses.

For additional information, write: The Orendorf Project, Upper Mississippi Valley Archaeological Research Foundation, 2216 West 112th Street, Chicago, IL 60643.

In California, UCLA Extension College, in cooperation with the University's Institute of Archaeology, offers a certification program that is notable both for its scholarly aspects and the excellence of its technical training. No matter your particular field of interest, you can select courses that should be fulfilling. And the course list from which you choose is, to a large extent, the course

"AMERICA'S   STONEHENGE"

MYSTERY HILL

North Salem, New Hampshire

DATES OPEN: (weather permitting)
DAILY—APRIL 1st through DEC. 1st

HOURS
SPRING & FALL—10:30 A.M. to 4:00 P.M.
SUMMER—9:30 A.M. to 5:30 P.M.

ADMISSIONS
Adults $2.50   Children (6-12) $1.00
Students (13-17) Military Personnel and
Senior Citizens $2.00
Children under 6 — FREE
GROUP RATES (20 or more)
Age 12 and under .75 — Age 13 and older $1.50
Schools — Thru 8th Grade .75 — 9th Grade and over $1.50

Group arrangements may be made by calling or writing:
MYSTERY HILL   NO. SALEM, N.H.
TEL. 603-893-8300

Your admission goes toward the preservation and further
research of this important archæological site.

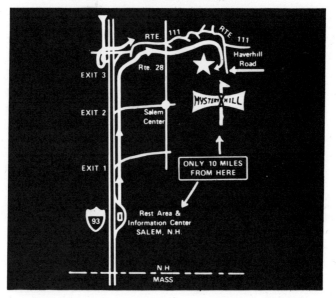

"America's Stonehenge" is what its supporters call Mystery Hill.

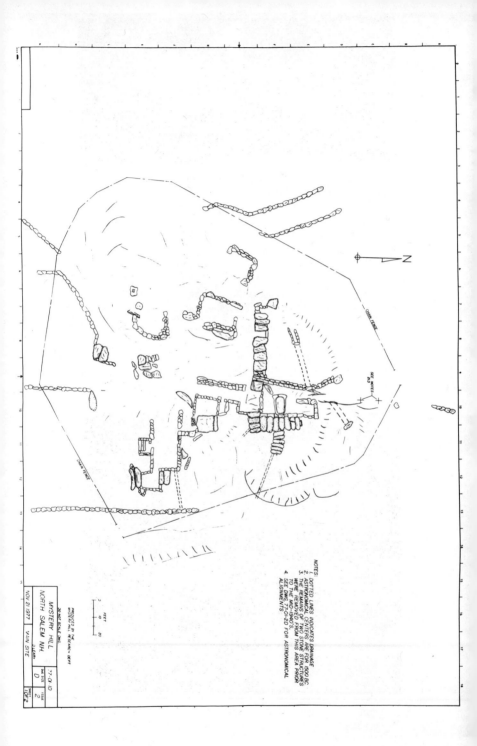

NOTES:
1. DOTTED LINES INDICATES DRAINAGE
2. ASTRONOMICAL CENTERS ARE FOR 1700 B.C.
3. THE REMAINS OF TWO STONE STRUCTURES WERE REMOVED FROM THIS AREA PRIOR TO THE MID-1940'S.
4. SEE DWG. 77-0-20 FOR ASTRONOMICAL ALIGNMENTS

SEE NOTES #3

STONE EDGE

STONE FENCE

N

FEET
20 0 5

PRODUCED BY THE
MYSTERY HILL RESEARCH DEPT.
DO NOT SCALE DWG.

MYSTERY HILL
NORTH SALEM NH
MAIN SITE

NOV 21 1977

DWG. NO. 77-0-10
DWG SIZE D
ITEM 2
SHEET 1 OF 2

Above, at Mystery Hill, this is called a Sacrificial Table. But is it merely a cider press? (George Sullivan)

Left, astronomical alignment stone—or a random boulder? (George Sullivan)

Oracle chamber—or a root cellar? (George Sullivan)

list that comprises UCLA's degree program, one offered by a staff of more then twenty archaeologists. Not only is the program a means of broadening your knowledge of archaeology, but it can lead directly to participation on a volunteer basis in one or more of the dozens of field research projects in which university archaeologists are involved.

To obtain a certificate, you must complete at least ten courses: five technical courses and five culture-area courses. The technical courses from which you choose include:

Strategy of Archaeology

Archaeological Research Techniques

Laboratory Analysis in Archaeology

History of Archaeology

Dating Techniques of Archaeology

Technical Skills in Archaeology

Introduction to Biostatistics

Introduction to Computing

Field Training: Archaeology

Fieldwork: Archaeology

Special Studies in Anthropology

Topic Orientation in Anthropology

The culture-area courses are:

Peoples of California: Prehistory

Archaeology of North America

Ancient Civilizations of Western Middle America

Ancient Civilizations of Eastern Middle America

Ancient Civilizations of Andean South America

Old Stone Archaeology

European Archaeology: Proto-Civilizations of Europe

European Archaeology: The Bronze Age

Origins of Old World Civilization

Egyptian Art and Archaeology

Art of the Ancient Near East

History of Ancient Egypt

History of Ancient Mesopotamia and Syria

Introduction to Near Eastern Archaeology

Archaeology of Mesopotamia

Archaeology of Palestine

Archaeology and the Minor Arts of Islam in the Middle Ages

Greek Art   The Early Art of India

Hellenistic Art   Archaeology in Early and Mod-
                                             ern China
Roman Art
                                         Special Topics in Archaeology
Classical Archaeology

To be admitted to the certificate program, you must demonstrate the ability to perform at what the university terms "the
upper division level." You do this by submitting one or more of
the following: a transcript of your college record, a brief state-
ment of purpose, and letters of recommendation. For more information concerning the program, write: Institute of Archaeology,
University of California, Los Angeles, 405 Hilgard Avenue, Los
Angeles, CA 90024.

Local community colleges are also beginning to offer an increasing number of courses covering one aspect or another of archaeology, and often their instruction involves methods and techniques. Not untypical is a program for "community avocational
archaeologists" given by Norwalk Community College in Norwalk,
Connecticut. Those certified through the program have sufficient
training to enable them to help in surveying the Connecticut area
for new archaeological sites, assist local historical societies in
the identification of materials in their collections, and aid local
professional archaeologists in excavating, keeping records, and
analyzing finds.

Other Field-School Opportunities

Scientists and scholars often need funds and volunteers to be
able to conduct their investigations. An organization called Earthwatch is helping to supply both. Specifically, the organization
enrolls members of the public who wish to make a financial contribution to a particular research project, in return for an opportunity to work on that project in the field as a research assistant.

Expeditions, usually two to three weeks in length, are open to
anyone, ages sixteen to seventy-five. No special skills are required;
participants are taught what they need to know in the field.

Expedition costs for an individual range from $450 to $1,000.
This contribution (which is tax deductible) covers expenses for

food, lodging (which may range from a tent to a comfortable guest house), ground transportation during the term of the expedition, and the use of equipment, tools, and scientific instruments. The contribution does not include transportation costs to and from your home to where you join the expedition at what is called the "staging area." You can become an Earthwatch member for $20. Membership entitles you to receive catalogues describing the forthcoming expeditions.

During one recent summer, a three-week expedition ($775) saw volunteers working along the banks of the Rio Motagua near the town of San Agustin Acasaguastlan in southeastern Guatemala under the supervision of archaeologist Gary Walters of the University of Missouri. Walters had previously found Mayan remains that possibly revealed a major source of pre-Columbian jade. The Earthwatch project was intended to define local culture and its geophysical boundaries in an effort to pinpoint the jade source. This involved excavation of the settlement and the jade workshops. "Participants should be in excellent physical condition," said a catalogue description of the project, "and prepared to work long hours in the hot sun."

Other projects have taken students to Mexico and El Salvador in Central America; to Ghana, Kenya, and Sudan in Africa; to Scotland, Ireland, England, and Greece in Europe; to Israel in the Middle East; and to Peru in South America.

Still others have been offered within the United States. For example, Dr. John McDaniel of Washington and Lee University has directed Earthwatch assistants in the excavation of Liberty Hall, an academy founded on Mulberry Hill near Roanoke, Virginia, by Scotch-Irish settlers in 1776. Archaeologists working there are seeking to establish what life was like for young scholars and instructors in a frontier community of the 1700s.

Earthwatch participants, housed in comfortable campus dormitories, helped in excavating, surveying, photography, the interpretation of geological data, and the preparation of drawings. Some evenings were spent in the laboratory, analyzing and classifying recovered artifacts. The three-week expedition cost $650.

Other expeditions within the United States have included these sites: Baker Cave, Texas, a project directed by Dr. Thomas R. Hester of the University of Texas and Dr. Robert F. Heizer of the University of California; western Connecticut, with work supervised by Dr. Roger Moeller of the American Indian Archaeological Institute; St. Mary's City, Maryland; Drakes Bay, California; and the Mogollon Pueblo, New Mexico.

For more information, contact Earthwatch, 10 Juniper Road, Box 127, Belmont, MA 02178.

The American Indian Archaeological Institute is another private organization that offers practical instruction in field archaeology. Located in Washington, Connecticut, the institute attracts pilgrims from as many as a dozen different states. Volunteer excavators have contributed meaningfully to the institute's field research program.

Actually, its field schools are only one aspect of the institute's program. At its research and visitors' center, the AIAI presents exhibits and education programs for the general public, and offers library facilities to serious students. A site reconstruction adjacent to the center illustrates excavation procedures and the methods used in discovering and interpreting artifacts.

The history of the institute serves as an interesting example of what can be accomplished by a dedicated and enthusiastic band of amateur archaeologists. In the late 1960s, seven residents of the village of Washington, population, thirty-three hundred, founded the Shepaug Valley Archaeological Society to seek out arrowheads and pottery for the local historical society. For two summers, they dug at several sites they knew of in northwestern Connecticut. They found little. "Then, in 1970, the lid blew off," according to Edmund (Ned) Swigart, for twenty years a teacher at a local private school. "We put down a test square in the middle of what looked like dwelling sites and we found two levels of dwellings. They dated back to about 1500 B.C. They were, at the time, the earliest dwellings ever found in Connecticut."

Swigart and his colleagues were eager to have their discoveries properly researched and documented, and they wanted their finds attractively displayed. They began visiting museums in the east, from Boston to Washington, D.C. But everywhere they went, they were told the same thing: "We don't have the resources to do research for you. We don't have the space for displays."

Swigart realized that anything they wanted to have done, they were going to have to do themselves. In 1971, the institute was incorporated and a board of directors was formed that included a lawyer, a successful businessman, an engineer, a member of the state historical commission, a public relations specialist, a woman with experience in political organizing. Swigart himself became the president of the institute.

Fund raising was the next step. A goal of $300,000 was established. The Kresge Foundation offered a grant of $50,000 if the board could raise $250,000 within a year. Two days before the deadline, the board was $20,000 short of the $250,000. "All of a sudden we started getting letters from people we'd never heard of, with checks," Swigart says. "The father of a former student of mine sent a check for $10,000." At the final board meeting, they were still $6,000 short. But the meeting was interrupted by telephone calls from two foundations, one contributing $2,000 and the other $3,000. Then a board member nudged them over the top with $1,000. "We made it with two minutes to spare," says Swigart.

Swigart next turned his attention toward forming an advisory board to plan the museum. As a curator, he hired Roger Moeller, a bearded young man who had recently been awarded a doctorate in archaeology from the State University in Buffalo.

Ground was broken in 1974, and a modernistic, circular museum was staffed and in operation by the next year. It was forecast that the building would be spacious enough for ten years, and that a staff of two or three would be sufficient to handle activities. But by 1976, it was obvious that the museum had run out of space, and a new wing was added. The number of staff members grew to twelve. At a time when private institutions everywhere were struggling with economic pressure that threatened their survival, why should a museum dedicated to Indian archaeology in western Connecticut continue to thrive? Swigart says this: "I guess there was an enormous void nobody knew about. There was apparently a real need for an archaeological center in this area. People support it. They want to dig into the past."

The institute gained widespread prominence late in 1977 when Dr. Moeller and a team of volunteers found clear-cut evidence of human habitation in Connecticut far earlier than had previously been believed.

Excavating on a site in a field adjacent to the Shepaug River in Washington Depot, Connecticut, a volunteer worker found a Clovis spearpoint, typical of those used by hunters who followed the retreating glaciers north during the last Ice Age. "It was the group's first day in the field," Dr. Moeller recalls, "and I had just finished showing them the proper way to use a trowel and described the sound a trowel makes when it scrapes against flint. I had turned my back and I heard a ringing sound. Andy [Postman] picked this thing up between his thumb and forefinger and said, 'Is this anything?' Later in the day, we found the other half about an inch away."

Carbon-dating tests later confirmed that the point dated back 10,190 years (plus or minus 300 years B.P.), or to approximately 8240 B.C. The oldest previous discovery in Connecticut dated to 3000 B.C.

The Washington Depot project also produced evidence that seemed to disprove the long-held theory that Indians in the area traveled to the Hudson River Valley for the flint they needed for their arrowheads and spearpoints. On a hunch, Steve Post, another of the institute archaeologists, went wading in the Shepaug River during a lunch break, and he came back with two big chunks of flint that had washed down from a mountain ridge somewhere.

Later in the year, archaeologists and volunteers began scouring the Shepaug Valley for the source of that flint. Above Bee Brook, a tributary of the Shepaug, in the town of Marbledale, they found deposits of flint close-by local marble formations. In some cases, the flint had a right-angle facet, indicating the stone had been cut away.

During the summer of 1978, institute archaeologists and volunteer workers conducted a wide-ranging survey program to establish new sites, both prehistoric and historic. More than fifty sites were found as a result of the project, and plans have been formulated to excavate many of them.

State-Operated Training Programs

Another excellent way to obtain archaeological training and experience is through a state certification program. These are usually offered in cooperation with the state archaeological society. Unfortunately, only a handful of states offer such programs, but out-of-state residents are welcome to enroll.

Perhaps the best-known program of this type is that offered

each summer by the Arkansas Archaeological Survey in conjunction with the Arkansas Archaeological Society. Every phase of the program is under the direct supervision of a professional. Training is offered in a wide range of archaeological activity, including excavation, site surveying, and laboratory processing. The program, which has been scheduled each year since 1964, is usually offered during the last three weeks of June.

The costs involved are minimal. You first have to become a member of the Arkansas Archaeological Society; that costs $6.00. Then there is a $5.00 registration fee for each participant, plus another $5.00 fee for each formal certification program in which you participate.

Recent training programs have been conducted on a site in the northwest corner of the state (not far from the borders of Oklahoma and Missouri). Some participants have camped—at no charge—in their own tents at a field adjacent to the site. A local school provided bathing facilities and an evening meal (for an additional fee). Children are welcome, as long as someone comes to watch them. Youngsters sixteen years old or younger who register for training must be accompanied by an adult.

The various seminars offered, each approximately twenty hours in length, are taught in three- to four-hour sessions and include lectures, demonstrations, and workshops. Normally, seminars are scheduled over a five-day period. As a textbook, *An Introduction to Prehistoric Archaeology* is recommended.

There are several levels of instruction. For beginners, there's the basic, or provisional, level, with three categories of instruction: site surveyor, crew member, and lab technician. In each course, you're closely supervised.

If you seek certification as a site surveyor on the provisional level, you must file reports on five sites based on your own reconnaissance. You must use standard report forms and each report must include a detailed map. All recovered material must be properly categorized with a site number on each artifact.

If you wish to be certified as a provisional crew member, you must take part in a minimum of forty hours of excavation work under professional supervision. You must demonstrate the ability to lay out a simple grid and properly record excavation data. You must be able to recognize and excavate at least two different types of sites, such as posthole or fire pit, and show the ability to properly cope with at least two different types of stratigraphic arrangements—natural strata, cultural strata, strata in middens, or various mound construction stages, et cetera.

To become certified as a lab technician on a provisional basis, you must perform a minimum of forty hours of laboratory work under supervision, demonstrating the proper techniques in washing, numbering, and rough sorting artifacts of various types—stone, shell, bone, ceramic, and so on. Naturally, artifacts recovered and records compiled are retained by the Arkansas Archaeological Survey for the benefit of the people of Arkansas.

For additional information on the program, write: Coordinating Office, Arkansas Archaeological Survey, University of Arkansas Museum, Fayetteville, AR 72701.

The Kansas State Historical Society and the Kansas Anthropological Association have recently undertaken a training program for association members that covers the basic techniques in what is termed "Plains Archaeology." Closely patterned after the Arkansas program, training in Kansas covers site surveying, excavation procedures, laboratory techniques, and the preparation of exhibits.

The program is expected to produce twofold benefits. For the trainee, it offers the opportunity to be exposed to and learn archaeological theories and procedures. The program will benefit the field of archaeology in general by increasing the number of individuals who are qualified to report sites, keep alert for areas of needed salvage, and generally assist in the collecting and recording of information.

For more information, contact the Kansas State Archaeologist, Kansas State Historical Society, Tenth and Jackson Streets, Topeka, KS 66612.

In Iowa, the office of the state archaeologist in cooperation with the state archaeological society has developed a certification program, the basic objective of which is to train individuals to assist career archaeologists in field and laboratory work. But it has produced several overriding benefits. It has served to increase the frequency of site reporting throughout the state and it has worked to upgrade the quality of information set down in such reports. It has also worked to impress upon beginners the importance of good planning, of properly conducting the site survey and the excavation itself. It has discouraged pothunting.

The program certifies each beginner in one of three categories:

as a site surveyor, field technician, or laboratory technician. Applicants must possess certain pieces of basic information, including the following:

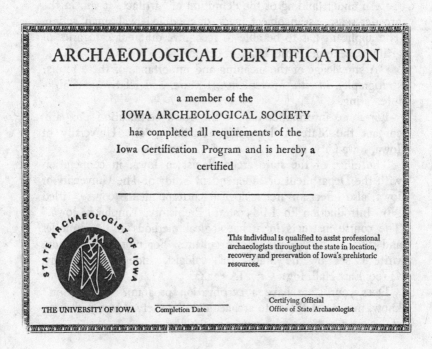

ARCHAEOLOGICAL CERTIFICATION

a member of the
IOWA ARCHEOLOGICAL SOCIETY
has completed all requirements of the
Iowa Certification Program and is hereby a
certified

This individual is qualified to assist professional archaeologists throughout the state in location, recovery and preservation of Iowa's prehistoric resources.

THE UNIVERSITY OF IOWA   Completion Date

Certifying Official
Office of State Archaeologist

IOWA ARCHEOLOGICAL SOCIETY

Member

CERTIFIED

State Archaeologist

Certifying Official

The University of Iowa

This certificate and ID card go to individuals completing Iowa's archaeological training program.

• An understanding of the definition of the term "site" in its broader sense, as being any place where there is evidence of human activity.

• An understanding of the definition of "artifact," again in the broader sense, as an object made or modified by human action. The applicant has to be able to recognize different categories of artifacts, ceramic, lithic, bone, et cetera.

• A knowledge of the meaning and importance of these terms: stratigraphy, *in situ*, provenience, feature, and relative and absolute dating.

For more information about the Iowa certification program, contact the State Archaeologist, Eastlawn, The University of Iowa, Iowa City, IA 52242.

The office of the state archaeologist in Iowa, in cooperation with the Department of Independent Study of The University of Iowa, also offers an archaeological correspondence course, titled "An Introduction to Midwestern Prehistory; Emphasis Iowa." The course instructs in archaeological methods and techniques and discusses Iowa's prehistoric cultures. For more information, write Office of the State Archaeologist, Independent Study, C-109, East Hall, Iowa City, IA 52242.

Does your state have a certification program? If you don't know, inquire at the state archaeological society. More and more states are adopting such programs each year.

Archaeology and the Federal Government

Several agencies of the federal government are involved in archaeological programs of one type or another, but most of the archaeological activity on the federal level is controlled and managed by the National Park Service (of the U. S. Department of the Interior). These efforts go back to 1945, a time when Congress began appropriating funds for the construction of a system of multipurpose dams in river basins throughout the country. Professional archaeologists realized that this construction program, plus the huge reservoirs that were to result, would obliterate hundreds upon hundreds of square miles of cultural resources. Out of this concern came the Interagency Archaeological Salvage Program, which involved the Bureau of Reclamation, the Corps of Engineers, the Smithsonian Institution, and the National Park Service, the coordinating agency for the program. In pursuing archaeological salvage operations, the Park Service drew upon the personnel, facilities, and resources of more than fifty colleges, universities, and museums.

Since that time, the Park Service's responsibilities have been broadened. The Reservoir Act of 1960 (Public Law 86-523) gave the Park Service major responsibility for the preservation of archaeological data that might be lost specifically through dam construction. In 1974, this law was amended with the passage of the Archaeological and Historic Preservation Act (Public Law 93-291) that placed upon the Secretary of the Interior, i.e., the Park Service, the responsibility of administrating a nationwide program for the recovery, protection, and preservation of scientific, historic, and prehistoric data, which might possibly be damaged or destroyed as a result of a wide range of federal construction activity. This activity includes not only dam construction, but pipeline and sewer construction, airport construction, power-line development, and all the rest.

This does not mean that the Park Service itself undertakes the recovery of endangered archaeological resources. Instead, it contracts with scientific and educational institutions to perform this work, then supervises their efforts. For more information on federal efforts toward the recovery and preservation of archaeological resources in your area, contact the office of the chief archaeologist of the National Park Service, or the appropriate regional office:

Office of Chief Archaeologist
Division of Archaeology and Anthropology
National Park Service
Department of the Interior
Washington, D.C. 20240

Southeast Archaeological Center
National Park Service
P.O. Box 2416
Tallahassee, FL 32304
   (Alabama, Florida, Georgia, Kentucky, Mississippi, North Carolina, Puerto Rico, South Carolina, Tennessee, Virgin Islands)

Midwest Archeological Center
National Park Service
2605 North 27th Street
Lincoln, NB 68504
  (Colorado, Iowa, Kansas, Missouri, Montana, Nebraska,
  North Dakota, South Dakota, Utah, Wyoming)

Arizona Archeological Center
National Park Service
P.O. Box 49008
Tucson, AZ 85717
  (Arizona, California, Hawaii, Nevada)

Regional Archeologist
Northeast Region
National Park Service
143 South Third Street
Philadelphia, PA 19106
  (Connecticut, Delaware, Illinois, Indiana, Maine, Mary-
  land, Massachusetts, Michigan, Minnesota, New Hamp-
  shire, New Jersey, New York, Ohio, Pennsylvania, Rhode
  Island, Vermont, Virginia, West Virginia, Wisconsin)

Regional Archeologist
Pacific Northwest Region
National Park Service
4th and Pike Building
1424 4th Avenue
Seattle, WA 98101
  (Alaska, Idaho, Oregon, Washington)

Regional Archeologist
Southwest Region
National Park Service
P.O. Box 728
Santa Fe, NM 87501
  (Arkansas, Louisiana, New Mexico, Oklahoma, Texas)

Archaeologically related activities conducted by the U. S. Forest
Service involve Forest Service land. When a road or other type of
construction is proposed for National Forest Service land, an archaeological survey of the area affected is undertaken, with the

work supervised by a professional archaeologist. If a site meets the criterion for the National Register, it is nominated. Provisions are made to protect and preserve the site.

The Forest Service also issues permits to educational or state organizations for archaeological research. Such work is also conducted by Forest Service staff archaeologists.

For more information on Forest Service activity, write: Chief, U. S. Forest Service, Department of Agriculture, Washington, D.C. 20250.

The Department of Housing and Urban Development and the Department of Transportation can also get involved in archaeological endeavors. Under certain conditions, the Department of Housing and Urban Development is authorized to make grants for surveys of archaeological sites and to fund, on a matching basis, technical assistance and investigation.

As for the Department of Transportation, it has been charged with the responsibility of making a special effort to preserve historic sites when undertaking construction activity, i.e., highway building. And "historic sites" can mean archaeological sites. Matching funds for archaeological research are provided a state highway department on the same basis as other construction costs.

Archaeology in Canada

Several years ago, near the town of Sheguiandah at the northern tip of Georgian Bay in the province of Ontario, archaeologists unearthed crude quartzite stone tools that have become the subject of considerable controversy. The artifacts were recovered amid what appeared to be an aggregation of glacial clay, rock, and sand. To the archaeologists who made the discovery, it looked as if the front edge of a glacier had pushed what had once been an ancient habitation site for a short distance.

If that is true, the implication is of great consequence. It means that the individuals who made those tools lived in Canada *before* the last of the glacial advances. The corollary is that man was living on this continent much earlier than believed. Indeed, Dr. Thomas E. Lee, who was in charge of the excavation, estimated the artifacts to be thirty thousand years old. Not all archaeologists agree with Dr. Lee's findings, however.

It is fitting that this discovery was made in Ontario, for the Ontario Archaeological Society (P.O. Box 241, Postal Station P, Toronto, Ontario M5S 2S8) is the most active organization of its type in all of Canada. With chapters in Ottawa, London, Windsor, and Simcoe County, the society provides personnel for excavations, sponsors symposiums, and offers training sessions in various aspects of archaeological research—pottery analysis, bone analysis, et cetera. The society publishes six newsletters and two attractive, informative journals each year.

A booklet titled *Archaeology and the Law in Ontario* is a well-written overview of archaeological activity in the province. It's free; request a copy from the Ontario Government Bookstore (88 Bay Street, Toronto, Ontario M7A 1Y7). The "Law" is only one of the booklet's concerns; it examines typical historic and prehistoric sites and surveys archaeological opportunities throughout the province.

The Manitoba Archaeological Society (Box 1171, Winnipeg, Manitoba R3C 2Y4) is very active, too, offering a variety of educational opportunities for members, including excavation work. The society conducts monthly meetings and publishes a quarterly journal. Its publication, *Ten Thousand Years; Archaeology in Manitoba,* is must reading.

In Manitoba, Ontario, and the other provinces, much of the archaeological fieldwork is sponsored by leading private or provincial universities. Write to them for information. For instance, one recent summer the University of Calgary sought volunteers for research and rescue work at Crows Nest Pass, Alberta, a possible Clovis site. The University of Manitoba offered field-school training at an early nineteenth-century fort. The principal universities are:

University of British Columbia
Vancouver, British Columbia
  V6T 1W5

University of Alberta
Edmonton, Alberta T6G 2E1

University of Calgary
2920 24th Avenue, N.W.
Calgary, Alberta T2N 1N4

McMaster University
Hamilton, Ontario L8S 4L8

University of Ottawa
Ottawa, Ontario K1N 6N5

University of Toronto
Toronto, Ontario M5S 1A1

McGill University
P.O. Box 6070
Montreal, Quebec H3C 3G1

University of New Brunswick
Fredericton, New Brunswick
  E3B 5A3

University of Regina
Regina, Saskatchewan S4S 0R2

University of Saskatchewan
Saskatoon, Saskatchewan S7N
  0W0

University of Manitoba
Fort Garry Campus
Winnipeg, Manitoba R3T 2N2

University of Winnipeg
515 Portage Avenue
Winnipeg, Manitoba R3B 2E9

University of Prince Edward Island
P.O. Box 1358
Charlottetown, Prince Edward
  Island C1A 4P3

Memorial University of Newfoundland
Elizabeth Avenue
St. John's, Newfoundland A1C
  5S7

OVERSEAS OPPORTUNITIES

> WANTED: *Person or persons wishing to spend summer vacations in foreign country performing tedious manual labor five days a week. Duties include digging up dirt with hand tools and sifting it; brushing small stone chips and ceramic pieces, and washing and sorting these items. Long hours. No pay.*

Unless you would consider answering an advertisement similar to the one above, forget about joining an overseas excavation team. Working conditions can be strenuous. Don't expect fine food, air conditioning, or even flush toilets. The only fresh meat may be local game. Water may have to be carried for miles. There may be no bathing facilities, except in the local river.

But there is the other side of the coin. Volunteers talk about the joy and awe of finding or even holding a tool that was used thousands of years ago. There's the fascination of putting together bits of stone and chips of pottery to add to the fund of human history.

The opportunities to learn and work overseas are somewhat comparable to those in this country. You can sign up for a field course in archaeology presented by an American college at the foreign site. Or you can join an excavation being underwritten by a foreign government or university as a volunteer. Some projects will be happy to take you on, even if you have had no field-school training; others won't.

There are fieldwork opportunities in just about every part of the

world. At some sites, important discoveries are waiting to be
made. Even in Egypt, where archaeologists have been working for
decades, there is still much remaining beneath the ground. The
graves of the priest-kings of Egypt's twenty-first dynasty, in the
tenth and eleventh centuries, and those of the thirtieth dynasty, in the fourth century B.C., have never been found. The best
prospects for future discoveries are believed to lie in the north of
Egypt, near the Mediterranean. Boston University offered a field
school in Marea, near Alexandria, during the summer of 1979.

The first real archaeological investigation in history is said to
date to 1719, when the Austrian Prince d'Elboef began to excavate the site of Herculaneum, an ancient city of Italy near Naples,
destroyed with Pompeii by the eruption of Mount Vesuvius in
A.D. 79. Since then, Roman archaeology has become well known
for its diversity. It can involve stratigraphic excavations based on
an analysis of pottery styles or the interpretation of great monuments of sculpture and architecture. One recent field school concerned the archaeology of a Neolithic site in Southern Italy, while
another emphasized measuring and drawing ancient Roman
buildings.

The ancient Greeks are said to be the first of the classical archaeologists. As soon as they began to speculate about their own
history, they started paying special attention to the monuments
and works of art about them. Recently, both the University of Illinois and Indiana University sought volunteers to work at sites in
Greece.

During recent summers, field schools were offered in Costa Rica
and El Salvador, in Jordan and Cyprus, in Tunisia, Spain, and
Yugoslavia. The greatest number of opportunities for overseas
fieldwork are in England and Israel. A section is devoted to each
of these countries in the pages that follow.

What expenses should you figure on? There's your tuition, of
course, if you sign up for a field school. There's your airfare.
You'll have to pay for your room and board, too, although this
may not amount to more than $10 or $15 a day. At some sites,
room and board are furnished without charge, although this usually only applies when the volunteer has useful skills to offer, skills
such as drawing, mapping, photography, or bone analysis, and
so on.

Sometimes there are daily transportation expenses getting to and from the site. And there can be weekend travel and entertainment expenses.

For up-to-date information on fieldwork opportunities overseas, obtain a copy of the *Fieldwork Opportunities Bulletin* mentioned earlier in this chapter. It is published each January by the Archaeological Institute of America (53 Park Place, New York, NY 10007), and it costs $3.50. It describes about one hundred field schools and opportunities for volunteer work, not only overseas, but in Canada and the United States as well.

The Archaeology Abroad Service provides similar information about archaeological projects in countries other than England. The organization maintains a file of volunteers, students, and specialists that excavation organizers often consult when recruiting personnel. Some organizers will accept persons with limited experience.

To obtain the AAS lists, send an international money order for the equivalent of two pounds (something less than $3.50; check with your bank) to: Archaeology Abroad Service, 31–34 Gordon Square, London WCIH OPY, England.

Bear in mind when selecting an overseas site that politics—international politics, that is—have to be considered. Certain developing countries, often potentially rich in artifacts, are reluctant to grant excavation permits. Their reasons cover a wide range. Some countries simply do not like the idea of Western scientists probing into their culture. Dr. Froelich Rainey, director of the University of Pennsylvania Museum, offers this explanation: "Westerners come in and poke around and study their culture as if they had some superior right to investigate these other people as little brown brothers or as some strange exotic people. The assumption that Western Europeans and Americans know better about archaeology than the so-called underdeveloped countries is anathema to most countries around the world these days."

Other nations are disturbed by the increasing number of incidents of archaeological looting. Most of the stealing is done by professional thieves, however. Professor Rainey blames it on inflation, on the fact that prices for ancient objects are being pumped up "beyond all reasonable value."

A nation's self-image can also be a problem. Archaeological and anthropological investigation can produce unflattering facts about a culture. When a country's leaders are seeking to build a glowing

self-image for the citizenry, they don't want archaeologists or anthropologists frustrating their efforts.

If you are planning to travel abroad, and the trip concerns archaeological investigation or education, you should be aware of
the Council in International Educational Exchange (777 United
Nations Plaza, New York, NY 10017). An organization whose
purpose it is to facilitate and encourage all aspects of educational
travel and exchange by students, teachers, and educational admin-
istrators, the council can help in arranging low-cost transportation
abroad, as well as travel within the countries of Europe, Asia,
Africa, and the Middle East. In addition, the organization provides access to inexpensive tours, car rentals, and insurance plans.

The council also administers "work abroad" programs through
which American college students can arrange for temporary jobs
in Britain, France, Germany, Ireland, and Israel.

The council publishes and copublishes more than thirty travel
guidebooks. They include *The Student Travel Catalog*, described
as the "how to" travel book for the academic community; *The
Whole World Handbook*; *A Student Guide to Work, Study, and
Travel Abroad*; and *The Student Guide to Latin America*.

Opportunities in Israel—Archaeology is a national pastime in
Israel. Excavations receive extensive press, radio, and television
coverage. The Department of Antiquities and Museums in the
Ministry of Education conducts nationwide surveys, protects ancient sites, arranges for the preservation and display of finds, and
provides assistance for local and foreign archaeologists. In addition to the Israel Museum and the Rockefeller Museum, a number of towns and villages maintain local collections, many of
which display the discoveries of amateur archaeologists from the
neighborhood.

Those supervising excavation sites in Israel have a reputation
for accepting persons with limited experience, and indeed, with
no experience at all. For a free list of current excavations, write
the Ministry of Education and Culture, Department of Antiquities and Museums, P.O. Box 586, Jerusalem, 9100 Israel.

Much of the archaeological work is centered in Jerusalem. "All
Jerusalem is ancient ground," says an Israeli archaeologist. "Wherever we dig, we find something."

It's true. Because of its enormous historical and religious
significance, Jerusalem has been one of archaeology's chief attrac-

tions for more than a century. However, because the city was in-habited by ancient civilizations on an almost layer-by-layer basis, added to the fact that many of the sites are sacred to one religion or another, problems of archaeological research are much more challenging than usual.

Some of the most exciting work concerns the excavation of the Second Temple of Jerusalem. Some two thousand years ago, Jesus Christ debated with the priests and scribes and overturned the tables of the money changers in this same temple. The temple structure was destroyed in A.D. 70, but Israeli archaeologists, helped by volunteer labor, have excavated the southern and west-ern walls that enclosed the temple site and also many of the struc-tures just outside them.

The Second Temple is actually the *third* Temple to have occu-pied the site. Solomon's Temple, the first, was demolished in 587 B.C. The second, a more modest structure, was destroyed about 20 B.C. Construction of what is now known as the Second Temple began at approximately that time. According to Josephus, the Jew-ish general and historian who lived from A.D. 37 to the end of the century, the temple was the crowning achievement of King Herod the Great, who built some of Israel's biggest and most enduring structures.

The Second Temple, which, like those that preceded it, occu-pied a hill with a commanding view of the city, was of enormous size. Construction began with the erection of four massive retain-ing walls, one of which, the western wall, was 1,620 feet long. The southern wall was 930 feet long. Once the walls were up, the area within was filled and leveled, making an area of about thirty-five acres.

Before archaeological excavation began, only the upper portion of the walls was visible. But in the more than decade of digging, the temple walls have been unearthed down to the level they were in Christ's time.

A flight of steps, each one over two hundred feet in length, which once led to a massive gate in the temple wall, has also been revealed. At the foot of the steps, there now lie the remains of a vast plaza, with what was once a bathhouse opening off of it.

All four gospels put Christ at the temple during the last week of His life. "There is a ninety per cent chance that Christ walked up those steps," says Mahen Magen, an Israeli archaeologist. It is

theorized that Christ, coming directly to the temple from the
Mount of Olives to the east, entered the plaza, climbed the stairs,
crossed the street, and passed through the gate. But before doing
so, He may well have stopped at the bathhouse for a ritual bath, a
custom followed by pilgrims before entering the temple's sacred
areas.

If this is true, if Christ did, in fact, ascend the temple stairs, if
He walked upon the stones that are outside the temple's southern
wall, then the site has exceptional importance. The most that can
be said for other sites and structures in Jerusalem, Bethlehem,
Nazareth, and other areas that latter-day Christians visit, is that
they *may* have been associated with Christ (the claims of the
travel brochures notwithstanding).

For instance, new archaeological evidence documents that the
stone floor of the Convent of Notre Dame de Sion, long regarded
as the floor of the structure where Christ was tried by Pontius
Pilate, was actually constructed about one full century after that
time.

Archaeologist Kathleen Kenyon, who, throughout most of the
1960s, conducted many excavations in and just outside Jerusalem,
was permitted to make one small excavation near the Church of
the Holy Sepulcher, the traditional site of Christ's burial. What
she found indicated that the site was outside the city's first-century
wall, where the New Testament fixed the place of burial. But the
church that now occupies the site prevented Kenyon or any succeeding archaeologists from digging for evidence that would defi-
nitely connect the site with Christ.

So the temple stairs and its adjacent plaza may be the only
places in Jerusalem of which archaeologists can say: "Christ
walked here." Volunteer work at the temple site is manual work—
shoveling, hauling dirt-filled baskets, and washing pottery shards.
It goes on just about all year round. Volunteers must be between
eighteen and thirty-five and be prepared to present a doctor's
certificate confirming their good health. The minimum work period is two weeks. The work day is long, from 7 A.M. to 6 P.M.,
and the site is active six days a week. It's not an assignment for
the soft or fragile.

If you're still interested, write The Temple Mount Excavations,
P.O. Box 7041, Jerusalem, Israel. Indicate your training, experience, and period of availability.

Other structures of Christ's time have also been excavated in Jerusalem, and it is reasonable to speculate that if they were not entered by Him, He at least saw them. Professor Nachman Avigad of Hebrew University, one of Israel's most noted archaeologists, has conducted excavations that have brought to light remnants of private homes in the western part of the city not far from the temple, and which were built some time during the first century before Christ. One, the dwelling of the Bar Kathos family, a name that was etched on a stone weight recovered in the ruins, proved a rich source of information and artifacts. The structure had six rooms on the lower floor and probably an equal number on an upper level. It yielded a small stone table with a decorated edge, a rare find, while a plaster fragment taken from another building was engraved with the representation of a menorah, one of the most ancient known examples. In still another house, a magnificent black-and-red mosaic floor was uncovered, its geometric patterns and colorful frescoes depicting floral scenes. The minutely carved columns found in some of the homes indicate they were flat-roofed structures, quite similar to those common to Greece of the same period.

Outside Jerusalem, one of the few structures archaeologists say may be associated with Christ is "Peter's house" in Capernaum, an ancient town on the northwest shore of the Sea of Galilee. In the New Testament, Capernaum is identified as a place of residence chosen by Jesus and is even termed "His own city" (Matt. 4:13; 9:1). At least five apostles, among the first ones, were fishermen of Capernaum.

Remains of a synagogue were excavated there in the early 1900s, and then cleared and partially restored by Franciscan fathers who owned the site. Dating to the late second or early third century, it is one of the best examples of early synagogues yet discovered. The walls of an upper gallery, probably reserved for women worshipers, are adorned with an elaborate stone frieze that depicts plants of the Holy Land; magic symbols, such as the hexagram and pentagram; and Jewish religious symbols—the Tabernacle, menorah, and Torah ark.

Recently, two Franciscan archaeologists excavated a house of modest size in Capernaum, one they have dated to the first century. It was later converted to a church. The archaeologists believe that it was so venerated because of its association with Peter and, possibly, Christ. Other experts aren't quite so sure. "Conceivable," says one, "but not proven."

A good number of American colleges and other institutions have been conducting archaeological research in Israel, and almost all have welcomed volunteer assistance. The Smithsonian Institution, for example, has undertaken an excavation at Tell Jemmeh (a tell is an ancient mound composed of the remains of several settlements), a site occupied from approximately 1800 to 200 B.C. Volunteers have been accepted for stays of four weeks or eight weeks. There's a $450 fee (for eight weeks) that goes toward food and living expenses, and, of course, you must pay your transportation to and from the site. For more information write: Dr. Gus W. Van Beek, Director, Tell Jemmeh Project, Department of Anthropology, Smithsonian Institution, Washington, D.C. 20560.

Hebrew Union College (Jewish Institute of Religion, 40 West 68th Street, New York, NY 10023) offers archaeological programs in Israel on a continuing basis. In 1979, the college sponsored an excavation in Tel Dam that required eighty volunteer workers. Instruction involved the use of archaeological data in historical reconstruction; and there were lectures, seminars, and field trips.

The University of Michigan (Department of Classical Studies); the University of Texas (Department of Anthropology/Archaeology); the State University of New York, Buffalo (Council on International Studies); Lake Forest (Illinois) College (Lahav Research Project); and Rockland Community College (Suffern, New York) are other American colleges and universities that have been conducting archaeological research and offering training programs in Israel.

Opportunities in England—If you plan to visit Europe, and want to join an excavation in London for a few days, a few weeks, or the entire summer, you're likely to find the welcome mat is out for you. The Department of Urban Archaeology of the Museum of London, involved in a continuing effort to explore and record the city's archaeological heritage, has gladly received visitors and volunteers at a medieval site near the Thames and also at a site near St. Paul's Cathedral where some first-century buildings have been unearthed. For more information, write: Brian Hobley, Chief Urban Archaeologist, Department of Urban Archaeology,

The Museum of London, 71 Basinghall Street, London EC2, England.

Other opportunities to take part in excavations throughout Great Britain are listed in the calendars issued monthly from March through September by the Council for British Archaeology (112 Kensington Road, London SEII 6RE England). An air-mail subscription costs $11; a surface mail subscription is $7.00. (You cannot purchase an individual month's listing separately.) Make your subscription payment by international money order or personal check.

When you receive a list, the next step is to pick out the excavation that suits you, then contact the director, making a formal application. When you write and apply, be sure to enclose at least two international reply coupons to cover return postage. As this suggests, the Council on British Archaeology is simply a coordinating service, meant to put you, the prospective volunteer, in touch with site directors.

Here are typical listings from recent bulletins:

Chester, Cheshire
    Greyfriars Court and other sites, mainly Roman and Medieval. Apply to: T. J. Strickland, Grosvenor Museum Excavations, 27 Grosvenor Street, Chester.

Holyhead, Gwynedd (Anglesey)
    Trefignath burial chamber, a megalithic chambered tomb. Apply to: C. Smith, Anglesey Excavations, Ancient Monuments Branch, DOE, Llansishen, Cardiff

Southampton, Hampshire
    Hamwih, continuation of the excavation of the Saxon port. Apply to: P. E. Holdsworth, SARC, 38 Upper Bugle Street, Southampton.

Beckford, Hereford, and Worcester
    Iron Age and Romano-British settlement. Apply to: J. Wills, Hereford and Worcester County Museum, Hartlebury Castle, Kidderminster, Worcester.

Noirmont, Jersey; Channel Islands
    La Cotte de St. Braelade, paleolithic cave site. Apply to: Professor C. B. M. McBurney, Department of Archaeology, Downing Street, Cambridge.

CHAPTER 6

Finding a Site

A number of years ago, in what was then the country of Palestine, a young shepherd made one of the most important archaeological finds of recent times. He had been grazing his goats and sheep beneath steep cliffs on the northwest coast of the Dead Sea, when he found that a goat had strayed up one of the narrow paths leading to the cliff summit. Following the animal, the boy came upon a small opening in the face of the cliff. Curious about it, he climbed in and found it was a cave. The floor was strewn with pottery and jars, storage vessels of some type, and many shards.

Fearful that supernatural spirits might be present, watching over their possessions, the boy climbed out of the cave without even examining the jars. But the next day he went back with a friend. When they reached into the jars, they found parchment scrolls wrapped in cloth. They brought them to a merchant in the town of Bethlehem. The merchant, suspecting that they might have some antiquarian value, brought them to his priest, Mar Athanasius Samuel. Soon after, scholars confirmed the importance of what came to be known as the Dead Sea Scrolls, which, along with scrolls later discovered, told of an ancient Essene community that existed from the second century B.C. to the third century A.D.

Chance finds of the type the young shepherd made still occur. A farmer plowing a field will unearth a treasure trove of projectile

Students (shown above) take surface samples within grid squares at University of Arizona Archaeological Field School. (Arizona State Museum, University of Arizona; C. Silver)

Decayed tops of stockade posts at Fort Necessity helped archaeologists correct historical misinterpretations. (National Park Service)

Beaches of St. Eustasius feature crumbling ruins of seventeenth- and eighteenth-century shops, warehouses, and other commercial structures. (George Sullivan)

St. Eustasius synagogue was built of yellow Dutch brick.
(George Sullivan)

Cannon litter a former fort site. (George Sullivan)

Artifacts are everywhere on St. Eustasius. Here, inverted bottoms from nineteenth-century rum bottles have been used to top stone fence. (George Sullivan)

points. A stream will wash away a layer of earth and expose carved stone. Potsherds will be revealed after a heavy rainstorm. But such occurrences are more the exception than the rule. Archaeological sites are usually "discovered" by careful research among historical records and documents and by painstaking field investigation.

Historical Research

A site can be a place or a plot of land where something is or was. A site can be a refuse heap or a building foundation, a fire pit or a burial place, a shrine or a storage chamber. It can be underground or underwater. It can be at the surface. It can be as big as a village, covering several square miles, or it can be the size of a single petroglyph-clad boulder.

No matter what type of site you plan to become involved with, the best way to start your research is by finding out what previous archaeological work has been done in the area. What sites have been excavated? What kinds of artifacts have been recovered? What findings have been reached?

Check with local colleges and universities for information of this type. Even local high schools, if they offer courses in archaeology, can be helpful. At Cheltenham High School, just north of Philadelphia, for example, teachers have supervised scores of excavations for students, and a wide array of Colonial artifacts have been recovered. Don't fail to contact your local archaeological society, of course. (Archaeological societies, and also colleges and universities most involved in archaeology on a statewide basis, are listed beginning on page 185.)

Another helpful starting point can be the local historical society. Every community in the United States founded before 1900 has an institution of one type or another that is meant to preserve local history and often to display related artifacts. This organization may be no more than a group of local residents who have gathered together books, records, and manuscript material concerning local history. Their artifacts display may consist of collections of arrowheads and random ceramic vessels donated by local citizens. The material may occupy only one room of a private home or town building, and you will probably need an appointment with an officer of the organization to get to see the material.

At the other end of the spectrum are institutions of impressive size, such as the New-York Historical Society, Chicago Historical Society, and the Historical Society of Pennsylvania (in Philadelphia). Each of these has scores of staff members and volunteer workers, and each offers library facilities, archives, a museum, and education programs.

No matter the size of the institution, a visit to your local historical society is certain to be time well spent. The staff is almost certain to be well versed in the archaeology of the area and will be able to provide you with important research material. In the state of Hawaii, for instance, the Maui Historical Society, located in Wailuku, maintains maps and records of all of the island's archaeological sites, and the files are constantly updated as new finds are made. Most archaeological investigations on the island, incidentally, are performed under the auspices of the Anthropology Department of Maui Community College. In Nova Scotia, the history section of the Nova Scotia Museum in Halifax performs a similar service, maintaining an inventory of archaeological sites and finds within the province. It also has a close working relationship with all professional archaeologists currently at work in Nova Scotia.

The Kentucky Historical Society is extremely interested in the preservation of the state's historic resources and plays an active role in the interpretation of artifacts and in archaeological training. It provides general reference works concerning archaeological surveys and excavations in the state; some of these sites are yet to be worked.

Such works as *Ancient History in Kentucky* (Constantine Samuel Rafinesque, Frankfort, 1824) and *Historical Sketches of Kentucky* (Lewis Collins, Covington, 1874) describe prehistoric and historic events and locations in the state's early history, and would prove extremely valuable to anyone seeking to pinpoint and evaluate a site for archaeological testing.

The Kentucky Junior Historical Society conducts archaeological excavations on sites in Frankfort and Shakerton for junior and senior high school members of the society. Involving about three thousand students, the program puts an emphasis on professionalism, training boys and girls in the proper techniques of excavation, writing reports, labeling artifacts, and so on.

If you want to find out the names of historical societies in your

area (there may be several), with information as to the major programs in which each institution is engaged, and the time period
covered by its collections, consult the *Directory of Historical
Societies and Agencies of the United States and Canada.* A publication of the American Association for State and Local History, it
is the best reference book available on historical organizations,
listing more than four thousand of them. Your local library undoubtedly has a copy.

Beginning with the 1975–76 edition, the directory contains a
special-interest index that serves as a key to the major fields of interest of each of the historical societies. It also gives the names
and addresses of the 172 historical properties maintained by the
National Park Service.

City, county, and state records can be helpful, too. Land grants
and deeds not only provide information as to the sequence of title
holders, but often give detailed specifications on buildings that occupied specific sites, including their size and locations, date of
construction, and materials used. Land features can be mentioned,
too.

Early fire insurance policies often contain maps, drawings, and
floor plans to identify the structure being insured. Court records
contain information relating to the collection of debts, disputes
over property lines, and marital strife.

Church vestry books offer data concerning the construction of
church buildings, their size and architectural features, and the
types of building materials used. Church registers list births and
deaths, baptisms and marriages.

Merchants' records list articles purchased, information that can
be helpful in identifying recovered artifacts. Any list of goods and
materials in stock can be helpful in the same way.

Old newspapers are always a great asset. Real estate adver-
tisements provide a careful description of houses for sale. Household items are sometimes richly described in classified adver-
tisements. News columns feature eyewitness accounts of fires,
floods, and other disasters. Drawings and, later, photographs depict what household items actually looked like.

Whatever source material you consult in the early stages of
your investigation, keep a careful record of it. In the case of
books, list the title, author, publisher, date of publication, the edition number, and the pages consulted. For periodicals, note the

name and date of the publication, the title of the article, and
the name of the author. Not only is such information important
should you have want to re-examine the material, but you'll want
to use the listing in preparing your final report.

Maps

At the same time you're working with your local historical society and archaeological society, you should also be obtaining detailed maps of the area. Excellent topographic maps are available
from the U. S. Geological Survey.

Each of these maps is a quadrangle which is bounded by paral-
lels of latitude and meridians of longitude. Quadrangles covering
7.5 minutes of latitude and longitude, the type you're most likely
to be using, are published at a scale of 1:24,000 (in which one
inch equals two thousand feet). Quadrangles covering fifteen
minutes of latitude and longitude are published at a scale of
1:62,500 (one inch equals one mile).

Printed in three colors, the maps are wonderfully detailed,
showing features of relief, such as hills, mountains, and valleys,
which are vital to anyone doing archaeological survey work; water
features, also vital; and cultural features, such as cities, towns,
roads, and railroads.

To obtain a map covering the area in which you are interested,
first get an index map for your state. On this, quadrangles are
outlined, named, and numbered. You simply order the quadrangle
you want. The date on which the area was last surveyed is also
given.

Map indexes are free. The maps themselves range in price from
$1.75 to $3.00.

Requests for indexes or maps for areas east of the Mississippi
River, including Minnesota, should be sent to the Branch of
Distribution, U. S. Geological Survey, 1200 South Eads Street,
Arlington, VA 22202.

Requests for indexes or maps for areas west of the Mississippi
River, including Louisiana, should be sent to the Branch of Distri-
bution, U. S. Geological Survey, P.O. Box 25286, Federal Center,
Denver, CO 80225.

USGS indexes and maps are also available on an over-the-counter basis from any Public Inquiries Office (PIO) and National Cartographic Information Center (NCIC) offices. The PIO addresses are:

7638 Federal Building
300 N. Los Angeles Street
Los Angeles, CA 90012

1045 Federal Building
1100 Commerce Street
Dallas, TX 75242

108 Skyline Building
508 Second Avenue
Anchorage, AL 99501

504 Custom House
555 Battery Street
San Francisco, CA 94111

8105 Federal Building
125 S. State Street
Salt Lake City, UT 84138

1028 General Services
Building Room 1C402
19th and F Streets, N.W.
Washington, D.C. 20244

1012 Federal Building
1961 Stout Street
Denver, CO 80294

U. S. Courthouse
West 920 Riverside Avenue
Spokane, WA 99201

USGS National Center
122201 Sunrise Valley Drive
Reston, VA 22092

Here are the addresses for the NCIC offices:

Western NCIC
345 Middlefield Road
Menlo Park, CA 94025

Eastern NCIC
Room 2B500
USGS National Center
122201 Sunrise Valley Drive
Reston, VA 22092

Rocky Mountain NCIC
Room 2206
Building 25
Federal Center
Denver, CO 80225

Mid-Continent NCIC
1400 Independence Road
Rolla, MO 65401

USGS maps are also available from some fifteen hundred private maps dealers. They are listed in the USGS indexes, or you can consult your Yellow Pages under "Maps."

Canadian maps that compare to USGS maps are available through the Canada Map Office, Department of Energy, Mines, and Resources (615 Booth Street, Ottawa, Ontario KIA OE9). In your letter requesting information, make reference to maps of the National Topographic System.

Other maps that you can obtain may be helpful in supplementing information on USGS maps. For example, a state highway office may have available local and county highway maps. The U. S. Army Corp of Engineers (The Pentagon, Washington, D.C. 20310) prepares detailed maps of local areas in connection with planned construction activities. So does the Bureau of Reclamation (Department of the Interior, Washington, D.C. 20240) and the Bureau of Soils (Department of Agriculture, Washington, DC 20250).

For maps of the national forests, contact the U. S. Forest Service (Department of Agriculture, Washington, D.C. 20250); for the National Parks, the National Park Service (Department of the Interior, Washington, D.C. 20240).

Aerial Photographs

Don't think that every piece of information concerning your area and the prospects it offers for an archaeological investigation are to be found in biographical research. There is a good deal that is likely to be omitted. Many archaeological sites, especially those dating to prehistoric times, are not mentioned in any records anywhere. Or if a particular site or settlement does happen to be referred to, there may not be sufficient information included to enable you to be able to pin down its location.

In such cases, you'll have to survey the area by yourself. Aerial photographs can be a good starting point. They can be extremely revealing, bringing to light ecological characteristics and topographic features that are not apparent at ground level, characteristics and features that can be used in pinpointing potential sites. When aerial photographs were taken for archaeologists in Wisconsin, they revealed effigy mounds built in the shapes of birds and animals. On the ground, their shapes could never have been perceived. Aerial photographs of the Estancia Valley in New Mexico showed the terraced beaches of huge lakes that had dried up thousands of years before. Archaeologists deduced that the areas photographed were once used by Paleo-Indian hunters, and subsequent ground surveys confirmed this.

You don't have to rent an airplane and hire an expensive photographer to get an aerial photograph of an area in which you're interested. Aerial photographs covering every square inch of the United States are available from the federal government, specifically from the National Cartographic Information Center of the U. S. Geological Survey (507 National Center, Reston, VA 22092). This agency maintains records of aerial photographic coverage of the United States and its territories, based on reports from other federal agencies, state government agencies, and private companies. From this fund of information, the Cartographic Information Center furnishes data on available photographs and the agency holding the film. The center also provides photos.

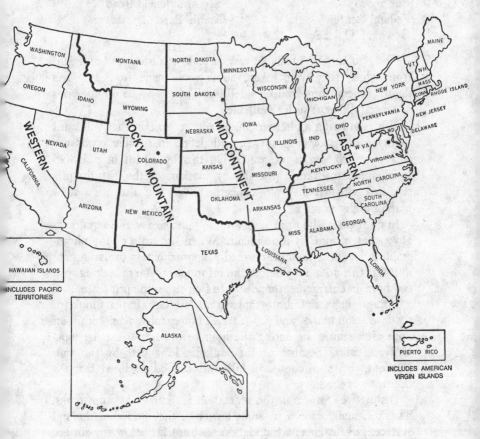

You can contact the National Cartographic Center itself, or one of the agency's regional offices (see map for regional boundaries). They are:

Eastern Mapping Center
U. S. Geological Survey
536 National Center
Reston, VA 22092

Rocky Mountain Mapping
  Center
U. S. Geological Survey
Box 25046
Federal Center
Denver, CO 80225

Mid-Continent Mapping Center
U. S. Geological Survey
900 Pine Street
Rolla, MO 65401

Western Mapping Center
U. S. Geological Survey
345 Middlefield Road
Menlo Park, CA 94025

The photographs available vary in scale according to the height from which they were taken. Some were made from low-level flights; others from orbiting satellites. There may be photographs of several different scales available.

When ordering a photograph, be sure to explain that you want it for an archaeological survey, and define in specific terms the area in which you're interested. Do this by means of a USGS topographic quadrangle (see above), marking on the map the precise area with which you're concerned. You can also use a state map or highway map.

In most cases, the print sizes are the same size as the aerial negative, that is, nine by nine inches. When the scale of the photograph is 1:24,000, the area covered is approximately twelve square miles. If this does not disclose the information you're seeking, you can have an enlargement made up to four times the print size.

Interpreting aerial photographs is no easy task. Experts look for shadows, crop marks, and soil marks. Photographs taken within an hour after sunrise or during the hour before sunset can be especially revealing because of the long shadows cast by the sun. Mounds, banks, ditches, and hill forts can be disclosed through the study of shadows.

Distinctive features in the vegetation are known as crop marks. They're usually caused by some structure that underlies the soil surface. For instance, a foundation wall not far below the surface is likely to severely limit the amount of water the soil can hold, thus retarding the growth of vegetation. In a color photograph, a strip of tan or brown within a wide swath of green would tip off the existence of the wall.

Or suppose there's an old irrigation ditch that's been filled in with loose soil. Plant life right above the ditch will probably be lusher and greener than surrounding plant life.

Soil marks occur on ground that has been cleared of vegetation or is unable to support it. A photograph of an expanse of bare land will sometimes show contrasting hues of soil. Where the soil has been turned over in the construction of earthworks, you can discern the difference between surface soil and subsoil. Filled-in ditches can be apparent because the soil used for the filling is likely to have a slightly different shading than surrounding soil. Cleared and uncleared land will show up differently. Land once farmed may be apparent by the absence of stones.

The area of the United States in which you're interested has also been photographed by the Earth Resources Technology Satellite and during the Apollo, Gemini, and Skylab programs, which were administered by the National Aeronautics and Space Administration. You can obtain photographs and data gathered during these programs. For information, write: Data Center, Earth Resources Observational Systems, U. S. Geological Survey, Sioux Falls, SD 57198.

Infrared photography is playing an increasingly important role in archaeological research. By showing the different heat capabilities of soil of various types, or by showing disturbances that have occurred in the earth, an infrared photograph can reveal ancient settlements beneath the earth's surface. Infrared photographs taken from satellites have already had practical application in this regard. The federal agencies listed above—the EROS Data Center and the National Cartographic Information Center—have available infrared photographs for some portions of the country.

Survey at Ground Level

Once you've obtained clues from photographs, written records, or whatever other sources you may be using, the next step is to survey the prospective site on foot. To perform the survey properly and prepare a formal report, you need, besides maps, a compass, a hand level (for measuring elevations), a cloth-measuring tape (one hundred feet or thirty meters), a six-inch rule (to aid in sketching maps), some small cloth, polyethylene, or paper bags (in which to put small artifacts you find), and a notebook and a few pencils.

You shouldn't have to spend any more than $10 for the compass. One in which the dial or needle is liquid-damped is easier to use.

You'll also undoubtedly need a couple of light digging tools, a trenching shovel, and a six-inch pointing trowel. You can buy the shovel in a hardware store or an Army surplus store. But be sure it's American-made. It should cost between $10 and $15. Some foreign-made shovels cost about half as much, but they break easily. The pointing trowel is used to remove dirt, or groundcover, that blankets archaeological features you may encounter.

A camera can be helpful, too. It's much easier to take a photograph of some object than to attempt to sketch it and describe it in writing. Another advantage is that you can study the photograph later, and perhaps discover something that you did not notice at the time you took it.

One word of preliminary advice: All land in the United States is owned. It is owned by an individual, a company, or a corporation; by a city, town, county, or some other local administrative authority; or by a state or the federal government. What this means is that you have to get permission before you conduct your survey.

In the case of privately owned land, explain to the owner exactly what you plan to do. Permission is almost certain to be granted. In other cases, written permission may be necessary.

The landowner and other people who live in the area may be able to provide you with helpful information. Tell them what you're seeking. Ask about fragments of pottery they may have seen, arrowheads, or building foundations.

During the summer of 1978, archaeological teams from the American Indian Archaeological Institute began concentrating on finding new archaeological sites, both historic and prehistoric, throughout the Housatanic Valley of western Connecticut. Staff members began the project by visiting the offices of tax assessors in every city and town along both the Housatanic and Shepaug rivers, obtaining property descriptions and other information for every tract of land. The measurements for each piece of property were then added to topographic quadrangles of the area.

The institute archaeologist then sent each property owner a questionnaire, requesting information about random artifacts that may have been recovered. The mailing was a big success. "We sent out almost five hundred questionnaries, and we got thirty or forty responses," says archaeologist Russell Handsman, a member of the institute staff. "The information helped us a great deal in establishing which sites were worthwhile investigating."

Institute archaeologists also gathered information from historical maps that they obtained from historical societies in the area. At the capital in Hartford, they consulted official state maps.

"Even arrowhead collectors helped us," Handsman says. "Some collectors recalled where they had found arrowheads as kids, and we tracked down these leads. Other people had large arrowhead collections, and could tell us where they had found each point."

The program was very successful. By the end of a summer of investigation, institute fieldworkers had established about fifty archaeological sites, all previously unrecorded.

When it comes to the physical features of an area, running water is what to look for first. Rivers and fast-flowing streams were extremely important in early American life, both before and after the arrival of the first Europeans, and archaeological sites are often established in association with them. Rivers offered fish of all types, including shellfish, provided a haven for waterfowl, served as a source of water for drinking and cooking, and were used in the irrigation of crops. Riverbanks were where beaver and muskrat were trapped. The flat terraces along the river were used for farmland.

Stands of timber along the river could be easily transported once cut. Riverbanks were sometimes the source of bog iron, which was used in the early stages of the iron industry. Clay for pottery making and for brickmaking was also dug from riverbeds.

Forts were erected along the rivers, for the military frequently traveled along inland waterways. Military fortifications were among the first sites excavated by American archaeologists. Such structures can be very old, actually predating the landing of the Pilgrims. Fort Raleigh on Roanoke Island in North Carolina was founded around 1585. The oldest masonry fort in the United States was built in St. Augustine, Florida, in the late 1600s.

American forts constructed in the seventeenth and eighteenth centuries were usually either four- or five-sided, with diamond-shaped bastions at the corners. Within each bastion the cannon were mounted. Sometimes such fortifications were built as earthworks; other times as stockades. In the earthwork type of structure, an earthen embankment rose from a deep ditch. Atop the embankment a low protective wall of stone would be built which contained the openings for the guns. The walls of the openings were slanted, so that the exterior dimensions were larger than those of the interior.

Stockades were built of heavy logs planted upright in the ground. The ditches into which the logs were placed were slanted on one side so the logs could be laid at a sharp angle, then tilted upright against the opposite and vertical side of the ditch. In the case of stockades where no upright timbers survive, rotted wood and earthfill can sometimes be discerned in a tracing four-sided or five-sided pattern.

Not only did rivers and streams serve the military, but they powered American industry from the earliest times. Even the smallest settlements had their own mills for the production of cornmeal and flour. Water-powered mills turned out barrel staves, ax handles, and even printed calico.

Early millsites can sometimes be detected by the presence of cut and dressed stone used in the mill foundation. Sometimes the remains of dams, wheel pits, or spillways can be found on the surface. Grindstones and millstones are found. Other evidence can include sawdust from a sawmill, charcoal from a powder mill, or nails from a nailery.

Small towns had several mills. Often, two mills would be built at a single dam, one on each side of the stream. Or one mill might be built just downstream from another. On large rivers, there might be as many as five or six mills drawing water from one dam.

Always check the riverbank itself. As the river cuts through the surrounding terrain, it can create stratigraphic sequences on either side of the bank. The information thus revealed can be comparable to what you get after digging a deep test pit.

Evidence of former Indian habitation is often revealed by finding a projectile point, that is, an arrowhead or a spearhead or some other distinctively worked artifact. But what you're more likely to find are the stone chips and flakes that were produced during the manufacturing process.

The North American Indians used many different kinds of stone in the manufacture of tools and implements. For axes, hammerstones, mauls, celts and other tools used in chopping or hammering, they used diorite, quartz, syenite, or granite—choosing whichever one happened to be the easiest to obtain.

In the case of objects that required a cutting edge, such as arrowheads, knives, or scrapers, very hard stone was used. This included quartz, chert, argillite, jasper, obsidian, chalcedony and flint. There is some confusion about the word flint, a fine, hardgrained quartz, for it is sometimes used in a generic sense to indicate quartz itself, chert, and other similar materials.

The archaeologist has to know each of these stones and the characteristics of each almost as thoroughly as a geologist does. He also has to know the technology used in shaping the stones.

Arrowheads, knives, scrapers, and drills were manufactured by a fracturing process in which small pieces or flakes were chipped from large stones. A hard stone, sometimes called a hammerstone, would be used to strike a second usually smaller stone.

Flake-producing fracturing process was used in the manufacture of arrowheads, knives, scrapers, and drills. (State of Iowa; Office of the State Archaeologist)

After a number of chips had been flaked away, a secondary flaking would be performed to finish the job. The tip of a bluntpointed punch, made of bone, antler, or hardwood, was placed at the spot where the flake was to be removed. The butt end of the punch was then hammered hard with another stone.

Artisans of the day worked rapidly. A projectile point or a knife could be turned out in about five minutes from a piece of quartzite, according to Paul S. Martin, writing in *Indians Before Columbus*. If the material happened to be obsidian, less than half the amount of time might be involved.

Axes, adzes, chisels, mauls, and manos, and other implements used in chopping, grinding, and crushing were usually made by pecking and grinding. Pecking was a process in which a very hard hammerstone was used to strike the surface of a second stone over and over again. Minute particles of the stone would be crumbled away with each blow. The rough surface of the stone was then ground smooth by rubbing it on a block of granite for several hours. To polish the stone, it was rubbed with quartzite.

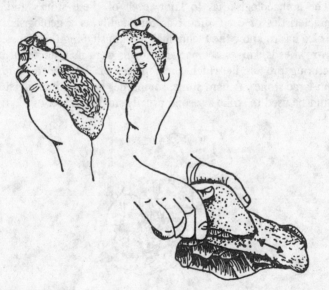

Pecking and grinding were used in making axes, chisels, and similar tools. (State of Iowa; Office of the State Archaeologist)

The North American Indians had several methods of drilling holes. A drill point of stone, copper, or horn would be mounted on a wooden shaft that was from about a half inch in diameter and from ten to twenty-four inches in length. The most common method of drilling was to simply roll the shaft between the palms while holding the tip in place at the point to be drilled.

There were also mechanical drills, one of which was the strap drill. A strap or cord would be wound once around the drill shaft at the center. Then the cord would be pulled, first in one direction, then the other, which caused the shaft to revolve. Someone else had to hold the shaft in place, or the driller had to do so by means of a mouthpiece.

A bow drill operated in much the same way. One turn of the bowstring was taken around the drill shaft, and then the string was refastened to the tips of the bow. To drill, the bow was drawn back and forth in somewhat the same manner a violinist draws *his* bow. The advantage of this method was that the driller could hold the shaft in place with one hand, while drawing the bow back and forth with the other; no outside help was needed.

There are other signs of manufacture and usage you should learn to recognize. A rounded stone used as a hammerstone is likely to be heavily scarred at both ends, the scarring resulting from the hammerblows. A stone with a deep and well-rounded depression in its surface may be a nutting stone, used to hold nuts as they were being cracked. A stone with a scarred flat face may have been an anvil stone. A rough cylinder-shaped stone of igneous material with a groove about its circumference may have been an ax head. The groove was used in securing the head to the handle. Stones of this type have been found weighing as much as twenty pounds. Other times the groove went only part of the way around the head, and occasionally there was no groove at all and the head would have a chisel shape. Such a tool was called a celt.

Also look for Indian beads. There were beads made of whole shells, parts of shells, animal teeth and claws, stone, ceramic material, and native copper. Glass beads the Indians obtained in trade.

Indian cookery often required the use of stones in one fashion or another, and thus fire-split rocks are frequently seen at habitation sites. Such stones were sometimes used to outline the hearth. Stews or soups were made by putting water and ingredients in a watertight vessel, and then dropping in hot stones right from the fire. In roasting, a fire would be built in a pit, allowed to burn down until only hot coals remained, and then a layer of stones was placed over the coals. The food to be roasted was placed on the stones.

Stones suffered from such use. The fire's heat would split them apart—into quarters, thirds, or halves. Look for these rugged-faced sections.

Stone axes were grooved so they could be hafted into wooden handles.
(State of Iowa; Office of the State Archaeologist)

Of all the organic refuse left behind by the Indians and colonists, none is more durable than the shells of the edible shellfish of the day, principally clams and oysters. Being composed of calcium carbonate, shells resist decomposition better than almost any other object of the past. Archaeologists have found oyster shells that are six thousand years old. They were weathered but still in whole condition.

Shells often serve as evidence of a former habitation site. Or, if they occur in large quantities, they can indicate the existence of an inn or tavern.

Shells aren't associated solely with salt water. The shells of freshwater mussels are fairly common along the Mississippi and Tennessee rivers and have even been found in Montana.

Of course, the type of evidence you'll be seeking depends on characteristics of the culture you're investigating. Generally speaking, however, any abnormal feature that disrupts the landscape is worth investigating. You never know what it might reveal. In centuries past, for example, one common method of getting rid of refuse was to dig a pit at some distance from one's home, and then simply dump the family trash into it. The pit might be as deep as eight or nine feet. Filling it would take several months. Once filled, it was covered over with soil and a new pit was dug. Depressions in the ground, caused by the trash settling, sometimes tip off where a trash pit is to be found.

A small ravine, a natural depression in the ground, or a crevice between rocks would also serve as a dumpsite in days gone by. Sometimes colonists would dump trash in between the outer walls of stone fences and cover it with rocks. Small porcelain fragments on the surface sometimes indicate these sites.

Privies were also used for trash disposal. Indeed, some seventeenth- and eighteenth-century privies have been found to contain historical treasures. Excavators who sifted through the debris found in two privies in Alexandria, Virginia, not long ago, uncovered what was termed one of the finest collections of eighteenth-century American ceramics ever assembled. In addition to several dozen big boxes of broken pottery and china, archaeologists, helped by a dozen volunteers, found twelve pairs of shoes, four pounds of printer's type, eyeglasses, watermelon and cherry seeds, and beef and pork bones.

Alexandria's eighteenth-century privies were lined with brick, similar to the way in which wells were lined, but they were built farther from the street than wells. Excavators had to dig approximately twenty-five feet down into the privies in order to reach layers of artifacts that dated to before 1840. Layers of items used after 1840 lay on top.

Ivor Noël Hume, director of archaeology at Colonial Williamsburg, called the find an important one because little is known about ceramics in America during the years immediately following the Revolutionary War. The ceramic material revealed information about the trade relationships, economic links, and cultural patterns of the period. For example, archaeologists were able to determine that although one would expect trade relations to have been severed between England and the United States after the war, this did not happen. Ninety per cent of the later eighteenth-century pottery and china found in the privies of Alexandria was imported from England.

How do you find a privy site? I once asked an archaeologist that question. "Through the determination of surface anomalies," he answered.

I looked at him quizzically.

"Just look around for a depression in the ground," he said with a grin.

Electronic Surveying Equipment

Once you've established in general terms where you believe a site to be, and you want to pinpoint exactly where to dig, any one of several electronic devices may be helpful to you. These instruments, widely used in petroleum and ore prospecting, enable you to get an idea of what lies below without having to break the soil surface.

One such device is called a soil-resistivity meter. It is based on the principle that moisture is a good conductor of electricity. Thus, the wetter the soil, the more readily electrical current will pass through it; and the drier the test area, the poorer the conductivity of the soil. In any type of ditch, pit, or gravesite, any place water tends to collect, resistance to electrical current will be weak. The resistance offered by a building foundation, a stone wall, or a well-trod footpath will be much greater. The soil-resistivity meter detects such abnormalities.

The device is not difficult to use. Two electrodes are driven into the ground some distance from one another, and an electric current is applied between them. Then two additional electrodes are thrust into the ground inside the first two, and these measure any abnormalities in the electrical field between the outer two electrodes.

The first commercial models of these meters were cumbersome devices, but in recent years they have become light in weight and eminently mobile, largely because of work performed by the Research Laboratory of the Ancient Monuments Department of the British Department of the Environment.

For additional information on this instrument and the other electronic devices mentioned in this section, contact a geological supply house. Look in the Yellow Pages of your telephone directory under "Geologists."

Or you can obtain a copy of The Geophysical Directory, a handbook that contains a comprehensive listing of all the companies and individuals directly connected with, or otherwise engaged in, petroleum exploration (and drilling and producing) in the United States and abroad. From it you can obtain a list of the manufacturers and dealers in the field of electronic surveying. The directory can be ordered from: The Geophysical Directory, Inc., 2200 Welch Avenue, Houston, TX 77019. It costs $12.

Magnetic Surveying

Archaeological sites can also be pinpointed by magnetic surveying, which is based on the principle that the earth's magnetic field is modified by different structures and types of buried remains. For instance, clay which has been heated (as in brick or pottery manufacture) acquires a magnetic force of its own which it retains after it cools. The result is that it can create a magnetic disturbance.

The instrument used to perceive these disturbances is a proton magnetometer. A systematic series of magnetometer measurements of a given area will reveal anomalies produced by the presence of buried hearths, furnaces, kilns, firepits, or building foundations.

Sophisticated magnetometer research has been conducted by the Midwest Archaeological Center of the National Park Service (Federal Building, Room 474, 100 Centennial Mall North, Lincoln NB 68508). Data collected by means of magnetometer surveys is processed by means of computer programs. These programs produce a variety of detailed maps, profiles, and three-dimensional views that can be easily interpreted. "This makes it possible to design excavations which maximize the amount of information recovered and minimize the area of disturbance," says Richard K. Nickel, a Park Service archaeologist associated with the project.

The Survey Report

Once a site has been surveyed, and it appears worthwhile to excavate, the next step is to record the survey data and submit it to the appropriate authority. State archaeological offices, educational institutions, and some private organizations have prepared survey forms to be used in filing site information.

First, the site has to be given some coded designation that can be used by you and archaeologists and researchists when referring to it. There are a number of systems used in numbering sites, and you should establish which one is used in your state. In most systems, the site number is made up of coded information that includes the name of the state, county, and a number indicating the site's place in a numerical sequence of sites discovered in the county. For instance, a site in Missouri might be designated 23CpG97. The number 23 is the code number for the state of Missouri, because it is the twenty-third state in the alphabetical order of states. The letters CpG stand for Cape Giradeau County, and the number 97 indicates that it is the ninety-seventh site to be officially recorded in that county by the Missouri Archaeological Society.

When Alaska and Hawaii were admitted to the Union, it threw this numbering system into confusion. It has been suggested that state numbers be replaced by the use of U. S. Postal Service state abbreviations, but no universal system has yet been adopted.

You also must prepare a map that pinpoints the site and file it with your report. (Use a felt-tip pen when drawing the map.) If you used the USGS quadrangle in finding the site, it's a good idea to make a Xerox copy of the area in which the site is located, and also submit that with your report. Or you can make a tracing of the area, including roads, rivers, houses, et cetera.

Usually the site is located according to township or range grids, and then by sections within one of those designations. The first section represents a one-mile square, and then that square is subdivided as many as four more times, with the site indicated each time. Map stores sell templates that aid you in drawing these sec-

Site No. __Ariz CC:5:6__   ARIZONA STATE MUSEUM ARCHAEOLOGICAL SURVEY

                26   NW   NW
T. _8S_ R. _25E_ Section _27_ / _NE ¼_ of the _NE ¼_. Map Ref. _USGS Mt. Graham 15' 1942_

                                                    ASM Map # 024367 (plotted)
U.T.M. Ref. __Zone 12, E-615500, N-3620000__   Co. _Graham_   Elev. _3850 feet_

                                                    United State Forest Service   and
Project _State Land Transaction_   Jurisdiction __State Land, leased by Ed Montierth__

Other Site Ref. __Marijilda Creek Ruin, US Forest Service # AR-03-05-04-1__

Site Type __Pueblo__   Cult. Affiliation __Salado__

Site Description: Material densely scattered around the major portion of site. Thins out at fringes. Ground stone frequent, but not over abundant. Plaza has several potholes w/ considerable amount of trash left behind. Pueblo is cobble masonry w/ some flat or tabular stones artistically arranged presenting a banded effect in room wall. One pothunted room has a ventilator shaft in south wall. Two or three of excavated rooms have large boulder boundaries.

Excavated rooms have standing walls 1-2 M high. Appears to be 3 sections to site.

Ceramics __Salado wares: red, corrugated, brown, Pinto Poly__   Colls. __No__

Other Items __Point, thinning flakes un-utilized, ground stone__   Colls. __No__

Site Dimensions __150(N-S) by 60(E-W) meters__   Depth __1-2 meters__

Site Condition: Several potholes in plaza and three rooms have been "excavated". Other than this site is basically undisturbed and a full scale excavation could be conducted with little loss due to pothunting.

Environmental Setting: Upper bajada just below canyon mouth. Site sits on cobble strewn terrace some 50ft above Marijilda Creek. Stream channel heavily wooded with tall oak & hackberry. Water coarse choked with desert broom. Stream channel naturally divided by site. Site covered with dense growth of mesquite & catclaw with much grass too. Water from stream divered to local reservoir by small cement ditch. Cattle roam State portion of site.

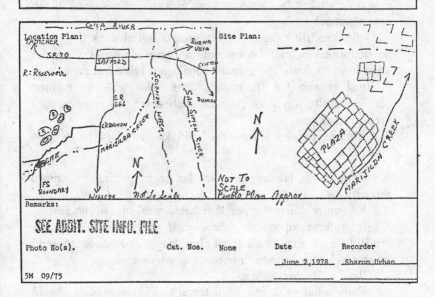

Location Plan:

Site Plan:

R: Reservoir

N

N

NOT TO SCALE
Pueblo Plan Approx

Not to Scale

Remarks:

SEE ADDIT. SITE INFO. FILE

Photo No(s).   Cat. Nos. __None__   Date __June 2, 1978__   Recorder __Sharon Urban__

5M 09/75

A state of Arizona site report.

130   *Discover Archaeology*

tions and subsections, with the patterns prepared in the same
scales as are used on USGS quadrangles. By dividing the section
into smaller and smaller units, you're able to locate the site with
absolute precision.

Your report should also include information as to the type of
vegetation in the area. Is it farmland, an open field, or heavily
wooded? Give a detailed description of the soil. Is it loose or hard-
packed?

Information as to previous excavations in the area should be
listed. Give the name and address of the property owner.

Describe any artifacts recovered; for example:

   Stone: 30 waste flakes, 2 projectile points, 1 biface
   Pottery: 2 late Woodland bodyshards, 6 Oneonta rimshards

Some site-record forms request information as to the depth of
the site. This can't be determined unless a test pit is dug or soil
samples are taken by means of a probe, a subject discussed in the
next chapter.

As the preceding pages suggest, archaeological work that must
be performed before the excavation begins demands a special
know-how. In Iowa, the state archaeological office has set certain
minimal criteria for those individuals who wish to become
certified as site surveyors. As a summation for this chapter, they
are reprinted here:

A site surveyor should have the basic skills and knowledge to be
able to:

• Contact the landowner-tenant before trespassing on private
property.
• Recognize different types of archaeological sites in the field.
• Interpret a topographic map, or, if no topographic map is
available, a soil map or an aerial photograph, and understand and
be able to locate a site to the nearest quarter section.
• Read a simple compass.
• Know what to collect from the site. (The candidate should
be aware that potsherds, bone fragments, and the like are just as
important as a complete projectile point.)
• Fill out a site form.
• Properly describe all artifacts found at the site and label them

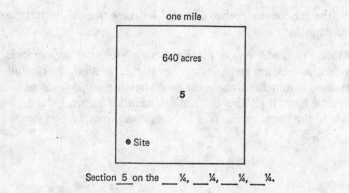

one mile

640 acres

5

● Site

Section _5_ on the ___ ¼, ___ ¼, ___ ¼, ___ ¼.

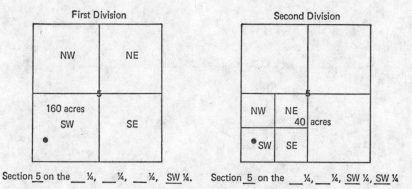

First Division

NW   NE

160 acres
SW   SE

Section _5_ on the ___ ¼, ___ ¼, ___ ¼, _SW_ ¼.

Second Division

NW   NE
      40 acres
●SW   SE

Section _5_ on the ___ ¼, ___ ¼, _SW_ ¼, _SW_ ¼

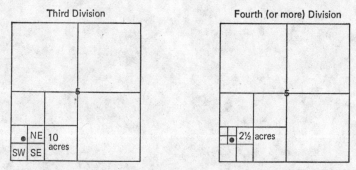

Third Division

● NE 10
SW SE acres

Section _5_ on the ___ ¼, _NW_ ¼, _SW_ ¼, _SW_ ¼.

Fourth (or more) Division

● 2½ acres

Section _5_ on the _SE_ ¼, _NW_ ¼, _SW_ ¼, _SW_ ¼.

Locating a site within a section. (State of Iowa; Office of the State Archaeologist)

with the catalogue number provided by the office of the state archaeologist.

Once the survey report has been completed, the archaeologist can begin making preparations for the excavation. A carefully prepared, comprehensive survey facilitates the work to come. At the same time, it justifies the work in scientific terms. Indeed, this phase of the investigation is as important as the excavation itself.

CHAPTER 7

In the Field

There are still countless individuals who believe that excavating consists of digging random holes in the ground with the intent of finding artifacts. Such conduct has nothing to do with archaeology.

Archaeological excavation is methodical and meticulous. You're compiling history. What you do in the field is much more like an autopsy than a construction chore.

But there is a fundamental problem. As you excavate in an effort to reveal the sequence of layers—the strata—you strip away the layers, and the stratification disappears. In other words, excavating, by its very nature, is self-destructive.

To solve this problem, archaeologists have developed a system that enables them to reconstruct—in theory, at least—the destroyed strata. They do this by regarding the excavation as being three dimensional, and compile their records accordingly. In specific terms, this means laying out a horizontal grid over the site to be excavated, and locating all recovered objects within the grid squares, as well as placing them in their related stratigraphic sections. (This is explained in detail later in this chapter.)

Of course, the ability to wield a shovel and trowel is important, but as the paragraphs above suggest, there is a great deal more you have to know. For the position of field technician, Iowa's Archaeological Certification Program expects individuals to have the skills and knowledge to be able to:

- Understand the use of a grid at an archaeological site.
- Understand the use of the metric system in the excavation of a square and in charting the provenience of artifacts within a square.
- Excavate a square by designated labels, keeping the walls straight and floors level.
- Recognize various categories of artifacts.
- Draw a basic wall profile.
- Map artifacts and features within the square.
- Use a trowel or shovel properly in skimming floor levels.
- Screen materials in the field.
- Understand the delicate nature of charcoal and the need for its careful recovery for carbon-14 analysis.
- Label level bags properly and identify artifacts.
- Keep daily excavation notes.
- Clean and care for field equipment.

Remember, this refers to the state of Iowa. Excavation work differs tremendously depending on where in the United States you happen to be digging. An Arizona archaeologist, visiting a friend in Oklahoma, was asked to help out on an excavation. As the party set out, the visitor was told they were going to spend the morning "desodding" the site. Only then could the actual excavation begin. "I didn't know what they meant," the archaeologist recalls. "I had never heard that word. In Arizona, even a *blade* of grass is cause for celebration."

Getting Ready to Dig

In some cases, it's necessary to probe a general area to establish exactly where to dig. It saves much time and effort if you know in advance exactly where the concentrations of occupational evidence are to be found. It's also helpful to get an idea of the stratigraphy of the area.

You can test a potential site in a number of ways. The most efficient method of finding a building foundation or a stockade postline may be by digging a long test trench through the area.

Test pits, however, are more common than trenches. A pit with one-meter sides will usually provide you with all the subsurface information you'll need. Sometimes smaller pits are dug. For instance, you may want to determine how the area between a pair of building foundations was once used, in which case you might dig circular test pits, each a foot or two in diameter, at measured intervals between the foundations. By then reading the variations in stratification between the test holes, you could probably detect different types of land use.

If the area to be tested is a very large one, using a soil auger is the most efficient method of testing. Such tools are about six feet in length, with a handle at the top mounted perpendicular to the shaft, giving the instrument a T shape. Using the auger, you collect soil samples from various sites and depths, and then analyze them for evidence of buried features. Posthole diggers are sometimes used in the same manner.

After the site has been pinpointed, the next step is to prepare a grid plan. This means staking out the site so that it resembles a very large sheet of graph paper. Establish squares that have either one-meter or two-meter sides, the latter if two people are going to be working in the excavation simultaneously.

If the area is level, you can lay out the grid with steel measuring tape, a compass, stakes, and a ball of twine. Usually, however, a plane table is used. The plane table is a portable surveying instrument that consists essentially of a drawing board and a ruler mounted on a tripod. You use the instrument in sighting and recording topographic details.

Begin by establishing a datum point—a fixed point within the site area. It can be a tree or a rock, or you can drive a stake deep into the ground near one corner of the site and use that as your datum point.

Use a compass in establishing a north-south line through the datum point, and then establish an east-west line at right angles to it. Once the north-south and east-west lines are established, lay out lines that are parallel to them to get your squares.

The best stakes to use are surveyor's stakes that are cut from two-by-two lengths of wood. Each stake should be about eighteen inches long. Stakes of this type give a broad, flat surface on which square-identification information can be recorded. Drive each stake to the depth of about one foot. When the stakes are in place, use the twine to lay out the grid.

Once the grid is staked out, draw a representation of it on graph paper, with one graph-paper square corresponding to a related square on the actual grid. Trees, streams, rivers, large rocks, and other topical features should be sketched onto the graph paper. Elevations, with reference to the U. S. Geological quad for the area, should also be recorded.

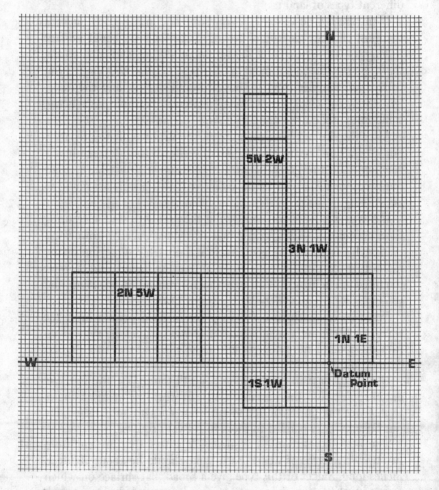

Grid plan as diagrammed on graph paper.

Once the site has been mapped in this fashion, identify the various squares, using the datum point as the point of reference. For instance, the square that is two squares north of the datum point and five squares west of it would be designated 2N5W (see illustration). This is one of several grid-identification systems.

The grid plan gives you a great deal of flexibility as you excavate the site. If you want to leave one square to work another, you can do so at any time. If you want to dig one square to a depth of four feet, but another square to the depth of only four inches, you can do so. All you have to do is be careful about identifying each artifact as to the square (and layer) from which it has been recovered.

You should also prepare a topographic map of the area, locating the site to be excavated in relation to roads, buildings, water features, highway survey points, and other such features. Both the topographic map and the grid plan become important features of your final report.

Tools for the Dig

What tools you use depends to a great extent on the type of soil in which you'll be working and the kinds of artifacts you expect to encounter. On one of the first digs in which I participated, the archaeologist in charge lamented the fact that he hadn't ordered a bulldozer to scrape away the two-and-one-half-foot layer of topsoil that covered the site. A *bulldozer*? I was shocked. But later I learned that a bulldozer can be a legitimate "tool" in the initial stages of excavation. Generally speaking, however, a shovel and pick and a variety of other smaller tools are the ones you'll be using most often. The shovel and pick are used in the first stages of a dig, when you don't expect to be finding anything. The trowel is used when you do.

For shoveling, most experienced archaeologists recommend a long-handled crescent-bladed shovel. In very sandy soil, however, a square-bladed shovel is more efficient.

For loosening ground that is too firmly packed for shoveling, you may have to use a pick. One end of the head is pointed, while the other end usually has a chisel edge. Naturally, you don't use a pick when you're expecting to come upon any artifacts.

If you find the standard pick to be too heavy and too ruthless a tool, you may be more comfortable using a hand pick, often called a mattock. The mattock blade is similar to the pick blade, pointed on one end, a chisel surface on the other; but the blade is much shorter. The handle is shorter, too, measuring only about fifteen inches.

When you're working in fairly loose soil or light rubble, consider a GI trenching tool. In one mode of use, it's a shovel, the blade small and rounded. However, by means of a locking nut, you can convert the instrument to use as a pick. The handle is only eighteen inches long, which means that the tool is a great deal more portable than a conventional shovel or pick.

You can buy a GI trenching tool at most any hardware store or Army-Navy surplus store. One costs $10 to $15. You'll also see Korean-made trenching tools that sell for as little as $3.00 or $4.00. But they're flimsy and quickly fall apart.

Even if your pursuit of archaeology is limited only to occasional summer weekends, you should own your own trowel. A trowel is to an excavator what a scalpel is to a surgeon.

While you are sure to know what a shovel and pick are for, you're much less likely to know how a trowel is used. It is not used for digging. Let me jump ahead a bit to explain what an excavated square looks like. Perfectly vertical sides and a flat bottom are two of its characteristics. Unless straight sides are maintained, you can't see and read the stratification. Well, the trowel is used in obtaining and maintaining the vertical surface. Gripping the trowel firmly, you sweep it toward your body, one edge scraping the wall on each pass. You never use the point.

The only type of trowel to consider is a diamond-shaped, flat-bladed mason's pointing trowel. The blade should be four to six inches in length. It may be helpful to have the point rounded off.

In some trowels, the blade and shank are welded into one piece. In others, the blade and shank are riveted together. Avoid the latter. A riveted trowel is not likely to last for much more than a week or so, while a quality welded trowel will give you years of use.

It's very fashionable these days to be seen using a six-inch Marshalltown pointing trowel. It's also practical, however. The Marshalltown trowel is made of quality steel, and the blade and

shank are one piece. While it costs a few dollars more than an ordinary trowel, it's worth it.

Once you've purchased a trowel, it's a good idea to paint the
handle a bright and distinctive color. This will help you spot the
instrument after you've laid it down, and it will also aid you in
identifying it from the trowels of other excavators. "Who's got
my trowel?" is a phrase you'll hear frequently on every dig.

For work in which the trowel is too heavy or unwieldy, a grape-
fruit knife is often used. An ice pick is also good for delicate work.

A whiskbroom is what you'll need for removing loose dirt from
the excavation sides. A metal dustpan is used to collect the
dirt dislodged by the whiskbroom. A paintbrush, the bristles two
to three inches in width, can be used instead of the whiskbroom.

A pair of pruning shears is invaluable in snipping small roots
that are encountered in the excavation. If the roots are big ones,
use two-handled lopping shears, a keyhole saw, or a small bowsaw.
You can use an ax on roots, of course, but in so doing you're going
to disturb a great deal of soil. You can damage artifacts, too. It's
best to use a gentler tool.

For measuring in connection with record keeping, you'll need a
steel pocket tape measure calibrated in centimeters with a minimum length of two meters. For making vertical measurements
from the edges of excavated squares, you'll require a line level
which is about three inches long with hooks on each end that
allow it to be suspended from a cord.

You may want to carry a pocket magnifying glass to examine
small objects that you find. You'll need a ballpoint or felt-tip pen.

The artifacts recovered from a particular square and layer are
kept together in bags. You can use polyethylene, cloth, or waxed-
paper bags. Last, you will need cardboard cartons in which to
carry and store the bags.

Excavating

An excavation may involve a refuse heap, a mound, a former
place of family habitation, or an entire town, but in each case the
basic plan is the same—to strip down the site, layer by layer.
There are really no set rules for doing this because no two sites are

ever exactly alike. It takes years of field experience before an individual can be considered skilled as a "dirt" archaeologist.

If you're following the grid system of excavation, and you've determined the size of each square, remember that you also have to allow for walls of dirt in between the squares. These walls, called balks, are necessary in order to permit the study of the stratigraphy of the square sides. The balks also permit individuals to walk about the site without tramping in the square bottoms.

How wide the balks should be depends on several conditions. Four-foot-wide balks may be all right, but if you're going to be working with a wheelbarrow, you no doubt will need to make the balks wider—and thus stronger—than four feet. If the soil is sandy, you'll also need wider-than-normal balks. The depth of excavation also has to be considered.

As mentioned earlier in this chapter, much of the excavation work is going to be done with a long-handled shovel. A technique called flat shoveling, or skim shoveling, is frequently used. In this, the blade of the shovel is held almost parallel to the bottom of the excavation, and the blade point is used to remove a very thin layer of soil.

Then each shovelful of dirt is spread over the floor of the square and examined for artifacts. Or the dirt is carried away for screening (see below). The trowel is used to keep the corners square and the sides straight.

When many artifacts are being encountered, or when the artifacts are particularly fragile ones, digging is done with the hand trowel or some other tool that enables you to work carefully. Even a dentist's pick might be used.

When an important artifact is encountered, it is carefully exposed, photographed *in situ*, and then its position is measured with reference to both the horizontal and vertical planes. This information, along with a description of the artifact, the date, the square number, the layer number, and the excavator's name, is entered onto an artifact record card. When the artifact is removed from the square, it is placed in a collection bag, usually with other artifacts from the same layer.

As the digger strips away the soil, he or she also has to be alert for features, that is, for distinctive aspects of the site fashioned by man. A hearth, a floor, or a posthole are examples of features. Abrupt variations in soil color often reveal them. When a feature is encountered, the excavator works carefully to expose it in its entirety and record it in its context.

Sometimes a grid frame is used in recording small features. This consists of a wooden frame of appropriate size—slightly more than one meter on each side, when one-meter squares are being excavated—with wires stretched in both directions at intervals of twenty millimeters so as to form a grid. When placed over the square being excavated, the grid frame permits more precise measuring and makes it easier to draw a scale sketch of the feature on cross-ruled paper.

Mounds are sometimes excavated, not by the grid system, but by what is called the quadrant technique. In this, the site is divided into four equal parts, and then the quadrants excavated alternately. Balks are left standing between the quadrants.

When the square or mound has been completely excavated, the walls are given a final and careful scraping with a sharp trowel or brushed with a whiskbroom so the strata become clearer. Sometimes wetting the walls with water from an atomizer accomplishes this.

The strata should then be photographed and a detailed scale drawing made of them. Each layer should be described as to its color and composition, and any unusual features should be recorded.

Stratigraphic photographs and drawings and other recorded information mentioned previously in this chapter go into the field catalogue. The field catalogue is to the excavation what a ship's log is to a voyage—a complete record. The notebook that is frequently used for this purpose is a standard surveyor's field book, known formally as an "engineering and science notebook." It is available in most well-stocked stationery stores. It is easy to handle, measuring five by eight inches. The water-resistant pages are bound in hard covers. One side of each page is lined and divided into columns, and you use it for notekeeping. The page opposite is graph paper, and on it you sketch artifacts or features or draw contour maps.

Screening

In theory, at least, there should be no need to use a screen, or, if one is used, nothing should ever be found in it. When you're

excavating, you're supposed to uncover artifacts *in situ*, then pinpoint their location and photograph them. Why, then, is a screen
necessary? It's necessary in those cases where artifacts are encountered in quantity and their placement within their respective
layers are not a critical matter.

In such cases, work can be speeded up by using a screen. Shovelfuls of dirt are thrown on or up against it. The dirt sifts
through; the artifacts remain on top.

There are many types of screens, ranging from small hand
screens to big motor-driven sifters that require a whole crew of
shovelers to keep them loaded. The most important feature in any
screen is the size of the mesh. Suppose you're digging a site that
contains tiny Indian embroidery beads. Then you'll need mesh
that's about the size of a window screen, and you'll have to use
water in sifting the dirt through. Usually, however, screens are
made of quarter-inch or half-inch mesh.

The hand sieve is simply a rectangular frame of three-quarter-
inch-by-three- or four-inch pine that measures about fourteen
inches by twenty inches. To some extent, the size depends on the
strength of the person doing the sifting. But when the screen gets
much bigger than fourteen inches by twenty inches, be prepared
to cope with a backache.

At most digs it's standard procedure to operate a central screen
manned by a screening crew. Such a screen is of good size, usually
measuring about three feet by five feet. In one system, the screen
is held parallel to the ground within a wooden frame that stands
on legs elevating it to about waist level of the workers. The frame
enables the screen to be rocked back and forth. The dirt shakes
through the screen; the artifacts remain on top.

A variation is to stand the screen on one end, tilting it about
forty-five degrees. Shovelfuls of dirt are then thrown against it.

One of the most practical screening systems utilizes a collapsible tripod from which a two-foot-by-three-foot sifting tray is suspended. The tripod itself is made of poles, each twelve feet in
length. The individual doing the screening simply grasps the tray
handles and shakes it back and forth. It's easy to do because the
tray's weight is carried by the tripod.

You can use this type of screening method in any terrain. If
you're working in a thickly wooded area, where it would be
difficult to carry the tripod in and out, you simply fell three sap-

lings to use as legs. And you don't have to take them with you when you go.

Another method of screening, called flotation, was initiated when archaeologists came to the realization that minute particles of food evidence—seeds and stem and bone fragments—were too tiny to be trapped by quarter-inch mesh. This method of screening is also known as water separation.

It involves the use of a washtub, the bottom of which has been replaced by $\frac{1}{16}$-inch mesh screen. When the tub bottom is held below water, usually a stream or river, the soil to be screened is poured slowly into the tub. At the same time, the tub is gently rotated. The soil sifts through, leaving the particle evidence. Sometimes a second person, using a tea strainer, scoops up the plant and bone remains, which tend to float to the top.

Using a Metal Detector

An electronic metal detector can perceive the presence of magnetic minerals—iron or black magnetic sand—and any metal that is capable of conducting electricity—lead, iron, brass, copper, silver, and gold. Such a device can play an important role in helping to excavate an archaeological site.

But the subject of metal detectors is a controversial one as far as archaeology is concerned. Most professional archaeologists look upon metal-detector users with complete disdain, and that is putting it mildly. These people, loosely classified as treasure hunters, are the people who have been ravaging public parks and national forests in their search for relics and old coins. They're the people who have been destroying ghost towns of the Old West for years. They're in the same category as pothunters.

There are some archaeologists, however, who are able to objectively evaluate the metal detector and the benefits it offers. Dr. James Moriarty (his doctorate is in anthropology), an associate professor at the University of San Diego and who teaches historical-site archaeology, is one. "I'm a scientist," he says. "I'd be a fool not to use the detector—or any other device that enables me and my students to do a better job of excavating and prepare a more adequate report."

It's after he's laid out his grid that Dr. Moriarty turns to the detector, sweeping it over the square to be excavated. Whenever the detector signals that a metal object lies below the surface, a small flag is planted at that point. No excavating has been done until the electronic survey has been completed and the entire square flagged.

"We thus get preknowledge of exactly where every metal artifact is located," says Dr. Moriarty. "We don't miss a thing once we start to dig.

"I'm a damn good archaeologist, and even without the use of a detector, there's not much chance I'd miss very much. But the detector increases your expertise."

Not only does the instrument enable one to find a greater percentage of artifacts, it also helps to prevent artifact damage. "Suppose you're digging a site and you come upon a buried piece of thin metal, perhaps a can that's been down there seventy or eighty years. A trowel used carelessly could penetrate the metal. But when you know the metal is there, you proceed with caution."

A detector can have safety value, too, Dr. Moriarty points out. "If there are buried electric cables, or other objects that are potentially dangerous, you can seek them out and establish where they are before you begin digging."

In the decade or so that Dr. Moriarty has been using detectors, he's tested several different types, but he has settled upon the Garrett Deepseeker, a stable and sensitive instrument, introduced in 1978.

Virtually all detectors look the same. Two sets of components are linked by a telescoping aluminum shaft. The unit's electronic circuitry—the batteries that power the instrument, the control knobs, a meter—is contained within a control case about the size of a shoebox.

At the other end of the shaft, there's a circular search head. It can be as small as a saucer or as big as a dinner platter. The search coils are contained within the search head.

There are two basic types of detectors—transmitter receiver (TR) and beat frequency oscillator (BFO). The TR type is the easiest to operate. It has two electronically balanced wire loops within its search head. One coil transmits signals; the other receives. The signals produce a uniform sound, unless something interferes with the signal. Interference can be caused by passing the search head over a piece of metal. The interference produces a tone change which the user hears as a high-pitched hum. The machine has, in essence, "detected" a metal object.

The BFO is a frequency-change instrument. When adjusted to a specific frequency, it produces a constant audible tone through the speaker, what users refer to as a "motorboating sound." It does indeed have a putt-putt quality to it. When the search head is passed over anything metal, the tone rises in pitch and the frequency of the beats increases.

While the detector's speaker system is usually adequate, experienced detector users recommend earphones. They plug into a control-box jack. Earphones enable you to be much more perceptive in detecting signal variations. They also block out the sound of high winds and/or other extraneous noises. And they discourage curious people from asking, "What are you looking for?"

Only the barest amount of technical skill is required to operate a detector. If you can tune in a radio, you should be able to use one. With the TR detector, you simply rotate the tuning knob until the tone is barely audible and the needle on the intensity meter just begins to move. Then you reverse the tuning knob slightly until the tone disappears and the needle rests on zero. Now the detector is ready for use.

With the BFO detector, you simply adjust the tuning knob until you get a continuous hum, which indicates it's ready for use.

The detector's search head is swung back and forth parallel to and about one or two inches above the ground. Most users swing the coil in a half-circle pattern. When the head passes over something metal buried beneath the surface, the speaker gives off its telltale sound or signal and the needle jumps.

TR units are sometimes referred to as "quick response" detectors. They're like light switches, either "on" or "off." There is no in-between. When the search head passes over a metal object, you get a sustained signal. When there's no metal, there's no signal.

But with the BFO detector, there is a direct relationship between what has been perceived by the search coil and the character of the sound produced. The beats increase in frequency and in loudness, in proportion to the amount of metal in the detectable field, until the machine's limit is reached. An experienced BFO user can "read" the sound variations and judge the size of the object being detected and, to a lesser degree, the depth at which it lies.

Another difference between TR and BFO detectors is apparent in those areas of the country where the soil is very high in mineral content. In some Rocky Mountain states, for example, deposits of black magnetic sand are widespread. If you use a TR detector over mineralized ground, you get audio and visual responses, even though no "metal" may be present. Obviously, this renders the unit almost useless. BFO detectors, on the other hand, can be tuned in such a way that their usefulness is not impaired.

During the mid-1970s, a third type of detector was introduced, the very-low-frequency (VLF) detector. It immediately began supplanting many of the TRs and BFOs then in use. With a VLF unit, it's possible to tune out ground-mineral interference. They also have the reputation of being able to probe deeper than either of the other instruments. VLFs have found widespread use in Europe and have been used by archaeologists there at a good number of sites.

It's this type of detector that Dr. Moriarty has been using. A multifunctioning thumb switch mounted in the handle makes it possible to choose the mode of operation wanted. Press the switch to the left and the detector has VLF capability; press it to the right and it's a conventional TR instrument.

No matter what type of detector you decide upon, the matter of search coils is critical. Search coils vary from three to twenty-four inches in diameter. Coils with the smaller diameters, from three to eight inches, say, are for detecting objects of every size at shallow depths, that is, at depths of up to two to three feet. Coils from eight to twenty-four inches are for detecting large objects at deeper ranges, to about eight feet.

If you're simply searching for small random artifacts, perhaps nails, boundary stakes, farm tools, or miscellaneous hardware, you'll be best served by using a smaller coil. It will give you a sure and quick response.

But suppose you're searching a large area for a long-buried refuse pile (which may be tipped off by the zinc tops of canning jars), and you know it is down deep. Then one of the bigger heads is what to use. I once accompanied an amateur archaeologist on a search for cast-iron scraps from what he believed to be the location of an eighteenth-century foundry on the banks of the

Westfield River in West Springfield, Massachusetts. He used a
TR detector with a twelve-inch coil. In less than fifteen minutes,
he found the first of several big chunks of cast iron, which were at
depths of between two and three feet. These led to the discovery
of the foundation of the foundry itself. Later, archaeologists
found artifacts that indicated that the foundry was actually an armory, which turned out bullets and guns used by the colonists
during the Revolutionary War. Were it not for the detector and
the scrap metal it "found," the story of the armory, important
in local history, might never have been made known.

Fortunately, coils are interchangeable. You can replace a small
one with a large one, and vice versa, and do it in about the same
amount of time it takes you to put fresh batteries in a flashlight.

In some BFO detectors, you can get coil versatility by using an
independently operated dual coil. This consists of a small-
diameter coil that is mounted within the circumference of a larger
coil. One such unit, manufactured by Garrett Electronics, is made
up of a coil that is five inches in diameter and is inside a twelve-
inch coil. A control-panel switch enables you to select the coil you
want to use.

Before you buy a detector, be sure to check the efficiency of the
search head. I'm not referring here to the quality of the elec-
tromagnetic field that is produced (although that is vital, since it
determines how deep the unit will search), but about the size and
configuration of that field. Let me backtrack for a minute. TR
search heads contain two types of loops. One transmits, the other
receives. In some TR units, the total response area—that is, the
area that produces the signal—is limited to an area that is the
same size as the receiving coil. If the receiving coil is only the size
of a silver dollar, which is not uncommon, you are not going to
have a very efficient unit.

In other TR models, the transmitting and receiving coils are
larger, and mounted side by side. Detectors of this type give opti-
mum efficiency. Such coils are sometimes called "full response"
coils.

The difference in the two types shows up quickly in use. When
the response area is limited in size to the diameter of the receiving
coil, it takes a greater number of passes, of sweeps, to cover a
given swath of ground.

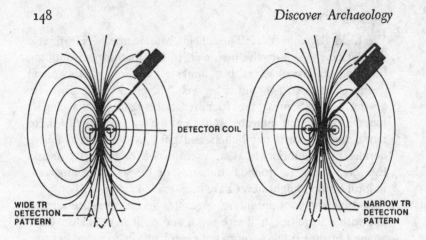

DETECTOR COIL

WIDE TR
DETECTION
PATTERN

NARROW TR
DETECTION
PATTERN

Narrow search pattern (right) limits area you can cover on each sweep. (Garrett Electronics)

The disk-shaped coil housing prevents you from telling one type from another by means of visual inspection. So, before you purchase a detector, try this test: Tune it in so it will respond to a small coin. Lay the unit on a desk or table. Take the coin, place it flat against the bottom of the search coil and slide it in a zigzag pattern over the coil surface. The wider the area of response, the better the search coil's detection pattern.

All coils should be checked for electrostatic shielding. With some you get signal interference, evidenced by a random crackling sound, like static, when the head is passed through wet grass or weeds. This won't happen if the coils are properly shielded. Check with your dealer to be sure you're getting this feature. Mere waterproofing isn't enough. The coils must be especially shielded from electrostatic interference.

If you believe what you're looking for to be buried very deeply, from five to ten feet or even deeper, what you have to get is an unusual type of TR unit, one referred to as a "double box" detector. Much heavier and bulkier than the conventional TR detector, it consists of two large boxes (each almost the size of a portable-typewriter case) that are mounted at opposite ends of a metal shaft. The unit is carried by means of a shoulder strap. One box contains components that transmits the electronic signal; the other receives. Signal interruption is reported to the operator by means of a meter or, audibly, through earphones. There is no speaker system. Detectors of this type cost around $500.

Be careful when you shop. Some detector companies produce inferior equipment. A detector may work well in the store, but you won't be able to detect a cast-iron cooking pot at a depth of three inches in the field.

Detector dealers are listed in your Yellow Pages under "Metal Detecting Equipment." Often detectors are also sold by dealers in electronic equipment, and some department stores stock them. You should expect to pay from $300 to $400 for a quality detector.

Here are some of the names of the leading detector manufacturers:

Compass Electronics Corp., 3700 24th Avenue, P.O. Box 366, Forest Grove, OR 97166

Garrett Electronics, 2814 National Drive, Garland, TX 75041

White's Electronics, Inc., 1011 Pleasant Valley Road, Sweet Home, OR 97386.

Write for free information on the various models each firm offers.

Two different TR detectors are available in kit form from Healthkit Electronics (Benton Harbor, MI 49022). Each requires from eight to ten hours to build. By doing your own assembly work, you save $30 to $40 on a detector with a retail price of about $150.

Metal objects can also be detected with a divining or dowsing rod of one type or another. Bent wire coat hangers are the most frequently used instrument of this type. If you're a skeptic, consider that Ivor Noël Hume, director of the Department of Archaeology at Colonial Williamsburg, in his book, *Historical Archaeology*, says that coat-hanger dowsers "serve a useful purpose and are included in every Williamsburg archaeologist's box of tricks." I have included them here, not so much in Noël Hume's testimony, but because I have seen their ability demonstrated.

Test the rods yourself. There's no cash investment. All you need is a wire coat hanger. Untwist it until you have a straight length of wire. Then cut it at the midpoint. Now you have two pieces of wire, each about two feet long. At a point about six inches from the end of each length, bend the wires to form a ninety-degree angle. These are the dowser handles.

To test your divining "power," hold a rod in each hand, grasping the short ends. Walk forward slowly, positioning your hands in front of your body, the knuckles just touching. The rods should be parallel to one another and parallel to the ground. As you approach a buried metal object, the tips of the wires will slowly begin to veer toward one another and then will cross. Stop walking. Dig at the spot where the rod handles point. There should be metal there.

Ivor Noël Hume calls this "archaeological dowsing." The method has been used, he says, "to approximately locate objects as small as a paper clip and as nonferric as a lead bullet." But the principal application of dowsing rods is in locating fragile metal objects during an excavation, so that they can be approached with caution by the diggers. Dowsing rods have also proven useful in locating buried utility lines, which must be avoided by the excavators.

The great failing of dowsing rods is that they don't work for everyone. Experiments conducted by Noël Hume demonstrated that the rods reacted for about eight out of ten men, but for only three out of ten women. He offered no explanation for the higher success rate among males.

Dowsing rods are not new. Not by any means. Their use was mentioned as early as 1556 in *De re metallica,* a treatise prepared in Latin by Georgius Agricola, wherein rods were cited as being useful in detecting mineral ores of various types. European explorers and colonists spread use of the rods to North and South America, Australia, and parts of Africa and Asia.

What makes the rods work? Whole books have been written in an effort to answer that question.

I recall the first time I saw the power of the rods demonstrated. When the dowser had finished and I was properly impressed, I asked him, "Why do the rods swing like that?"

He shrugged. "I don't know," he answered. "But what difference does it make? They just do."

Keeping a Photographic Record

You should supplement your written account of the excavation with photographs that give a visual representation of work as it progresses and the artifacts that are recovered. Develop a serious-minded attitude toward such photographs. You're not merely "taking pictures"; you're creating a photographic record. This means that you have to think in imaginative terms before you click the shutter. It also means that you have to handle yourself and your equipment in a professional manner. And it means that you should have equipment that enables you to produce professional-looking photographs. Forget about snapshot photographs. Forget about snapshot cameras, too. Think in terms of a 2¼-by-2¼-inch twin-lens reflex camera. A camera of this type employs a matched pair of lenses, one mounted atop the other, that work in unison. The top lens focuses an image onto ground glass where you view it, while the bottom lens puts the image on the film.

There is one problem with cameras of this type. In close-up photographs, there can be a slight difference between what you see on the ground glass and what ends up on the film. This condition is known as parallax. But the several advantages of the 2¼-by-2¼-inch twin-lens reflex outweigh this drawback.

One advantage is cost. You can purchase a quality camera of this type for about $100, or for about one-third the cost of a 35-mm single-lens reflex camera (discussed below). The negatives that the 2¼-by-2¼-inch camera produces (it uses 120 film) are large enough so that you can enlarge any small portion of the negative without getting any of the graininess which is sometimes associated with film that is 35-mm in size. At the same time, the 2¼-by-2¼-inch camera is almost as portable as the 35-mm camera.

The 35-mm camera that I'm referring to is a single-lens reflex, or SLR as it is sometimes called. As with the twin-lens reflex, you view the image the lens projects on ground glass at the back of the camera, where you are able to see which objects are in focus and which objects aren't. A clever mirror system, with the mirror placed at a forty-five-degree angle inside the camera behind the lens, reflects the image from the lens onto the ground glass. When you trip the shutter to make the exposure, you also, by the same finger pressure, spring a release that swings the mirror out of the way so the image can be projected to the film. Nikon, Canon, Minolta, and Pentax are the best known of the companies that make and market cameras of this type.

As a general rule, 35-mm single-lens reflex cameras offer lens aperture and shutter-speed control systems that are more sophisticated than those common to twin-lens reflex cameras. And

35-mm cameras are well known for their ability to accommodate lenses of various sizes, and they are also compatible with a wide range of other accessories. But in archaeological photography, accessories and lots of lenses are not critical items.

One accessory you do require, however, is a tripod. If you try to hand hold the camera, no matter the type you're using, you're going to get camera movement, resulting in some blurriness, however slight. Lightweight tripods, the legs made of tubular aluminum, are sturdy and portable.

The tripod also helps you to be a more careful photographer, and carefulness is a quality to cultivate. When you're using a tripod and you look through the viewfinder and something is in the image that shouldn't be there, maybe an unsightly root, you can leave the camera where it is and go up to the excavation and trim the root away. Unless you're using a tripod, you can't do such manicuring. You can, of course, but not without beginning from scratch in framing and composing your picture. What is said above rules out the use of a monopod, the one-legged stand that some photographers prefer to the tripod because of its greater portability.

Filters are important, too. Unless you use a filter, you may lose the definition between layers when photographing site stratifications. The problem is that several different soil layers within the same surface being photographed may all have the same tonal qualities. What a filter will do is increase the contrast between layers. Of course, you have to know what filter to use. This knowledge usually comes from experience. A green filter is a good all-purpose filter, and the best color with which to experiment. If you're photographing a brick wall, try an orange filter to bring out the detail.

Your photographs should always include a measuring device of some type, the most common being a ranging pole. Made of fiberglass, and available in interlocking pieces, the ranging pole is marked in the increments being used. If you're working in the metric system, the pole is marked in meters and millimeters. Ranging poles are frequently used in documenting the depths of an excavation and, in such cases, are placed vertically against the surface being photographed. A ranging pole may also be laid flat across an object, such as a foundation.

Each of your photographs should also be slated in order to identify it. The slate can be a real slate—a blackboard, that is—on which you write in chalk the identification number of the site, the square being excavated, the date, and any other information you deem important. Instead of a blackboard, you can use one of the various types of felt-backed boards and white plastic letters sold by photographic supply stores.

Some archaeologists eschew the use of slates and felt-backed boards, "menu boards" as they are sometimes called, in favor of keeping a detailed photo register. "The slate or board always obscures something in the photograph," says one archaeologist. "For that reason, a detailed description of the photograph, properly recorded, is better." Not only does the description give a detailed account of what is being photographed, but it also can contain technical information as to the shutter speed an F stop employed.

PHOTO REGISTER

B/W or Color

No._____   Description of View_____

_____

_____

Compass Orientation_____

Shutter Speed_____   F-Stop_____

Use a form similar to this one, and you won't have to slate your photos. (National Park Service)

In photographing inscriptions, archaeologists try to get strong side lighting on the object, which may mean having to photograph within an hour or so after sunrise or about an hour before sunset. Of course, side lighting can also be provided artificially. Strong side lighting assures long, bold shadows, giving distinction to the inscribed designs.

Sometimes the grooves are filled with chalk or charcoal before the photo is taken. Chalk stands out better in the print, but some experts disapprove of the use of chalk because it gives the inscription a flat and artificial appearance, which charcoal doesn't.

Replicating Inscriptions

Inscriptions are often replicated, that is, copied or duplicated. This facilitates study and research.

Replication often begins by making an imprint of the inscription on aluminum foil. There's no "special" foil for the purpose. Any of the brands available at the supermarket can be used.

The foil is impressed into the inscribed surface with the fingers, then beat lightly with a stiff nylon brush. This forces the foil into all the minute details of the inscribed surface.

The final step is to carefully peel away the foil and place it in a wooden box or other rigid container. It has to be kept perfectly still. Any crinkle is a disaster.

Often a cast of the foil will be made in plaster of Paris, which can be obtained from a building-materials firm or a medical supply house. The foil is turned upside down on a workbench. Three layers of plaster are used in making the casting. The first layer is formed out of a thin, yet creamy mixture, of plaster and water, plus a pinch of alum. The mixture is carefully spooned onto the foil until it is completely covered. Then dry plaster powder is sprinkled onto the wet plaster, which dries it out. A sifter or sieve is used in applying the dry plaster.

It takes about fifteen minutes for the first layer to harden. The same technique is used in applying the second layer. The third layer is formed from a thicker, creamier mix. It, too, must be carefully applied; otherwise, the first two layers can crack. The third layer should bring the casting to a thickness of about one inch. When it hardens and the foil is peeled away, the result is a perfect replica of the original inscription.

Latex rubber, which can be obtained from hobby and model-construction supply shops, can also be used in replicating inscriptions. Portability is the advantage that latex has. After you've made a latex replication, you can roll it up and tuck it under your arm without damaging it.

The problem with latex is that you need warm and dry conditions to assure that the material will harden within a reasonable amount of time. If it should happen to be cool and damp, it can take several days for the latex to become thick and leathery.

The latex is usually applied with a brush. But if you're working with a horizontal surface, you can pour it on. Some experts prefer forming the replication out of two layers, applying the second as soon as the first has dried.

When the final layer appears to have dried, one edge is carefully pulled away. If the inner surface of the latex is dry, it is likely that the entire sheet is ready to be lifted off. Latex doesn't leave the slightest mar or mark on the surface of the original object.

CHAPTER 8

In the Lab

While excavation and fieldwork are usually taken as the most exciting and glamorous aspects of archaeology, they are only the first steps. Once the remains have been found, they have to be classified and interpreted, and that's what laboratory work is all about.

It's generally estimated that for every hour the archaeologist spends in the field, he works three hours in the laboratory. During those hours, he seeks to answer these questions about each artifact:

What is the object?

For what was it used?

When was it made?

How was it made?

What happened to it from the time of its manufacture until it was recovered at the site?

What information does it give about the site? In particular, does it help to date the site?

What significance does the object have? Was it merely a household utensil or was it important to some occupation or profession? Is it a religious object? Is it a work of art? If so, what aesthetic principles does the object express?

Above, recovered timbers from the
Tiger, which burned off Manhattan
Island in 1613.
(Museum of the City of New York)

Left, urban archaeologist
William Asadorian,
an expert on clay smoking pipes.
(George Sullivan)

These artifacts were recovered during the construction of the World Trade Center in New York City. (Port of New York Authority)

Wooden water pipe; this section is lead-lined. (Chase Manhattan Bank)

These Paterson mills are part of the city's Historic District.

Tiered cast-iron fire tower in New York's Mount Morris Park has been cited for architectural significance. (George Sullivan)

Sorting and Washing

The first steps in the laboratory process are sorting, washing, numbering, and mending. In each of these phases, artifacts from the same layer are kept together. A misplaced artifact can change the interpretation of an entire level or feature.

In the first sorting, the artifacts are usually classified by the material from which they're made. These classifications include ceramic material, glassware, stone, metal, wood, cloth, and leather. Faunal remains are another classification. This term refers to bone, horn, shell, and other animal parts.

Many of these materials require special treatment. Most wood objects recovered during an excavation will be in a waterlogged state. The drying process must be retarded; otherwise, the wood is likely to crack or warp. Try wrapping the object in wet newspaper or packing it in a box of wet sand. Another method is to place the object in a tightly sealed plastic bag. If you can extend the drying-out period for as much as six months, you may be able to prevent any damage from occurring.

Dry wood should be treated with linseed oil, then placed in a sealed plastic bag. Dry leather should get the linseed oil treatment, too.

Most metal objects that you recover are likely to be made of iron. When iron artifacts come out of the ground, they are invariably heavily caked with corrosion and bear only the vaguest resemblance to their original shape. A cannonball looks like a misshapen rock. A knife blade has about the same dimensions as a sash weight. The first step is to determine how much damage has been done, that is, how much of the original object has been eaten away. X rays can distinguish between corrosive lumps and real metal, but an easier, less expensive, and still adequate method involves a strong magnet. Go over the entire object with the magnet, judging the amount of attraction you get. If the pull is very weak, you can conclude the object is worn away to its core. If you have a long and lumpish piece of corroded metal and you get a strong pull at one end but little or none at the end opposite, you may have a knife blade that is in good shape at one end but in poor condition at the other. This knowledge helps you when you start cleaning the object. Wherever it is in poor condition, you cannot clean too deeply.

To remove rust from an iron artifact, use a small metal instrument, such as a dissecting needle or a hooked needle of the type used in crocheting. You can speed the process by using an electric-powered rotary brush or an electric engraver's tool. Modern archaeological laboratories have available electrolytic tanks and vacuum desiccators for use in the restoration of iron artifacts.

Most sites where iron objects are found will also yield artifacts of copper and brass, although they are almost certain to be much fewer in number. You can usually recognize a copper or brass artifact by the greenish coating of encrusted material that surrounds it. The thickness of the layer and the amount of damage that has been wrought usually vary with the amount of moisture in the soil. Wet soil usually means much corrosion and much damage.

Proceed with caution when attempting to clean any heavily corroded artifact. Not only do you have to contend with the outer encrustation, composed of copper carbonates, but also with a layer of cuprous chloride which may exist beneath the surface of the metal. If you're working with a copper coin, this means that if you remove the chloride layer, you also remove the coin's lettering and surface design. You end up with a copper disk.

When you're confronted with this problem, immerse the coin in a solution that is four parts sodium bicarbonate and five parts sodium carbonate, with enough water to make it a 5 per cent solution, recommended by Ivor Noël Hume in his book, *Historical Archaeology*. This treatment will not actually remove the carbonate or chloride layers, but it will soften them to a degree that they can be washed away under tap water. Use a wooden toothpick to dislodge the most stubborn encrustations.

After you have removed the layers, washed the coin thoroughly, and dried it, it's a good idea to coat it with silicone. The silicone halts decaying and corrosion.

Tarnished lead and pewter artifacts can be cleaned by immersing them in a mixture of boiling lye and zinc. If the objects are heavily corroded, however, there is little you can do to salvage them. Because of corrosion, the objects are likely to be reduced to powdery form.

Tarnished silver can be cleaned by immersing the artifacts in a solution consisting of twenty-five parts ammonia and seventy-five parts water. Leave the artifacts in the solution overnight. Then finish the cleaning job with a good silver polish.

Shards of pottery and glass and pieces of clay pipe should be washed in running water while being scrubbed with a nail brush or toothbrush. But sort through the potsherds first, culling those that might suffer damage. Washing Oriental porcelain can be ruinous to the decoration, and with some early delftware the glaze gets spoiled.

Those potsherds that will withstand washing should be washed one by one. If you were to visit a major archaeological excavation on a rainy day when digging has been suspended, you're likely to find staff members engaged in potsherd washing. It's not a task that can be done on a mass-production basis. Every grain of dirt must be removed from the edges of each shard; otherwise, the pieces can't be glued together. Holding a shard under a running tap of water while scrubbing it with a brush is about the only way to do this. Soap and detergent aren't needed.

Numbering and Mending

Once the artifacts are completely dry, they are returned to their original labeled bags, which are transferred to the numbering bench. The coded number to be applied to each artifact usually includes the site designation, the feature designation, and the level number, with a diagonal slash dividing the last two. Thus, level 12 of feature N.1 at the PII site yields this artifact number: PII N1/12.

Artifacts should be numbered in the most inconspicuous possible place. Ceramic and glass shards can be numbered along the edges, and bottles in their bases. Numbers should be as small as possible, while still remaining readable.

Some artifacts, such as clear glass, must be primed before the number can be applied. As a primer, apply a narrow swath of clear nail polish.

The best type of pen to use for numbering is a Rapidograph, available at art supply stores. Get an "o" size point. Use India ink; for very dark-colored artifacts, use white ink.

The Rapidograph may cause you some problems. If you put the pen down, even for just a few minutes, the ink in the tip dries, and it clogs as a result. You have to disassemble the pen and unclog the tip under running water to get the ink to flow again. It's a messy job. But you can prevent the ink from drying by inserting the tip in a ball of wet cotton. Once you have inked the number on the artifact and allowed the ink to dry, then coat it with clear nail polish so the ink won't smear.

After you've finished numbering, the next step is to sort the artifacts into various subdivisions and reconstruct those pieces for which you have a sufficient number of shards. Ceramic material, for instance, can be sorted by color and type. It can be a formidable task. During one recent summer, an archaeologist in New York City recovered several thousand creamware shards from a building site that was being excavated in Lower Manhattan. At first glance, they all seemed to be exactly the same type. But on close examination, important differences could be detected. There were many color variations, with some shards tending toward white, while others were more yellow. The first sorting was by tonal differences.

Within each color grouping, there were other variations. Some pieces matched up according to tiny bubbles or other imperfections in the glaze. Others could be separated by their particular thicknesses. A shard from a cup was not nearly as heavy as one from a dinner plate. Body pieces were distinct from bases. Rim pieces could be easily identified.

So it was not just a job of sorting; he had to keep resorting and resorting. Eventually, he got the shards grouped by individual vessel. Then it was a matter of mending them.

Mending pottery is not difficult to do as long as you are patient and don't attempt to reconstruct an entire dish or bowl in one session. Use a household cellulose glue, such as Ross Household Cement or Duco Cement. You can buy it in either a hardware store or a five-and-ten. Avoid epoxy glues, even though they provide a stronger bond. That very strong bond creates a problem. Make a mistake and you have to live with it. Sometimes newly bonded fragments become unaligned and dry that way. Then you have to break the pieces apart and redo the job. But with epoxy glues, there's no breaking the pieces apart on the old lines. Test samples of ceramic vessels mended with epoxy glue have been dropped on concrete, and while they did shatter, they shattered into new fragments. The old fragments held together. When you're using household cement and pieces get out of alignment, you can easily break them apart. When you do this, be sure to rub the edges of the glued sections with acetate (nail polish remover will do) to remove the old cement before regluing.

Simply follow the directions on the glue tube when doing repair work. Begin at the base of the object and work toward the top. Apply a coat of glue to each of the two surfaces being joined, allow it to dry for about five minutes, and then join them. Swab any surplus glue away with acetate. Let the two joined pieces stand at least overnight, then add the next piece.

More often than not, you'll be lacking pieces of the puzzle. Chunks of the rim may be missing, or body parts, or the base may not be complete. In such cases you may want to restore the vessel using plaster of Paris. First, back the cavity to be filled with overlapping strips of heavy paper that you glue together so they match the contour of the adjoining pieces. Or you can use modeling clay.

Mix the plaster of Paris to the proper consistency, then pour it into the cavity, smoothing it so that it takes on the same curve as the vessel exterior as it sets. A sculptor's knife will help you to get the plaster smooth. Afterward, you can smooth it with fine sandpaper. Wipe away any plaster that gets on adjacent pieces before it dries. If you have never used plaster of Paris before, do some test pours first.

If you're skilled in the use of a potter's wheel, you can restore a vessel to its original form even if you have only a portion of the genuine vessel. The first step is to prepare a duplicate of the original in new clay. The genuine section is then set in position within the newly formed vessel as the wheel is turned. Gradually work the section into the clay. Such restoration work is said to be archaeologically valid as long as you have at least one third of the original vessel.

After some projects, you're going to end up with many hundreds of shards that have no relationship to one another, and also have no significance insofar as your interpretation of the excavation is concerned. Be careful how you dispose of these shards. You don't want to confuse anyone. One archaeologist, working amid the pueblo ruins of New Mexico, came upon a pile of shards in one of the rooms he was excavating. As he kept digging, the pile kept getting bigger and bigger. It eventually numbered more than ten thousand pieces. When he reached the bottom of the pile, he found a vinegar bottle, and inside the bottle was a note. It explained that the shards were from an excavation done many years before at another part of the ruins, and it was signed by the archaeologist in charge.

Dating

Once the artifacts have been classified as to type, they are dated, another step toward the final goal of interpretation. In this phase, the archaeologist may call upon one or more specialists. Petrologists and mineralogists provide information about tools and implements made of stone. A botanist can tell the archaeologist about plant life. An archaeologist concerned with prehistory may require the services of a paleobotanist. A linguist, a historian, or an expert on ceramics manufacture can contribute useful information. Even a folklorist may be called upon.

Archaeologists recognize two types of dating, relative dating and absolute dating. Relative dating is really not dating in the true sense of the word, but merely the placement of one body of materials in a time frame relative to another group of materials. Thus, an excavator will say that an assemblage of materials he identifies as A is older than assemblage B or C, and assemblage C is not as old as B.

Stratigraphy is the essence of relative dating. By determining the succession of layers in an excavation, the archaeologist can establish the chronology of the layers relative to one another.

What the archaeologist strives to do is to turn the relative chronology into an absolute chronology, fixing a specific time for each layer. Absolute dates are those given in terms of years ago or years old. Your birth date is an absolute date. So are A.D. 1904, A.D. 1492, and 36 B.C.

In establishing a relative chronology for the various layers, it is usually assumed that the oldest layer is at the bottom. But it doesn't always work out that way. A Staten Island, New York, archaeologist recalls a site in which the surface was littered with the oldest artifacts, ones that dated to the seventeenth century. Subsequent layers were in reverse time sequence. Investigation disclosed a bulldozer had overturned the soil to a depth of several feet in the preparation for the construction of a housing project.

Of course, stratigraphic interpretation has no validity unless all the artifacts found in the same level are contemporaneous. One of the most noted archaeological frauds involved the planting of faked remains with a stratigraphic level of known antiquity. I'm referring to the Great Piltdown Hoax. Charles Dawson, an English lawyer and amateur paleontologist, "discovered" fossils in an early Pleistocene gravel pit in Piltdown, Sussex, between 1909 and 1915. At this particular stage in archaeological development, only a small handful of man-resembling creatures had been discovered and authenticated, and Piltdown man quickly won professional endorsement. Britons hailed the discovery with great enthusiasm, for now they could point to ancestors as old as Neanderthal man, an extinct species that also lived during the Pleistocene Age, the remains of which had been found in Germany in 1856.

As the years passed, however, Piltdown man came to be looked upon with suspicion. He had the jaw of an ape and the cranium of a man. Nothing that looked like that was ever found again, whereas discoveries made in other parts of the world gave evidence that prehistoric creatures developed manlike jaw structures long before their skulls expanded to anything resembling their present size. Then in 1953 these suspicions were confirmed when testing revealed that the Piltdown jaw was that of a nineteenth-century ape, and, while the skull was a human fossil, it was not a very old one. In a word, Piltdown man was a fake.

A footnote was recorded in 1978. James Douglas, a professor of geology at Oxford University, who died that year, left behind a tape recording in which he claimed a colleague, a Professor William Sollas, had faked the Piltdown fossils in an effort to embarrass Sir Arthur Smith Woodward, keeper of geology at the British Museum. Charles Dawson, the aforementioned "discoverer" of the Piltdown remains, conspired with Professor Sollas, according to Professor Douglas. The conspiracy was successful, for Woodward was one of those who had stamped the find as authentic.

Pottery Analysis

Pottery survives. Shards are recovered at almost every prehistoric and historic site. Sometimes they are even strewn about the surface. The variety of materials, styles, and pottery-making tech-

niques enables the archaeologist to develop detailed interpretations about such remains. "In some regions," according to
Field Methods in Archaeology, "the great body of present archaeological knowledge derives almost entirely from the area's pottery."

Trying to establish the origins of English pottery making is
something like trying to determine when soccer was first played.
After all, kicking a ball around is not to be construed as a particularly innovative art. Anyone at almost anytime could have "invented" soccer. The same applies to firing clay.

Historians say that pottery that is of English manufacture probably dates to as far back as the thirteenth century. Fragments of
earlier dates have been found from time to time, but they so lack
in completeness and character that they fail to establish a national style.

When the first colonists arrived in America, they brought what
pottery they needed with them. But they were not here very long
before they began making pottery of their own. One Dirck
Claesen established a kiln on Manhattan Island in the early
1650s, according to William C. Ketchum in his valuable handbook, *Early Potters and Potteries of New York State.* Before the
century ended, there were at least three other Manhattan potters
turning out an assortment of wares.

Using the same coarse red-bodied clays they used in the manufacture of bricks and roof tiles, the earliest colonial potters made
crocks for milk and butter and for storing fruits and vegetables,
jugs for vinegar and molasses, and bowls and dishware of various
types. These products were known as redware. They required only
the simplest kilns and equipment.

The origins of redware can be difficult to trace, particularly
when you're working only with shards. But since local potters
used local clays, and they differed somewhat from place to place,
you can sometimes identify an artifact by the shade and porosity
of the clay from which it's made.

Sometimes redware was decorated with designs applied by
trailing or pouring a thinned clay mixture of a contrasting color
over the surface of the dish or vessel. Or the "slip," as the watery
clay was called, would be applied by means of a quill. The slip
was usually yellow or white, but shades of green were also used.
Slipware was manufactured throughout the colonies, although it

is frequently associated with German settlers in Pennsylvania, in which case the designs were usually lively and imaginative. Redware of New England and New York usually had a staid quality.

Not long after they arrived, colonists in Manhattan discovered huge banks of white clay along the north shore of Staten Island and in the area that is now Bayonne, New Jersey. With white clay they could make stoneware vessels, which were superior to those of the porous and more fragile redware. Stoneware began to appear in Manhattan in the 1730s, long before it became available in New England. There, red clay had to serve almost exclusively. Understandably, New England potters became redware craftsmen of the highest order.

In time, stoneware was manufactured just about wherever white clay was to be found. This included areas in New York, New Jersey, Pennsylvania, Maryland, West Virginia, and Ohio. The pieces produced were usually gray or beige in color, finished with a salt glaze, and decorated in cobalt blue.

Again, local clays made for distinctive qualities. For example, early stoneware from Cortland and Homer in New York was often a burnt dull gray in color. Some stoneware from Morganville, New York, west of Rochester, had a light tan or rose finish.

Despite the efforts of native potters, the colonists continued to import pottery from England. Virtually all fragments of jugs and bottles found at Revolutionary War encampments, as well as those recovered from English military sites, are of foreign manufacture, indicating that even in the later years of the eighteenth century, American potters had not yet begun to catch up with the demand.

Throughout most of the northeastern United States, the remains of early potteries offer an excellent opportunity for archaeological investigation. This is particularly true in Pennsylvania and New York. Practically all of the earthenware kilns that operated in New York's smaller communities have yet to be excavated, and sometimes only a foot or so of topsoil covers them. Concentrations of potsherds and sometimes bricks lying on the surface, pushed up by frost and growing roots, indicate that something more is below.

Former buildings—the pottery shop and storage sheds—may be visible as overgrown mounds. The underground remains of most North American potteries usually consist of kilns and waster dumps. From an archaeological standpoint, the buildings usually are not as important as the kilns. Their brick or stone floors and their fireplace bases give an indication as to the kiln's shape and the type of draft system it had. Nearby the kilns there may be setting tiles, stilts, wedges, and saggers (which were protective clay casings in which delicate ceramic articles were fired), and other pieces of kiln hardware. These give evidence of the firing technique the potter used. There may even be shards that date to the final firing of the kiln.

Waster dumps, located near the kilns, offer a big challenge. They contain enormous quantities of pottery, discarded for one reason or another during production. It may be that the pieces were overfired in the first, or biscuit, firing. Occasionally, biscuit-fired earthenware was covered with a lead oxide glaze before being discarded, and the glaze will appear as a coating of orange-red powder on the recovered piece. The waster dump is also likely to contain misshapen pottery or shards of pots that became fused during firing. There can also be fractured pottery and pieces with pebbled, bubbled, or discolored glazes. The waster dump can be several feet deep and spread over the entire pottery yard.

No two excavators agree on the best method for digging waster dumps. It depends to a great extent on the conditions you face, that is, the size of the dump and the depth to which it goes. Some prefer to dig every shard to a depth of one meter. But to make something out of all the shards recovered, you may need an open area the size of Yankee Stadium. You also need a great deal of time.

A more efficient method involves working with a trowel in one hand and a roll of masking tape encircling the other wrist. You use the tape to reconstruct pottery pieces as you go along, putting each in a collection bag.

While redware and stoneware were made in colonial America from almost the earliest times, the manufacture of porcelain ware, or china, was slow to begin. After all, seventeenth- and eighteenth-century potters provided every type of ware a household of the day might require. China was considered a luxury, and these were not luxurious times.

By the end of the nineteenth century, however, things were different. Americans were ready and financially able to discard their crudely made dishes and mugs for porcelain. English potters became aware of this, and began producing enormous quantities of china for export to the American market.

The year 1756 is an important one in attempting to date pottery shards. That was the year that John Sadler, a Liverpool printer, applied for a patent in transfer printing, a process that enabled him to apply to earthenware and porcelain any design that could be printed on paper. The story goes that Sadler threw away some spoiled proofs that were still wet. Children found them amid the trash and began sticking them on broken pieces of pottery. Sadler noticed that the wet print left a faint impression on the surface of the pottery. From that he figured out how to transfer print.

He had to carry the process through an additional stage so that the design wouldn't appear in reverse. His solution was to first print on tissue and then transfer the tissue impression to the pottery. With Guy Green, another Liverpool printer, he set up a "Printed Ware Manufactory." In the patent application Sadler filed, he claimed that he and Green could print twelve hundred fireplace tiles in six hours, a remarkable feat when compared with standards of the day.

Sadler and Green did not manufacture pottery themselves, but decorated it for other potters of the period for a fee. According to Josiah Wedgwood's correspondence, Sadler and Green purchased pottery from Wedgwood, decorated it, and then sold it back to him for distribution. Sadler retired in 1770; Green continued to operate the firm until 1799.

Saltware was introduced in England late in the seventeenth century from Cologne, where the technique it represented had been used in the manufacture of stoneware jugs, bottles, and tankards. The process involved throwing salt into the kiln during firing. The salt vaporized and the vapor settled on the pieces to produce a thin and transparent salt coating, which, in the finished product, became an exceedingly hard glaze. When the salt-glaze treatment was given white stoneware, as was usual, it turned the product somewhat grayish. Another characteristic was a slight pitting in the surface of the piece, almost like the pitting on an orange skin.

Saltware pieces were exported to the colonies during most of the eighteenth century. Designs were usually simple geometric patterns, although flowers, leaves, and birds were sometimes also used. The finest pieces, turned out between 1720 and 1760, often featured an over-the-glaze decoration in enamel.

Creamware, introduced about 1760, eventually displaced both stoneware and saltware as an export item. Almost every colonial site dating to the eighteenth or nineteenth century yields creamware shards. They're hard-bodied, pleasant to the touch, and have a distinctive pale yellow glaze.

What American housewives of the early 1800s coveted most was Staffordshire porcelain that was transfer printed in deep cobalt blue. Frequently the pieces were decorated with an American scene—a public building, a park, a bench, a bridge, or an important historical event, e.g., the landing of the Pilgrims. Americans of the day held Lafayette in high esteem, so English potters flooded the country with dishware bearing his portrait.

Called Old Blue or Historical Blue, the first of these pieces were rather crudely made, and the indigo blue color was chiefly used to cover defects. It wasn't even real china, but earthenware with a china appearance. It cracked and chipped easily.

After 1830, the shade of blue lightened. Other colors began to be used—pink, red, green, and black. By 1850, colors in combinations were being used. American views were pretty much abandoned for those of the romantic East.

In the Staffordshire district of England lived the Wedgwoods, Enoch Wood and son, James and Ralph Clews, the Ridgways, T. Mayer, W. Adams, and other potters. They frequently stamped their names on the underside of their pieces. They also imprinted the names of their towns—Burslem, Longton, Hanley, Tunstall, and Stoke-on-Trent. Sometimes a shard will bear all or part of a potter's stamp or registry mark. There are several handbooks available in which these stamps and registry marks are identified and explained. One comprehensive listing is The Encyclopedia of British Pottery and Porcelain Marks, Geoffrey A. Godden, New York, 1974.

Typical eighteenth- and nineteenth-century pottery trademarks. (*George Sullivan*)

Staffordshire potters also exported brightly colored tableware, called spatterware. It was somewhat common along the Eastern Seaboard, but was more popular in Philadelphia than anywhere else. The spatter design was accomplished by tapping a brushful of paint against a newly formed piece. After 1845, the spattering was performed by a sponge process. The term spongeware is often applied to these later pieces.

Mocha ware was a distinctive type of banded creamware that originated in England in the late 1790s. Between the bright bands of orange or green that encircled a bowl, mug, or pitcher, lacy decorations resembling feathery ferns or seaweeds were added. No two were exactly alike. The term is said to be derived from Mocha, in Yemen, where moss agate resembling the ware is to be found.

The unique designs were obtained in an unusual way. After the background color, usually cream, had been laid and was still moist, the piece was turned upside down and dotted at intervals with a black-colored liquid made of tobacco juice, printer's ink, urine, and water. As soon as the mixture touched the moist paste, it flared into its distinctive shape.

Later examples of Mocha ware, those manufactured after 1840, had white as a background color instead of cream. Round handles replaced traditional strap handles.

Handbooks and articles explaining early pottery styles abound, and some are of excellent quality. While you'll want to consult those that refer to local pottery making, you also may be helped by these sources:

An Illustrated Encyclopedia of British Pottery and Porcelain, Geoffrey A. Godden, New York, 1966.

A *Picture History of British Pottery,* Grizelda Lewis, London, 1956.

Early Potters of New York State, William C. Ketchum, Jr., New York, 1970.

"Creamware to Pearlware; A Williamsburg Perspective," Ivor Noël Hume in *Ceramics in America,* Winterthur, Delaware, 1973.

Collectors Guide to Antique American Ceramics, Marvin D. Schwartz, New York, 1964.

A *Manual of Pottery & Porcelain for American Collectors,* John Treadwell, New York, 1872.

North Devon Pottery and Its Export to America in the 17th Century, Malcolm C. Watkins, United States National Museum Bulletin No. 225, Paper 13, Washington, D.C., 1960

Anglo-American archaeological sites often yield fragments of ceramic tiles used in fireplace facings or to simply line walls. Such tiles are usually associated with the Dutch, who began making them as early as 1550. Their first efforts offered a lead-glazed front over a reddish-gray body. They were decorated by means of a simple stencil filled in by hand painters. During the 1600s, they decorated them with a variety of designs, some floral in nature, some depicting landscapes, while others were based on biblical subjects. Later colors were usually blue and white, or reddish-brown and white. The tiles usually measured five by five inches. They were seldom marked.

It was inevitable that British pottery makers would enter the market—and they did. Around 1675, Liverpool potters began exporting tiles that were similar to those of Dutch manufacture. With the development of transfer printing in 1756 (see above), the importation of Dutch tiles declined in favor of those manufactured in England.

Tobacco Pipes

Besides pottery, early colonists also imported bricks and smoking pipes of white clay. Of these two, pipes are the more reliable in site dating.

The practice of smoking, introduced by the Indians, was very fashionable in England by the 1570s, and clay pipes were common. The smoking craze later became so intense that it took some three thousand English pipemakers to supply the demand. Pipes were also manufactured in Holland. So many manufacturers were necessary because pipes were smoked for a short period, then thrown away. Also, they were so cheap they could be purchased by almost anyone.

Pipe fragments are common to virtually every archaeological site in the eastern United States. Sometimes these fragments take the form of bowl shards, but more often they're stem fragments. As many as two thousand such fragments were recovered from archaeological sites in the Jamestown and Plymouth Colony areas. In New York City, turn over a few spades full of earth from almost any site below Wall Street, and you are likely to find a pipe fragment or two.

Methods used in dating pipes relate to the size of the pipe bowl and the diameter of the bore within the stem. And these factors, in turn, related to the availability of tobacco. After tobacco was introduced into England in the sixteenth century, it remained in short supply for years. Pipe bowls of this period are relatively small, while the bores are large. The smoker packed the bowl, lit the tobacco, and then quickly gulped in the smoke in two or three quick inhalations. Quite understandably, the term used for smoking during the 1700s was "drinking."

As tobacco became more plentiful, pipe bowls became bigger. Because they were bigger, they burned hotter. To keep the hot bowl away from the smoker's face, the stems were made longer. And to cut down on the amount of unburned particles filtering into the smoker's mouth, the size of the bore was reduced. In the earliest pipes, the bores are $\frac{9}{64}$ inch in diameter. They got smaller at a fairly uniform rate.

There are two excellent studies that explain how to date pipe-stem fragments. They are:

"Dating Stem Fragments of Seventeenth and Eighteenth Century Clay Tobacco Pipes," J. C. Harrington, *Quarterly Bulletin*, Archeological Society of Virginia, Vol. 9, No. 1, September 1954.

"A New Method of Calculating Dates from Kaolin Pipe Stem Fragments," Lewis R. Binford, *Southeastern Archaeological Conference Newsletter*, Vol. 9, No. 1, June 1962.

These studies led to the development of this chronological chart, which gives time periods for various bore diameters:

Diameter	Dates
9/64	1590–1620
8/64	1620–1650
7/64	1650–1680
6/64	1680–1720
5/64	1720–1750
4/64	1750–1800

Suppose you've excavated a site that has yielded stems with bores that measure from $\frac{5}{64}$ inch to $\frac{6}{64}$ inch. That would seem to indicate that the site was occupied between 1680 and 1750.

In measuring bore diameters, you can use a set of six drills which range in size (in increments of $\frac{1}{64}$ inch) from $\frac{4}{64}$ inch to $\frac{9}{64}$ inch. Insert the bits one by one until you find the one that fits. If you have a sizable number of pipe-stem pieces, this can be tedious and time-consuming. Edward J. Lenik, a well-known New Jersey amateur archaeologist, has devised a more efficient way of measuring bore diameters. He invented what he calls a "step gauge," a pencil-sized steel rod that incorporates the six different measurements in one tool. You insert the tip of the gauge into the bore, and push it in as far as it will go. When it will go no farther, you read the gauge, and that's the size of the bore.

Pipes can also be identified by makers' trademarks and other decorations and designs that appear on both the bowls and stems. Sometimes even the manufacturer's name is given. There are several monographs on this subject. They include:

"Makers' Marks on Clay Tobacco Pipes Found in London," D. R. Atkinson, *Archaeological News Letter* (London), Vol. 7, No. 8, April 1962.

"The Tobacco Trade as It Appeared on the American Scene in New York up to the Nineteenth Century; Its origins and Its Physical Evidence Seen from Documentary Evidence and Excavated Clay Pipes," William Asadorian, 1973 (on file at the New-York Historical Society).

"The Rise and Fall of the Clay Pipe," Roger Fresco-Corbu, *Country Life*, Vol. CXXXV, No. 3507, May 21, 1964.

Building Materials and Styles

Bricks or, more precisely, brick sizes have also been used to date archaeological sites. But they haven't been used very often. They're simply not a reliable guide.

While it is true that royal statutes were issued in England that sought to regulate brick dimensions, the sizes of molds varied, both in England and America. Variations also occurred because there was a greater amount of shrinkage in some clays than in others.

So called "statute brick" measures 9 by 4½ by 2½ inches. But countless buildings known to be English built have yielded a smallish, tightly grained brick that measures 7½ by 3½ by 2 inches. Were such bricks, the statute brick or otherwise, made in England? No one can tell for sure without a comparative analysis of the clays used.

Dutch bricks are more trustworthy. The Dutch, who were the most skilled of all European brick masons, brought their art to New Amsterdam shortly after the colony was founded. They were the first to build with glazed brick and tile, and the first to make brick in a variety of colors. Usually it was yellow, but it was also produced with a greenish hue, in purple, red, or salmon pink. The Dutch produced different colors by varying the temperature in the kiln and the amount of baking time. Of course, the presence of one type or another of salt in the clay also affected color.

Dutch bricks often measure 7⅛ by 3¼ by 1¾ inches, but examples are sometimes recovered that are no more than 5¾ inches in length and 2¾ inches in width.

This variation in sizes has been known for some time. Richard Neve, in the 1736 edition of his *Builder's Dictionary*, had this:

> *Dutch*, or *Flemish-bricks* I am informed that they are 6¼n. long, 2½ broad, and 1¼n. thick; another tells me they are 6n. long, 3n. broad, and 1n. thick; for my part, I never measured any of them.
>
> They are of yellowish Colour.
>
> The paving with these *Bricks* is neater and stronger than common. They must be laid in sand.
>
> They are commonly used here in *England*, to pave Yards and Stables withal, and they make a durable Pavement, and being laid Edge-ways, look handsomely, especially if laid Herring-bone fashion.
>
> They are also used in Soap-boilers Vats, and likewise in making of Cisterns.

According to a Dutch trade association, De Nederlandse Baksteenindustrie, yellow bricks for export were fired in kilns near Gouda from soft mud dredged from the nearby IJssel River. They were yellow because of the high lime content of the mud. They were brought to America as ballast in Dutch ships during the seventeenth and eighteenth centuries. But Dutch bricks or the fragments you find shouldn't necessarily be taken as being two hundred or three hundred years old. The kilns at Gouda continued operating well into the twentieth century, and, according to a spokesman for the De Nederlandse Baksteeindustrie, "In the near future, there is a very good chance that this type of brick manufacturing will resume."

Not only bricks, but brickwork can sometimes be used in dating a site. You need to know some terminology, first. Suppose you're dealing with American brick, which usually measures 2 by 4 by 8 inches. If an individual brick has been laid across a wall rather than parallel to it, and you're looking at an exposed face that measures 2 by 4 inches, then that brick is called a "header." If the brick is laid parallel to the wall so that you see a 2-by-8-inch exposed face, the brick is a "stretcher."

English foundations built in the seventeenth century display alternating horizontal rows—called courses—of headers and stretchers.

With Dutch- or Flemish-built structures of the eighteenth century, headers and stretchers alternated in each course.

American bricklayers of the nineteenth century did it another way. Five or six rows of stretchers would be laid atop one another, and then a row of headers would be introduced.

Two helpful studies on this topic are:

American Building Materials and Techniques from the First Colonial Settlements to the Present, Carl W. Condit, Chicago, 1968.

Comments on Virginia Brickwork before 1800, Hubert A. Claiborne, Walpole Society, Portland, ME., 1957.

Bottle Identification

Shards of glass or chunks of bottles or flasks can also be used to establish the date for a site, because bottles have gone through well-defined stages of development. From 1790 through the early decades of the nineteenth century, bottles were made in a one-piece dip mold. The body was formed by blowing, while the neck, mouth, and shoulder were hand-formed. A telltale horizontal mold mark can sometimes be seen at the shoulder, and, of course, there's a pontil mark within the recessed bottom. Any bottle with this mark—a jagged ring of glass—was made before 1860.

Around 1810, the three-part mold was developed, and bottles formed from it have a horizontal mold line on the lower portion of the body, and two vertical mold lines just above. There are no mold lines on the lip, which was hand-formed.

The two-piece mold was introduced in the 1840s. It produced bottles with two vertical mold lines running from the base to the upper neck. The first lettered bottles date to the 1860s. Frequently used for patent medicines, they were often square or rectangular in shape, with recessed panels on one or more sides within which raised letters appeared, spelling out what the bottle contained and the name of the manufacturer.

Bottle-making machines began to appear in the late 1800s. A semiautomatic bottle machine turned out bottles with mold lines running up to the lip. Michael Owens was granted a patent on his fully automatic bottle-making machine in 1903, which produced (and continues to produce) bottles with mold lines running all the way up the sides to the tip of the lip.

Bottle collecting is one of the most popular of all hobbies, perhaps exceeded only by stamp collecting and coin collecting, so there is an enormous amount of literature on the subject. For a rundown of what's available, obtain the catalogue published by the Bottle Digger's Library, Old Bottle Magazine, Box 243, Bend, OR 97701.

Coins

Establishing a site's date by means of a recovered coin would seem to be the simplest method of all. But watch out; coins can be misleading. For example, Roman coins have turned up in Tennessee, Florida, Texas, and Arizona. A Carthaginian coin was reportedly found in Arkansas not long ago. Do these coins give evidence of ancient transoceanic contact? It's not likely. Research conducted by Dr. Jeremiah Epstein, an anthropologist at the University of Texas in Austin, concluded that many such coins are most likely lost souvenirs of World War I and World War II. "If the Romans ever got to America," says Dr. Epstein, "we haven't got any evidence of it."

The finding of a Roman "follis" of the period of Emperor Constantine the Great (A.D. 306–337) in an Indian mound was what started Dr. Epstein collecting reports of other Roman-coin discoveries. He advertised in coin publications in an effort to find people who had recovered coins or lost them. Finds were reported from many different areas, in what Dr. Epstein said were "obviously historical contexts," such as a Baton Rouge, Louisiana, bus station, and the officers' club of an Abilene, Texas, Air Force base. A letter writer from Africa reported losing a coin while skiing in Colorado. Dr. Epstein said that the number of reported finds increased after 1914, apparently by virtue of returning servicemen losing coins picked up in foreign countries.

In other cases, the coins reported to be Roman were actually something else. One was a token from the 1893 Colombian Exposition. An "ancient Jewish shekel" turned out to be a commemorative coin given Jewish immigrants to the New World.

As for the Roman follis discovered in the Indian mound, Dr. Epstein said it was an example of "reverse stratigraphy," a phenomenon in which an object from some other archaeological site is carried down below earlier ones, often by a burrowing animal.

Petrological Analysis

The archaeologist specializing in prehistory may turn to his colleagues in geology, petrology, or metallurgy for assistance in analyzing material from which recovered artifacts are made. Significant findings have been made through petrological analysis. In the early 1920s, for example, H. H. Thomas, of the Geological Survey of Great Britain, was able to demonstrate that the huge stones used in the construction of Stonehenge had been quarried in the Prescelly Mountains of north Pembrokeshire, and he established that the stones had been transported the two hundred miles from west Wales to the Salisbury Plain almost two thousand years before the birth of Christ.

Petrological analysis was relied upon during the summer of 1978 when Thomas Ullrich, a graduate student in archaeology at the University of Massachusetts, found fluted stone fragments, each about two inches long, similar in appearance to arrowheads, at an Indian campsite in Deerfield, Massachusetts. The analysis showed that the fragments were made from banded chert, a siliceous rock common to the Lake Champlain area of Vermont. This evidence helped to establish that the artifacts belonged to nomadic hunters who roamed the area during the Paleo-Indian period, eight thousand to ten thousand years before.

Other Dating Techniques

In sophisticated laboratories, professional archaeologists have several other methods for establishing absolute dates. They are radioactive carbon dating, dendrochronology, and thermoluminescence.

Radioactive carbon dating, developed in 1948, by Willard F. Libby, a University of Chicago scientist, had a revolutionary effect upon archaeological interpretation. It is based upon the principle that all plants and animals, while they are alive, take in small amounts of the radioactive form of carbon known as carbon 14. When they die, this intake ends, and the radioactive isotope starts to decay at a constant speed. Because the ratio of radioactive carbon to normal carbon decreases at a precise and calculable rate, measurements of the ratio can provide the age of nearly all once-living finds.

Since it was first developed, the methodology of radioactive carbon dating has been greatly improved. It is now possible to establish absolute chronologies that go back forty thousand years. Libby received the Nobel Prize in 1960, the first time any scientist at all connected with archaeology had been so honored.

Incidentally, carbon-14 dates are sometimes given in terms of "B. P.," meaning "Before Present." In order for the dates to have uniformity the "Present" in Before Present has been established as A.D. 1950.

Dendrochronology, the science of dating trees by counting their rings, known at least since the time of Leonardo da Vinci, was adapted for archaeological purposes by Andrew E. Douglass, an American astronomer and physicist. Douglass became intrigued by the fact that the rings of any given tree are unequal in size and form, and also differ in color. Through Douglass' work, it became possible to draw up a master chart of tree rings through the centuries. By comparing the rings of old datable trees used in the construction of homes and buildings with the master chart, it became possible to formulate their age, and thus date the site. Through dendrochronology, it is now possible to date American prehistoric sites as far back as the third and fourth centuries B.C.

Dendrochronology has played an important role in establishing dates for a major excavation in London along the Thames River waterfront, which goes back to Roman times. Roman builders used timbers of mature oak of a size rarely seen today, some with over two hundred and fifty years of growth. Archaeologists figured out they had started growing at the beginning of the first century B.C., and they were thus able to establish a dendrochronological sequence for early Roman London.

In recent years, a new technique for dating pottery has been developed. Called thermoluminescence, it is based on the principle that a very slight glow starts to build up in pottery the instant it is fired because of radioactive processes. By heating a few specks of a pottery sample, and using sophisticated measuring devices, university scientists say that they can calibrate the glow with enough accuracy as to determine when the artifact was made.

University of Pennsylvania archaeologists have used thermoluminescence to formulate new theories concerning the development of basic metallurgical techniques. In the village of Ban Chiang in northwest Thailand, where they have been excavating an ancient burial mound, these archaeologists recovered bronze artifacts and clay pots. By thermoluminescence dating, they established that the artifacts were made about 3500 B.C. If this is true, it means the artifacts are five hundred years older than any found in the Middle East. Historians have long held that the skills implicit in alloying copper and tin to get bronze were developed in the Middle East and transmitted to Asia and Europe. Now it's theorized it may have been the other way around.

Photographing Artifacts

Although done indoors under studiolike conditions, the photographing of artifacts requires just as much care and concern as site photography. Such photographs must show an exact likeness of the artifact; there can be no distortion. And each photo must show as much detail as possible.

Often artifacts are photographed from directly overhead, with the camera mounted on a tripod or stand. Lighting the artifact can be tricky. Sometimes it's necessary to eliminate shadows to show every facet of the artifact in sharp detail. Other times, a shadow may be useful. For example, in photographing a well-worn coin, a shadow may help to make clearer the areas of relief.

All of this presupposes that you're going to be using floodlights and spotlights (as opposed to flash or available light). A good basic lighting kit might include three reflector-type photoflood bulbs (or three photoflood bulbs plus metal reflectors) to give broad beams of light from different directions. You also should have one reflector-type spotlight (or small spotlight unit) to provide a narrow beam of light. You need three clamp-on units, each consisting of a socket, electrical cord and plug, and a gripping device. You need light stands and extension cords.

If you're working at home, be a bit wary about how much power you're going to be using. Since most household fuses are rated at 15 amperes and the average household circuit carries a current of 110 volts, this means you cannot use any more than 1,650 watts. (This figure presupposes that no other household appliances are going to be drawing from the same circuit.) To be on the safe side, keep your wattage below 1,500 watts. This means, for example, that you could use two 500-watt bulbs and one 250-watt bulb without undue concern.

Just as important as your floods and spots are the methods you use to control the light each throws. There is what is known as a barndoor, a set of metal flaps mounted on a reflector and used to control the breadth or width of a beam of light. There is also a snoot, a cone-shaped device that directs a beam to a small, specific area. (You can make a snoot from black construction paper and masking tape.) While you may be able to get along without a snoot or a barndoor, you surely will need a diffusing screen of some type. A diffusing screen is simply a piece of muslin, cheesecloth, spun glass, or fiberglass, or some other like material, stretched across a frame and placed in front of a beam. It breaks up the light, making it less directional, softer. You can easily make your own diffusion screens. Experiment with different materials.

One problem with lights is the heat they generate, and the harmful effect it can have on the objects being photographed. Intense heat can cause fragile pottery to crack or it can discolor delicate fabrics. When you are planning to photograph a fragile artifact, use a substitute item of the same size and shape—a "stand in"—while you are composing the picture and focusing.

You'll also need some background paper. When photographing a dark object, use a light blue or light gray background. It will show up as white in the photograph. When photographing an object that's white or a very light color, switch to a dark background. Black velvet has been used successfully in such cases.

Each photograph you take should have a measuring instrument in the picture, a small rule calibrated in centimeters or inches. The size of the artifact can then be established at a glance.

The Final Report

The last step is to prepare a comprehensive report on the work performed, the artifacts unearthed, and what findings you've established. While reports differ widely—depending on the nature of the investigation, the kind of site it is, and the number of people involved—they all have several of the same basic features. The report opens with introductory pages explaining how the site was found, why it was deemed important enough to investigate, and what was learned as a result of the excavation.

Succeeding pages outline what is known about the history of the site. If there is a building or buildings involved, you can include some architectural history of the area, so as to put the structure being studied in its proper context.

The site is described in detail and the method of excavation is explained. Artifacts recovered are presented in drawings and photographs, and each is briefly and concisely described. I've included samples of such descriptions here. These are from the National Park Service's archaeological report on the Franklin Court excavation in Philadelphia.

> V-868 Plain glazed earthenware jug or bowl. Local. Base only.
> Similar to V-867. ± 4″ diameter.
> 1730–1760 by context.
> Feature 22, Context III, FC-678-10

University of Arizona offers field-school instruction each summer at this site on Fort Apache Indian reservation near Cibecue, Arizona. (Arizona State Museum)

Left, student assists archaeologist in setting up a mapping frame at Catholic University summer field school at Thunderbird-Paleo Indian complex near Front Royal, Virginia. (Catholic University of America; Joan Walker) Right, an Earthwatch participant trowels some flakes from a lump of peat at Machrie Moor, Scotland. (Earthwatch)

Excavating an Iron Age pot in Zambia. (Earthwatch)

Excavations along the southwest corner of the wall surrounding the Temple Mount in Jerusalem. (Consulate General of Israel in New York)

Right, excavations revealed these remains of fifth- to sixth-century monastery at Beisan, Israel. (Consulate General of Israel in New York)

Below, archaeological excavations at Tel-el-Sultan, Israel. (Consulate General of Israel in New York)

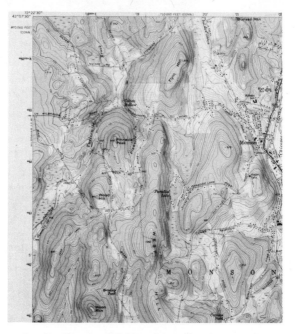

Section from a USGS topographical map (for an area near Monson, Massachusetts).

Typical aerial photograph provided by National Cartographic Information Center of the Department of Interior. (National Cartographic Information Center)

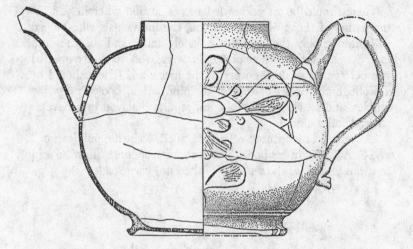

A drawing from the Franklin Court report. This was described as: "Scratch blue stoneware teapot. Floral description. Nearly whole. 4" high. 1745–1760." (National Park Service)

V-869 Unglazed earthenware flower pot. Probably local. Rim fragment only. Red body with applied fillet banding.
late 18th–19th c.
Feature 22, Context I, FC-655-23

V-870 Unglazed earthenware flower pot. Base only. Probably local. Red body, wheel thrown.
19th–20th c.
Feature 22, Context I, FC-640-1

V-871 Unglazed earthenware dish. Probably local. Probably intended for flower pot holder. 7" diameter, 1½" high.
late 18th–20th c.
Feature 22, Context I, FC-647-14
                               FC-650-27

V-872 Unglazed earthenware. Flat bottom and straight sides. Thickly potted and crude. Possibly a sagger, unused. 10" diameter.
1730–1760 by context.
Feature 22, Context III, FC-676-51

In the final pages of the report, you present your interpretations, your conclusions.

There should be an acknowledgments section wherein you list the names of those who assisted you, the individuals who helped with the survey, the excavating, cataloguing, and all the rest. Don't overlook the owners of the property, who may have granted you permission to do the work in the first place. There should be a bibliography, a list of sources of information, books, magazine articles, and previous archaeological reports that you may have as background material.

"An excavation without a final, detailed, scientific publication," says S. A. Pallis in his book, *The Antiquity of Iraq*, "must be said to mean to science the same as if it had not been made."

CHAPTER 9

For More Information

The pages that follow will help you to get information and advice on archaeological facilities and activities in your state.

Whatever your interest—getting training, serving as a volunteer worker, or simply gathering information—begin by contacting your state archaeological society. The state archaeologist, if your state has one, is another good starting point.

To familiarize yourself with work that is underway, or work that has been completed, you may wish to visit one or more of the archaeological sites mentioned. Most of these present displays of artifacts and explain local history. It's a good idea to contact the site supervisor in advance, to determine hours of admission and fees that might be involved. In the case of a national historic site, make contact through the regional branch of the National Park Service (addresses on pages 95–96). In the case of a state-operated facility, contact your state division of parks and recreation.

Virtually every state has enacted laws regulating the disturbance of archaeological resources on state land and, in some instances, on private land, and these are briefly summarized.

Legal restrictions that may apply to archaeological research on state-owned land are usually to be found in the antiquities code of the state. In some states, the code is very restrictive; in others, it encourages research, and in some cases may even provide funding. However, in most cases where funds are available, they are meant for professional archaeologists associated with state colleges. Often the antiquities code applies not just to state land, but to privately owned land which has been designated as having historical importance.

Virtually all states demand that you obtain permission in advance before you begin digging on state land. Other features of the antiquity codes include the following: In Alabama, "only residents living in the state may actually excavate." In Arizona, "all artifacts and other materials must be turned over to the State Museum." In Maine, "permits for excavation are allowed, but the state is the beneficiary of all finds." In Oklahoma, a license must be obtained for excavation. In Utah, a permit must be obtained.

Public Archaeology, by Charles R. McGimsey III (Seminar Press, 111 Fifth Avenue, New York, NY 10003), is an excellent handbook on the subject. It describes and discusses legislation affecting archaeological research in each of the fifty states. The volume also makes recommendations concerning state-directed programs in archaeological research and preservation, recommendations that follow those adopted by the state of Arkansas (Dr. McGimsey is director of the Arkansas Archaeological Survey), one of the most enlightened of all state programs.

Other measures taken to preserve the nation's cultural heritage include the National Historic Preservation Act of 1966, which pledges federal assistance toward preservation efforts undertaken by state and local governments. The legislation also expanded the National Register, the official inventory of the nation's properties —objects, buildings, sites, and districts—that merit preservation by virtue of their archaeological, architectural, or cultural importance. The program had its beginnings in 1960. A cumulative listing of all National Register properties is published each February in the Federal Register (available from the Superintendent of Documents, U. S. Government Printing Office, Washington, D.C. 20402). Don't look upon the National Register as an all-embracing source of information concerning significant and potentially significant archaeological sites, however. States and local authorities often do not nominate sites for Register listing unless provision has been made for their protection from possible vandalism and other damage.

The federal assistance provided for, under the terms of the Historic Preservation Act of 1966, often takes the form of matching

funds to be used to conduct surveys for locating sites to be placed
on the National Register, and also to acquire and preserve the
sites. The program is administered by the National Park Service.

You can supplement the information contained in this chapter
by obtaining the annual listings of fieldwork opportunities published by these organizations:

Archaeological Institute of America
53 Park Place
New York, NY 10007

Society for American Archaeology
1703 New Hampshire Avenue,
N.W.
Washington, D.C. 20009

The SAA's listing is free. The listing published by the AIA,
titled *Fieldwork Opportunities Bulletin*, costs $3.50.

ALABAMA

Contact:
Department of Sociology and Anthropology
University of Alabama
University, AL 35436

Alabama Archaeological Society
7608 Teal Drive, S.W.
Huntsville, AL 35802

Chapters in: Albertville, Auburn, Birmingham, Gadsden,
Huntsville, Mauville, Mobile, Montgomery, Moundville,
Muscle Shoals, Noccalulu, Selma, Sheffield, and Tusca-
loosa.

Sites to visit:
Mound State Monument, National Historic Landmark, near
Tuscaloosa.
Russell Cave National Monument (Paleo-Indian), near Bridge-
port.

Source Material:
Journal of Alabama Archaeology, semiannual publication of the
Alabama Archaeological Society (address above).

Handbook of Alabama Archaeology, Part 1, Point Types, $7.35; *Part 2, Uniface Blade and Flake Tools,* $2.25. Order from: Alabama Archaeological Society, University of Alabama (Drawer BA, University, AL 35486).

Recent fieldwork opportunities offered by:

Sociology Department, Auburn University (Montgomery, AL 36109).

Relevant legislation:

The state maintains an exclusive right to explore, excavate, and survey all aboriginal works and antiquities within the state. Nonresidents are not permitted to excavate, nor may antiquities be removed from the state.

ALASKA

Contact:

Douglas Reger
State Archaeologist
State of Alaska
Department of Natural Resources
323 E. Fourth Avenue
Anchorage, AK 99501

Recent fieldwork opportunities offered by:

Anthropology Program, University of Alaska (Fairbanks, AK 99701).

Relevant legislation:

No one is permitted to excavate, remove, or disturb archaeological materials without first obtaining a permit from the office of the state archaeologist (address above). Permits require a level of professional competence gained normally only after receipt of a master's degree in anthropology with archaeological emphasis.

ARIZONA

Contact:
Arizona Archaeological and Historical Society
Arizona State Museum
University of Arizona
Tucson, AZ 85721

Arizona Archaeological Society
P.O. Box 9665
Phoenix, AZ 85020

> *Chapters:*
> Cochise (P.O. Box 477, Douglas, AZ 85607)
> Desert Foothills (P.O. Box 1864, Cave Creek, AZ 85331)
> Phoenix (9310 Briarwood Circle, Sun City, AZ 85351)
> Verde Valley (P.O. Box 1057, Sedona, AZ 86336)
> Yavapai (P.O. Box 828, Prescott, AZ 83602)
> Yuma (P.O. Box 4997, Yuma, AZ 85364)

Sites to visit:
Casa Grande Ruins National Monument (Hohokam Indians), Coolidge.
Kinishba Pueblo (Mogollon, Anasazi Indians), near White-river.
Kinlichee Tribal Park (Anasazi Indians), near Window Rock.
Navajo National Monument (Anasazi Indians), near Tuba City.
Pueblo Grande (Hohokam Indians), Phoenix.
Toltec Indian Mounds State Park, near Scott.
Tuzigoot National Monument (Hohokam), Cottonwood.
Wupatki National Monument (Paleo-Indian), near Flagstaff.

Source material:
The Kiva, a quarterly publication of the Arizona Archaeological and Historical Society; contains articles on archaeology in the Southwest, with occasional pieces on ethnology, geology, and history.

An Introduction to the Study of Southwestern Archaeology,
A. V. Kidder, Yale University Press, 1962.

Prehistoric Indians of the Southwest (Fifth edition), H. M.
Wormington, Denver Museum of Natural History, 1961.

Southwestern Archaeology, J. C. McGregor, University of Illinois Press, 1955.

Recent fieldwork opportunities offered by:

Department of Anthropology, Northern Arizona University
(Flagstaff, AZ 86011); research and survey at historic site near
Little Colorado River.

Department of Anthropology, Arizona State University
(Tempe, AZ 85281), Payson area; occupation from A.D.
1000–1300.

Relevant legislation:

No one is permitted to excavate archaeological material on
state-controlled land without first obtaining a permit from the director of the Arizona State Museum (address above). Permits are
granted only to scientific and educational institutions.

ARKANSAS

Contact:

Hester A. Davis
State Archaeologist
Arkansas Archaeological Survey
Coordinating Office
University of Arkansas Museum
Fayetteville, AR 72701

Arkansas Archaeological Society
University of Arkansas Museum
Fayetteville, AR 72701

Northwest Arkansas Archaeological Society
P.O. Box 1154
Fayetteville, AR 72701

Source material:

The Arkansas Archaeologist, bulletin of the Arkansas Archaeological Society (address above).

Arkansas Amateur, monthly bulletin of the Northwest Arkansas Archaeological Society (address above).

Miscellaneous research reports and publications available from the Arkansas Archaeological Society and Northwest Arkansas Archaeological Society. Write for free publications lists.

Indians of Arkansas, Charles R. McGimsey III, 1969, $1.00, Arkansas Archaeological Survey (address above).

Recent fieldwork opportunities offered by:

Arkansas Archaeological Society (address above); training programs in archaeological techniques—site surveying, excavation, recording field data, preparing reports, laboratory work, et cetera. Also research at Toltec Indian Mounds State Park.

Department of Anthropology, University of Arkansas (Fayetteville, AR 72701); field school involving ceremonial center of Coles Creek culture at Toltec Indian Mounds State Park.

Relevant legislation:

Under the terms of the act establishing the Arkansas Archaeological Survey, the state holds the exclusive privilege of conducting archaeological investigation on state-owned land, and seeks to discourage fieldwork on privately owned land, except when conducted in accordance with the provisions of the law.

CALIFORNIA

Contact:

Society of California Archaeology
Department of Anthropology
California State University
Fullerton, CA 92634

Department of Parks and Recreation
P.O. Box 2390
Sacramento, CA 95811

Archaeological Research Facility
University of California, Berkeley
Berkeley, CA 94720

Los Angeles Archaeological Survey
University of California
Los Angeles, CA 90023

Institute of Archaeology
UCLA Extension
10995 Le Conte Avenue
Los Angeles, CA 90024

Pacific Coast Archaeological Society
Box 926
Costa Mesa, CA 92627

San Diego County Archaeological Society
Box 187
Encinitas, CA 92024

San Luis Obispo Archaeology Society
P.O. Box 109
San Luis Obispo, CA 93406

Sites to visit:
Big and Little Petroglyph Canyons, Naval Weapons Center, China Lake.
Coyote Hills Regional Park (Costanoan Indians), Fremont.
Inscription Canyon (Petroglyphs), near Barstow.
Mission San Antonio de Padua (Hispanic period, 1771–1850), Jolon.
Mission Valley (Prehistoric), San Diego.
Petroglyphs near Bishop, Bishop.

Source Material:
The California Archaeologist, the *Newsletter,* and *Method and Theory in California Archaeology;* publications of the Society of California Archaeology (address above).

Recent fieldwork opportunities offered by:
Los Angeles Archaeological Survey, University of California (address above).

Social Sciences Department, California Polytechnic State University (San Luis Obispo, CA 93407); field school at Mission San Antonio de Padua, Jolon; site dates from 1771 to 1834.

Anthropology Department, Cabrillo College (6500 Soquel Drive, Aptos, CA 95003); field school at Fort Ross historical site.

California State University/Chico (Chico, CA 95926).

California State University/Long Beach (Long Beach, CA 90801).

California State University/Sacramento (Sacramento, CA 95819).

California State University/San Diego State University (San Diego, CA 92182).

California State University/San Francisco State University (San Francisco, CA 94132).

Relevant legislation:

Excavation and removal of archaeological materials from state land is prohibited, except by permit obtained from the Director, Department of Parks and Recreation (address above).

COLORADO

Contact:

Colorado Archaeological Society
Department of Anthropology
University of Colorado
Boulder, CO 80302

State Historical Society of Colorado
Colorado State Museum
East Fourteenth Avenue and Sherman Street
Denver, CO 80203

Sites to visit:

Lowry Pueblo Ruins (Anasazi Indians), north of Cortez.
Mesa Verde National Park (Anasazi Indians), between Cortez and Mancos.

Source Material:
  Southwestern Lore, quarterly publication, Department of Anthropology, University of Colorado (address above).

Recent fieldwork opportunities offered by:
  Department of Anthropology, University of Denver (Denver, CO 80208).

Relevant legislation:
  All materials with historic, prehistoric, scientific, or archaeological value occurring in the state belong to the state. Permits for survey, excavation, and the removal of materials are issued to qualified institutions by the Historical Society of the State of Colorado (address above).

CONNECTICUT

Contact:
  The Archaeological Society of Connecticut, Inc.
  Central Connecticut State College
  1615 Stanley Street
  New Britain, CT 06050

   Federated organizations:
      American Indian Archaeological Institute (Box 252, Washington, CT 06792).
      Archaeological Associates of Greenwich (Bryan Drive, Greenwich, CT 06870).
      Albert Morgan Archaeological Society (c/o Charles Rignal, 185 Hubbard Street, Glastonbury, CT 06033).
      New Haven Archaeological Society (c/o David Thompson, 403 Bethmore Road, Bethaney, CT 06525).
      Norwalk Community College Archaeology Club (33 Wilson Avenue, Norwalk, CT 06854).
      Archaeological Society of Southern Connecticut (P.O. Box 654, Old Lyme, CT 06371).
      Fort Stamford Restoration (c/o Elizabeth Gershman, 86 Saddle Hill Road, Greenwich, CT 06870).

Southeastern Connecticut Archaeological Community (c/o Earl Claypool, 23 Plymouth Road, Stamford, CT 06906).

State Archaeologist
University of Connecticut
Storrs, CT 06268

Source Material:
Newsletters and publications of the Archaeological Society of Connecticut (address above).

An Introduction to the Archaeology and History of the Connecticut Valley Indian, William R. Young, editor, 1969, $3.00; available from Springfield Museum of Natural Science (Chestnut Street at the Quadrangle, Springfield, MA 01103).

Recent fieldwork opportunities offered by:
American Indian Archaeology Institute (Box 252, Washington, CT 06792).

Department of Anthropology, Central Connecticut State College (New Britain, CT 06050).

Relevant legislation:
Minimal.

DELAWARE

Contact:
Daniel R. Griffith
Archaeologist
Bureau of Archaeology and Historic Preservation
Division of Historical and Cultural Affairs
Hall of Records
Dover, DE 19899

The Archaeological Society of Delaware
P.O. Box 301
Wilmington, DE 19899

Chapters:
Kent County Chapter, 52 S. Old Mill Road, Dover, DE 19901
Minguaanan Chapter, State Road, Box 310, Avondale, PA 19311
Tancopanican Chapter, 15 Myrtle Avenue, Claymont, DE 19703

Sussex Society for Archaeology and History
R. D. #3
Box 190
Laurel, DE 19956

Bureau of Archaeology and Historic Preservation
Hall of Records
Dover, DE 19901

Site to visit:
Island Field Site (Archaic Indian), near Dover.

Source Material:
Publications of the Archaeological Society of Delaware and the Sussex Society of Archaeology and History (addresses above).

A *Brief Prehistory of Delaware,* Ronald A. Thomas; A *Handbook of Delmarva Archaeology,* Cara L. Wise; *Delaware Archaeology* (discontinued series). Available for reference through Delaware archaeological societies or through Island Field Museum (Route 2, Box 126, Milford, DE 19963).

Recent fieldwork opportunities offered by:
Bureau of Archaeology and Historic Preservation, State Division of Historical and Cultural Affairs (address above); surveys and evaluation of extant cultural resources, including archaeological sites, in three areas: Route 40/I-95 corridor, Atlantic coast drainage, and Dover and environs.

Relevant legislation:
No one is permitted to "excavate, appropriate, injure, or destroy" any aboriginal site on state-owned or -controlled land, except by permission of the governor (or a person duly authorized by the governor). Permits are granted only to colleges, universi-

ties, museums, and other recognized scientific institutions. Excavation on private land is discouraged, except when in accordance with the spirit of the law.

FLORIDA

Contact:
  L. Ross Morrell
  State Archaeologist
  Division of Archives, History, and Records Management
  Department of State
  State of Florida
  The Capitol
  Tallahassee, FL 32304

  Florida Anthropological Society, Inc.
  Room 130
  Florida State Museum
  University of Florida
  Gainesville, FL 32611

     Chapters in: Miami, Hollywood, Fort Walton Beach, Cocoa, Tampa.

  Pensacola Historical Society
  Old Christ Church
  405 S. Adams Street
  Seville Square
  Pensacola, FL 32501

  Suncoast Archaeology Society, Inc.
  2216 Third Street, N.
  St. Petersburg, FL 33704

  Tallahassee Historical Society
  Florida State University
  Tallahassee, FL 32306

Sites to visit:
  Crystal River State Archaeological Site (mound builders), Crystal River.

Lake Jackson Mounds State Archaeological Site, National Historic Landmark, near Tallahassee.

Madira Bickel Mound State Archaeological Site, near Bradenton.

Temple Mound Museum and Park, National Historic Site (Paleo-Indian), Fort Walton Beach.

Source Material:

The Florida Anthropologist, quarterly publication of the Florida Anthropological Society (address above).

Florida Anthropology, Charles H. Fairbanks, editor; 1958, $2.00; available from the Florida Anthropological Society (address above).

A Guide to the Identification of Florida Projectile Points, Ripley P. Bullen, 1975, $2.00; available from Pensacola Historical Society (address above).

Indians of the Florida Panhandle, Yulee W. Lazarus, 1968, $1.00; available from Pensacola Historical Society.

Recent fieldwork opportunities offered by:

State Division of Archives, History, and Records Management (address above) in cooperation with local chapters of the Florida Anthropological Society; sites in Dade and Brevard counties.

Department of Anthropology, University of South Florida (Tampa, FL 33620).

Relevant legislation:

The Florida Division of Archives, History, and Records Management (address above) holds title to and is charged with administering and protecting all historical and archaeological remains abandoned on state-owned land. The division issues permits for excavation and surface reconnaissance on state land to qualified institutions.

GEORGIA

Contact:

Society for Georgia Archaeology
c/o Patrick H. Garrow

Senior Archaeologist
Earth Systems Division
Soil Systems Inc.
525 Webb Industrial Drive
Marietta, GA 30062

Augusta Archaeological Society
2206 Mura Drive
Augusta, GA 29208

Northwest Georgia Archaeological Society
Shorter College
Rome, GA 30161

Augusta Richmond County Museum
540 Telfair Street
Augusta, GA 30901

Sites to visit:
Etowah Mounds Archaeological Area, National Historic Land-
mark, near Cartersville.
Kolomoki Mounds State Park, National Historic Landmark,
near Blakely.
Ocmulgee National Monument (Paleo-Indian), Macon.
Rock Eagle Effigy Mound, near Eatonton.
Track Rock Archaeological Area, Chattahoochee National For-
est (petroglyphs), near Blairsville.

Source material:
Archaeological Survey of Northern Georgia, Robert Wauchope
(available from the Society of American Anthropology, 1703 New
Hampshire Avenue, N.W., Washington, D.C. 20009).

Recent fieldwork opportunities offered by:
Department of Anthropology, University of Georgia (Athens,
GA 30601); excavation at prehistoric Dyar Mound and Village.
Department of Anthropology, University of Florida (1350 General Purpose Building, Gainesville, FL 32611); salvage and field
school at Wallace Reservoir, mid-nineteenth-century watermill
hamlet.

Department of Sociology Anthropology, West Georgia College (Carrolton, GA 30118).

Relevant legislation:
Excavation and removal of materials from state-owned land is prohibited, except by permit granted by the Historical Commission (address above). The commission urges private landowners to allow only qualified individuals to conduct archaeological investigation. Legislation also provides that the Historical Commission can pay a "finder's fee," the amount to be established by the commission, to persons who report the discovery of archaeological sites.

HAWAII

Contact:
Department of Land and Natural Resources
Division of State Parks
P.O. Box 621
Honolulu, HI 96809

Relevant legislation:
Permits for archaeological excavation are issued by the Department of Land and Natural Resources (address above) to recognized educational and scientific institutions.

IDAHO

Contact:
Idaho Historical Society
610 Julia Davis Drive
Boise, ID 83706

Society for Historical Archaeology
Department of Sociology/Anthropology
University of Idaho
Moscow, ID 83843

Sites to visit:
  Alpha Rock Shelter (cave paintings), Shoup.
  McCammon Petroglyphs, near Pocatello.
  Weis Rock Shelter (Historic Indian), Cottonwood.
  Wilson Butte Cave (Prehistoric), near Wilson Lake Reservoir.

Relevant legislation:
A permit must be obtained from the Idaho Historical Society
before archaeological investigation can be pursued on state land.
Permits are granted only to those applicants deemed qualified by
virtue of professional training or experience.

ILLINOIS

Contact:
  Illinois Archaeological Survey
  109 Davenport Hall
  University of Illinois
  Urbana, IL 61801

  Illinois State Museum
  Spring and Edwards Streets
  Springfield, IL 62706

  Southern Illinois Historical Society
  Southern Illinois University
  Carbondale, IL 62901

  Upper Mississippi Valley Archaeological Foundation
  2216 West 112th Street
  Chicago, IL 60643

Sites to visit:
  Cahokia Mounds State Park, near East St. Louis.
  Dickson Mounds Museum of the Illinois Indian, near Lewis-
  town.
  Kincaid Mounds Area (Mississippian Indian), Massac and
  Pope counties.
  Koster Site (to Paleo-Indian), Kampsville.

Orendorf Site (Mississippian Indian), Fulton County.
Pere Marquette State Park (mound builders), near Alton.
Starved Rock State Park (Archaic), near Ottawa.

Source material:
Various publications offered by Illinois Archaeological Survey
(address above; write for publications list, enclosing self-addressed
stamped envelope).

Recent fieldwork opportunities offered by:
Kampsville Archaeological Center (Northwestern Archaeological Program, 2000 Sheridan Road, Evanston, IL 60201);
open to all interested students, regardless of prior archaeological
training.

The Upper Mississippi Valley Archaeological Research Foundation in Cooperation with Western Illinois University, College of
Arts and Sciences, Sociology and Anthropology (Macomb, IL
61455); Orendorf Site, one of a series of political and ceremonial
centers which flourished in the Central Illinois River Valley at
different times between A.D. 1050 and 1550. Orendorf was one of
the largest of these towns, covering thirty acres of habitation area.

Department of Anthropology, University of Missouri-Columbia
(210 Switzler Hall, Columbia, MO 65201); research at nineteenth-century Mansion House, Nauvoo, Illinois.

Relevant legislation:
Archaeological resources on state land are considered "in re-
serve" for the state. The particular department of the state having
jurisdiction over a specific land area can issue permits to "competent persons" to conduct archaeological investigation on the land.
The Illinois State Museum (address above) reviews permit applications.

INDIANA

Contact:
Indiana Society of Archaeology
590 N. Washington Street
Scottsburg, IN 47170

Indiana Historical Society
315 West Ohio Street
Indianapolis, IN 46202

Glenn A. Black Laboratory of Archaeology
Indiana University
Bloomington, IN 47401

Sites to visit:
Angel Mounds State Memorial, National Historic Landmark, near Evansville.
Fort Quiatenon (Historic, 1717–1791), Lafayette.
Mounds State Park, near Anderson.

Source material:
Prehistoric Antiquities of Indiana, Eli Lilly, Indiana Historical Society, 1937; *An Introduction to the Prehistory of Indiana*, James H. Keller, Indiana Historical Society, 1973, $1.00.

Recent fieldwork opportunities offered by:
Glenn A. Black Laboratory of Archaeology, Indiana University (Bloomington, IN 47401).
Department of Anthropology, Ball State University (Muncie, IN 47306).
Department of Sociology/Anthropology, University of Notre Dame (Notre Dame, IN 46556).

Relevant legislation:
Minimal.

IOWA

State Archaeologist
Eastlawn Building
The University of Iowa
Iowa City, IA 52242

Iowa Archaeological Society
The University of Iowa
Iowa City, IA 52242

Quad City Archaeological Society
4106 El Rancho Drive
Davenport, IA 52806

Sites to visit:
Effigy Mounds National Monument, near Marquette.
Fish Farm Mounds, near New Albin.
Pikes Peak State Park (mound builders), near McGregor.

Source material:
Newsletter and various journals published by Iowa Archaeological Society, including, *The Surface Collector, Historic Sauk
Indian Art and Technology, Identifying Iowa Projectile Points,*
and *The Mound Builders; An American Myth.* Write for free
publications list. Enclose self-addressed stamped envelope.

Recent fieldwork opportunities offered by:
Iowa Archaeological Society (address above), sites near Milford
(in cooperation with the University of Iowa) and Logansport (in
cooperation with Iowa State University).

Relevant legislation:
Minimal; no provision for the granting of permits for archaeological investigation.

KANSAS

Contact:
State Archaeologist
Kansas State Historical Society
10th and Jackson Streets
Topeka, KS 66612

Kansas Anthropological Association
Route 2
Beloit, KS 67420

Department of Anthropology
University of Kansas
Lawrence, KS 66044

Sites to visit:

Indian Burial Pit; National Historic Landmark, near Salina.

Hillsdale Lake Project (Archaic Indian through Historic), near Hillsdale.
Inscription Rock (petroglyphs), near Ellsworth.

Source material:

An Introduction to Kansas Archaeology, Waldo Wedel, Bureau of American Ethnology, Smithsonian Institution, Washington, D.C. 20560.

Various publications of the Kansas State Historical Society and Kansas Anthropological Association (addresses above).

Recent fieldwork opportunities offered by:

Kansas Anthropological Association (address above); Tobias Site, Rice County.

Department of Anthropology, Wichita State University (Wichita, KS 67208); research and survey work at Hillsdale Lake Project, about 130 sites.

Relevant legislation:

Permits for archaeological excavation, including the removal of material from sites, are to be obtained from the Kansas Antiquities Commission, which is composed of the state archaeologist, the secretary of the State Historical Society, and the heads of the department of anthropology at the principal state universities. Such permits are granted to educational or research institutions and to public organizations judged to be professionally competent.

KENTUCKY

Contact:

Department of Anthropology
University of Kentucky
Lexington, KY 40506

Department of Anthropology
University of Western Kentucky
Bowling Green, KY 42101

Archaeological Survey
University of Louisville
Louisville, KY 40208

Kentucky Archaeological Association, Inc.
Department of Anthropology
Western Kentucky University
Bowling Green, KY 42101

Chapters:
   Louisville Archaeological Society, c/o Lewis Soule, 2906
   Brinkley Way, Apartment 2, Louisville, KY 40218

   Bowling Green Chapter of the Kentucky Archaeological
   Association, c/o Department of Sociology and Anthropology, Western Kentucky University, Bowling Green, KY
   42101

Kentucky Historical Society
Old State House
P.O. Box H
Frankfort, KY 40601

Site to visit:
Mammoth Cave National Park (Archaic Indian), near Bowling
Green.

Source material:
Prehistoric Indians of Southern Kentucky, Jack M. Schock,
1978, $3.50; available from Department of Sociology and Anthro-
pology, Western Kentucky University (address above).
A *Bibliography of Kentucky Archaeology*, Mary L. Bowman,
1973; available from Kentucky Archaeology Association (address
above).
Various publications and bulletins of the Kentucky Archaeological Association.

Recent fieldwork opportunities offered by:
Department of Sociology and Anthropology, Western Kentucky University (address above).

Relevant legislation:
Permits to conduct archaeological investigation on locally, state-,

Right, excavation work is frequently meticulous work. (Catholic University of America; Joan Walker)

Below, a Marshalltown trowel. (George Sullivan)

A student profiles and maps archaeological section at Grasshopper Pueblo, University of Arizona Archaeological Field School. (Arizona State Museum, University of Arizona; C. Silver)

Left, this is skim shoveling. (George Sullivan) Right, features like these have to be described and their positions carefully plotted. (Catholic University of America; Joan Walker)

Grid frame helps in plotting small features. (Earthwatch)

This efficient sifting system utilizes collapsible tripod from which screening tray is suspended. (George Sullivan)

Left, analyzing and weighing lithic material collected from excavation, University of Arizona Archaeological Field School. (Arizona State Museum, University of Arizona; C. Silver) Right, a partially mended nineteenth-century creamware bowl. (George Sullivan)

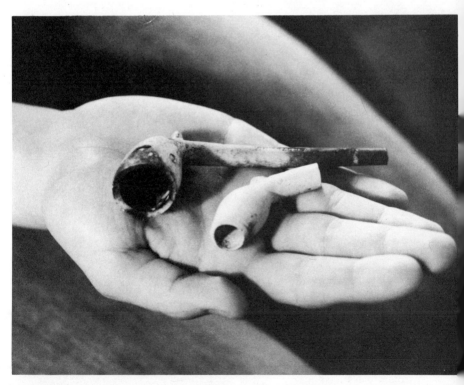

Small-bowled pipe dates to mid-seventeenth century. Bigger bowl indicates pipe of more recent manufacture. This one dates to 1880s. (George Sullivan)

or county-owned land are issued by the Department of Anthropology, University of Kentucky (address above). Only professional archaeologists representing educational or research institutions are granted such permits.

LOUISIANA

Contact:
Louisiana Archaeological Society
Department of Sociology and Anthropology
University of Southwestern Louisiana
Lafayette, LA 70503

Department of Geography and Anthropology
Louisiana State University
Baton Rouge, LA 70803

Sites to visit:
Marksville Prehistoric Indian Park State Monument (mound builders), near Marksville.
Pargood Landing Site (Late Woodland Indian, Mississippian, Historic), Monroe.

Recent fieldwork offered by:
Geosciences Department, Northeastern Louisiana University (Monroe, LA 71201); research at Pargood Landing site.
Department of Anthropology, Tulane University (New Orleans, LA 70118).

Relevant legislation:
Minimal.

MAINE

Contact:
Maine Archaeological Society
Box 133
Stillwater, ME 04489

Department of Sociology and Anthropology
University of Maine
Orono, ME 04473

Maine State Museum
State House
Augusta, ME 04430

Site to visit:
Damariscotta River Shell Mounds, Damariscotta.

Source material:
Various publications of Maine Archaeological Society (address above).

Recent fieldwork opportunities offered by:
Department of Anthropology, University of Southern Maine (College Avenue, Gorham, ME 04038).

Relevant legislation:
Permits for excavation on state land are to be obtained from a committee composed of the director of the State Museum, the senior archaeologist at the University of Maine (address above), and a representative of the state agency having jurisdiction over the land involved. Archaeological materials on state lands are regarded as state property; thus, artifacts recovered must be given over to the state museum for permanent custody.

MARYLAND

Contact:
Tyler Bastian
State Archaeologist
Division of Archaeology
Maryland Geological Survey
The Johns Hopkins University
Baltimore, MD 21218

Archaeological Society of Maryland, Inc.
c/o Mary Lathroum
729 Hollen Road
Baltimore, MD 21212

Department of Anthropology
University of Maryland
College Park, MD 20742

> *Chapters:* Anne Arundel County, Baltimore County, Catons-
> ville, Central (Baltimore area), Hartford County, Lower
> Delmarva (Somerset, Wicomico, and Worcester counties),
> Northeastern (northern Eastern Shore), Pikesville-Milford
> (northwest suburban Baltimore high schools), South-
> western (Washington, D.C., and Maryland suburbs).

Source material:
Biannual journal and various publications of the Archaeological
Society of Maryland; publications list can be obtained from Paul
Cresthull, editor, *Maryland Archaeology* (721 Hookers Mill Road,
Abingdon, MD 21009).

The Prehistoric People of Accokeek Creek, Robert L. Stephen-
son, 1959, $1.00; available from the Alice Ferguson Foundation
(Accokeek, MD 20607).

A Brief Survey of Prehistoric Man on the Delmarva Peninsula,
Ronald A. Thomas, 1974, 50¢; available from Island Field Museum (Route 2, Box 126, Milford, DE 19963).

Recent fieldwork opportunities offered by:
State Archaeologist, Division of Archaeology, Maryland Geological Survey (address above); Fort Frederick, Catoctin Iron Furnace, and tentatively, Point Lookout Civil War camp and prison.

Archaeologists, St. Mary's City Commission (Box 26, St.
Mary's City, MD 20686); research concerning Maryland's first
capital.

Staff Archaeologist, Maryland Historical Trust (21 State Circle,
Annapolis, MD 21401).

Department of Anthropology, George Washington University
(Washington, D.C. 20052); research and field school at Abell's
Wharf site.

Relevant legislation:

No one can "excavate, appropriate, injure, or destroy" any archaeological site on land owned or controlled by the state without obtaining a permit from the office of the state archaeologist, Maryland Geological Survey (address above). Permits are issued to individuals or institutions who, in the survey's judgment, are found "qualified to conduct an excavation to gather objects and material of historical or archaeological value or interest."

MASSACHUSETTS

Contact:

Maurice Robbins
State Archaeologist
Bronson Museum
8 North Main Street
Attleboro, MA 02703

Massachusetts Archaeological Society
Bronson Museum
(address above)

Sites to visit:

Cape Cod National Seashore (Archaic to Woodland Indian), Eastham.
Dighton Rock State Park (petroglyphs), Assonet.

Source material:

Biannual bulletin published by Massachusetts Archaeological Society (address above).

An Introduction to the Archaeology and History of the Connecticut Valley Indian, William R. Young, editor; Springfield Museum of Science, 1969.

Recent fieldwork opportunities offered by:

Public Archaeology Laboratory, Brown University (Providence, RI 02912); sites along Route 495 in Norton and Taunton.

Institute for Conservation Archaeology, Peabody Museum, Harvard University (Cambridge, MA 02138).

Department of Anthropology, Machmer Hall, University of Massachusetts (Amherst, MA 01003); survey and excavation of prehistoric sites in Connecticut River Valley.

Archaeological Field School, Harvard Summer School (20 Garden Street, Cambridge, MA 02138).

Relevant legislation:

The state archaeologist (address above) is responsible for the preservation and protection of the state's archaeological resources. He is empowered to issue permit for exploration and field investigation. All specimens collected through such activity become the permanent property of the state.

MICHIGAN

Contact:

State Archaeologist
Michigan History Division
Department of State
Lansing, MI 48918

Michigan Archaeological Society
Museum of Anthropology
University of Michigan
Ann Arbor, MI 48104

Michigan Archaeological Association
Department of Anthropology
Western Michigan State University
Kalamazoo, MI 49001

Department of Anthropology
Michigan State University
East Lansing, MI 48823

Sites to visit:

Fort Gratiot (Historic, 1814–79), Port Huron.
Historic Fort Wayne Museum (mound builders), Detroit.
Isle Royale National Park (Paleo-Indian), Houghton.
Norton Mounds National Historic Landmark, near Grand Rapids.

Source material:

Michigan Archaeology, quarterly publication of the Anthropology Department, Michigan State University (East Lansing, MI 48823).

Relevant legislation:

The state reserves the right to explore and excavate all archaeological sites on state-owned and state-controlled land. Permits to conduct archaeological investigation must be obtained from the Director, Department of Natural Resources (Lansing, MI 48918).

MINNESOTA

Contact:

State Archaeologist
Department of Anthropology
University of Minnesota
Minneapolis, MN 55455

Minnesota Archaeological Society
Buildings 25–27, Fort Snelling
St. Paul, MN 55111

Minnesota Historical Society
1500 Mississippi Street
St. Paul, MN 55101

Sites to visit:

Mounds Park, St. Paul.
Pipestone National Monument (to Historic Indian), near Pipestone.

Source material:

Minnesota Archaeologist, quarterly publication of the Minnesota Archaeological Society (address above).

Various publications of the Minnesota Historical Society (address above); write for publications list, enclosing self-addressed stamped envelope. Publications include:

The Prehistoric Peoples of Minnesota, Elden Johnson, 1969, $1.50.

The Jeffers Petroglyphs Site; A Survey and Analysis, Gordon Allan Lothson, 1976, $3.75.

Recent fieldwork opportunities offered by:
Minnesota Archaeological Society (address above).
Hamline Field School; Hamline University (St. Paul, MN 55104).

Relevant legislation:
The state declares all archaeological sites on state lands to be under its jurisdiction, and discourages field archaeology on private lands. Permits to conduct archaeological investigation on state lands are to be obtained from the Minnesota Historical Society (address above).

MISSISSIPPI

Contact:
Mississippi Archaeological Association
115 Wiltshire Boulevard
Biloxi, MS 39531

   Chapters:
   Gulf Coast (Route 7, Box 148, Ocean Springs, MS 39564).
   Clarksdale (615 Oakhurst Ave., Clarksdale, MS 38614).
   Winterville Mounds (Route 2, Box 146, Shaw, MS 38773).

Department of Archives and History
State of Mississippi
P.O. Box 571
Jackson, MS 39205

Sites to visit:
Bynum Mounds, near Tupelo.
Emerald Mound, near Natchez.
Owl Creek Indian Mounds, Tombigbee National Forest, near Old Houlka.
Winterville Mounds State Park, near Greenville.

Source material:

Newsletter published by Mississippi Archaeological Association (address above).

Archaeological survey reports published by Mississippi Department of Archives and History (address above).

Recent fieldwork opportunities offered by:

Department of Anthropology, Mississippi State University (Mississippi State, MS 39762).

Relevant legislation:

Legislation enacted in 1970 declares that all archaeological objects and artifacts, "as well as archaeological sites of every character," that are located on state land, belong to the state and may not be "altered, damaged, destroyed, salvaged, or excavated" without a permit. Such permits are issued by the Department of Archives and History (address above).

MISSOURI

Contact:

Missouri Archaeological Society
15 Switzler Hall
P.O. Box 958
Columbia, MO 65201

Sites to visit:

Graham Cave State Park, National Historic Landmark (Paleo-Indian), near Danville.

Lyman Archaeological Research Center and Hamilton Field School, National Historic Landmark, near Marshall.

Towosahgy State Park (Mississippian Indian), near East Prairie.

Washington State Park (petroglyphs), near Desoto.

Source material:

Various publications of the Missouri Archaeological Society (address above), including *The Missouri Archaeologist*. Write for free publications list, enclosing self-addressed, stamped envelope.

Relevant legislation:
Minimal.

MONTANA

Contact:
Montana Archaeological Society
Department of Anthropology
University of Montana
Missoula, MT 59801

Department of Anthropology
Montana State University
Bozeman, MT 59715

Site to visit:
Pictograph Cave State Monument, near Billings.

Source material:
Archaeology in Montana, publication of the Montana Archaeological Society (address above).

Recent fieldwork opportunities offered by:
Dr. Larry A. Lahren (Box 1218, Livingston, MT 59047); research and survey work at various sites in Montana and Wyoming.

Relevant legislation:
Permits for excavation are required. They are issued by the commissioner of public lands upon the recommendation of the state historical society. Excavation of an archaeological site on state land without a permit can be deemed a misdemeanor.

NEBRASKA

Contact:
Nebraska State Historical Society
1500 R Street
Lincoln, NB 68508

Department of Anthropology
University of Nebraska, Lincoln
Lincoln, NB 68588

Source material:
   Chapters in Nebraska Archaeology, E. H. Bell, editor; available
from University of Nebraska (address above).

Recent fieldwork opportunities offered by:
   Department of Anthropology, University of Nebraska, Lincoln,
NB 68588.
   Nebraska State Historical Society (address above).

Relevant legislation:
   Minimal.

NEVADA

Contact:
   Nevada Archaeological Survey
   University of Nevada
   Reno, NV 89507

   Nevada Historical Society
   1650 North Virginia Street
   Reno, NV 89503

Sites to visit:
   Lake Mead National Recreation Area (petroglyphs), near Las
Vegas.
   Red Rock Recreation Area (petroglyphs), near Las Vegas.
   Valley of Fire State Park (Anasazi Indians), near Overton.

Relevant legislation:
   Excavation of archaeological sites on state land is prohibited
unless a permit has been obtained from the Nevada State Museum. Such permits are granted only to trained persons representing scientific or educational institutions.

NEW HAMPSHIRE

Contact:
New Hampshire Archaeological Society
Averill Road
Brookline, NH 03103

Sites to visit:
Newington Site (early Colonial), Newington.
Weirs Beach (Paleo-Indian and Woodland), Laconia.

Source material:
Various publications of the New Hampshire Archaeological Society (address above), including *The New Hampshire Archaeologist.*
Colby's Indian History, Solon Colby, 1975, Walker Pound Press, $10; available from the author (65 Park Street, Exeter, NH 03833).
The Neville Site, Dina Dinauze, 1976, Peabody Museum Monograph, $8.95; available from Kenneth Rhodes (19 Fairbanks Street, Manchester, NH 03103).

Recent fieldwork opportunities offered by:
Department of Anthropology, Franklin Pierce College (Rindge, NH 03461).
Archaeological Research Services (424 Social Science Center, University of New Hampshire, Durham, NH 03824); research and survey work at Colonial Newington; also at Weirs Indian site.
Frederick J. E. Gorman, Director, Archaeological Laboratory, Boston University (232 Bay State Road, Boston, MA 02215); research at New England glassworks, 1780–82.

NEW JERSEY

Contact:
Archaeological Society of New Jersey
Room 106

Humanities Building
Seton Hall University
South Orange, NJ 07079

   Chapters:
   Abnaki, Salem County (Garrison Road, R.D. 1, Monroe-
ville, NJ 08343).
   Monmouth County (407 Sunset Avenue, Asbury Park, NJ
07712).
   Minisink, Sussex and Warren counties (4 Ashford Street,
Newton, NJ 07860).
   Southern New Jersey (316 Middlesex Street, Gloucester, NJ
08030).
   Unami, Middlesex, Monmouth, and Mercer counties (95
Broad Street, Matawan, NJ 07747).

Bureau of Research-Archaeology
Department of Education
State Museum
P.O. Box 1868
Trenton, NJ 08625

Department of Anthropology
Rutgers University
New Brunswick, NJ 08903

Site to visit:
Paterson Historic District (1780s to present), Paterson.

Source material:
Various publications of the Archaeological Society of New Jersey (address above).
   Archaeology of New Jersey, Volumes I and II, Dorothy Cross;
available from Bureau of Research-Archaeology (address above).
   Weekends in the Soil, Edward J. Lenik, $4.00; available from
the Archaeological Society of New Jersey.

Recent fieldwork opportunities offered by:
Roger L. Holzen, Redevelopment Division, Department of
Community Development (100 Hamilton Plaza, Paterson, NJ

07505); research, survey, and salvage work at nineteenth-century Paterson site.

Relevant legislation:
  Minimal.

NEW MEXICO

Contact:
  State Archaeologist
  Laboratory of Anthropology
  Museum of New Mexico
  Santa Fe, NM 87501

  Archaeological Society of New Mexico
  Box 3485
  Albuquerque, NM 87110

  Department of Anthropology
  University of New Mexico
  Albuquerque, NM 87106

Sites to visit:
  Albuquerque Petroglyphs, near Albuquerque.
  Aztec Ruins National Monument (Anasazi Indians), Aztec.
  Bandelier National Monument (Anasazi Indians), Projoaque.
  Chaco Canyon National Monument (Anasazi Indians), near Bloomfield.
  Gila Cliff Dwellings (Mogollon Indians), near Silver City.
  Gran Quivira National Monument (Mogollon Indians), near Carrizozo.
  Pecos National Monument (Anasazi Indians), near Santa Fe.
  Quarai State Monument (Historic, seventeenth-century Spanish), Punta de Aqua.
  Sandia Man Cave (Clovis), near Albuquerque.
  Three Rivers Petroglyphs, near Carrizozo.

Source material:
  Various publications of the Archaeological Society of New Mexico (address above).

Recent fieldwork opportunities offered by:

Archaeological Society of New Mexico (Harry L. Hadlock, P.O. Box 397, Fruitland, NM 87416); excavation of Pueblo Indian site on outskirts of Gallup, New Mexico.

San Juan Valley Archaeological Project, Eastern New Mexico University (Portales, NM 88130).

Department of Anthropology, Adams State College (Alamosa, CO 81102).

Department of Anthropology, Northern Arizona University (Flagstaff, AZ 86011).

Relevant legislation:

Permits to excavate or carry on other archaeological activities must be obtained from the Cultural Properties Review Committee, which consists of seven members, including the state archaeologist (address above), state historian, and other professional archaeologists appointed by the governor. Only museums, colleges, and universities, or other historic, scientific, or educational institutions, can be granted such permits.

NEW YORK

Contact:

State Archaeologist
State Education Department
New York State Museum and Science Service
University of the State of New York
Albany, NY 12234

New York State Archaeological Association
c/o Dr. Elizabeth M. Dumont
29 Highridge Road
Monroe, NY 10950

    Chapters in: Saratoga Springs, Syracuse, Norwich, Amherst, Southold, Middletown, Rochester, Rhinebeck, Binghamton, Otego, Fonda, and New York City.

New York Institute of Anthropology
34–15 94th Street
Jackson Heights, NY 11372

Rochester Museum and Science Center
657 East Avenue
Box 1480
Rochester, NY 14603

Site to visit:
Ostego County Site (Middle Woodland Indian), near Coopers-town.

Source material:
The Bulletin, publication of the New York State Archaeological Society, issued by the Rochester Museum and Science Center (address above).
The Archaeology of New York State, William A. Ritchie, the Natural History Press, New York, 1969.

Recent fieldwork opportunities offered by:
New York State Institute of Anthropology (34–15 94th Street, Jackson Heights, NY 11372); research, survey, and salvage at various sites in Queens and Schoharie counties, involving Archaic to Woodland periods.
Department of Anthropology, State University of New York at Albany (Albany, NY 12222); research and survey work in Lake George area, involving Paleo-Indian to Late Woodland periods.
Department of Anthropology, State University College at Oneonta (Oneonta, NY 13820); research and survey work in Ostego County, involving Middle Woodland site.
Public Archaeology Facility, Department of Anthropology, State University of New York at Binghamton (Binghamton, NY 13901); investigation and evaluation involving several historic and prehistoric sites.
Department of Anthropology, State University of New York at Buffalo (Buffalo, NY 14214); research and survey work in western New York state.
Department of Anthropology, State University College at New Paltz (New Paltz, NY 12561); research and survey work at prehistoric sites in lower Hudson Valley.
Department of Anthropology, City University of New York, Convent Avenue and 138th Street. (New York, NY 10031); research, survey, and salvage work at various historical sites in New York City area.

New School for Social Research, 66 West 12th Street, New York, NY 10011.

Relevant legislation:
No person is permitted to "appropriate, excavate, injure, or destroy" any object of archaeological or paleontological interest located on lands owned by the state without the written permission of the commissioner of education.

NORTH CAROLINA

Contact:
State Archaeologist
Research Laboratory of Anthropology
University of North Carolina
Chapel Hill, NC 27514

Archaeological Society of North Carolina
(address above)

State Department of Archives and History
Division of Historic Sites
P.O. Box 18
Raleigh, NC 27514

Sites to visit:
Oconaluftee Indian Village (prehistoric, historic), near Cherokee.
Town Creek Indian Mound State Historic Site, National Historic Landmark, near Mount Gilead.

Source material:
Southern Indian Studies, publication of Archaeological Society of North Carolina (address above).

Relevant legislation:
The excavation or destruction of archaeological material on state-owned or controlled land is prohibited without a permit from the director of the State Museum or the Department of

Archives and History (address above). Private landowners are urged to seek professional guidance when archaeological materials are found on their property.

NORTH DAKOTA

Contact:
   Survey Archaeologist
   State Historical Society of North Dakota
   Liberty Memorial Building
   Bismarck, ND 58505

   Department of Anthropology and Archaeology
   University of North Dakota
   Babcock Hall
   Grand Forks, ND 58502

Sites to visit:
   Fort Clark Historic Site (Mandan Indian Village), Fort Clark.
   Huff Indian Village Historic Site (Mandan Indian Village), Huff.
   Molander Indian Village Historic Site, near Price.
   Slant Indian Village (Mandan Indian site), Fort Lincoln State Park.

Source material:
   North Dakota History; Journal of the Northern Plains, quarterly publication of the State Historical Society of North Dakota (address above).

Relevant legislation:
   A permit to investigate or excavate on state land must be obtained from the State Historical Society Board (address above). Issued only to "qualified persons," such permits cost $5.00 per year for one site and $2.50 for each additional site. A one-year renewal costs $2.00. If the site is on state land, all objects recovered must be deposited with the Historical Society. The preparation of a final report is another requirement.

OHIO

Contact:
    Department of Archaeology
    Ohio Historical Society
    I-71 and 17th Avenue
    Columbus, OH 43211

    Regional Archaeological Preservation Office
    Department of Anthropology
    College of Social and Behavioral Sciences
    Ohio State University
    213 Lord Hall
    124 West 17th Avenue
    Columbus, OH 43210

Sites to visit:
    Campbell Mound, Columbus.
    Flint Ridge Memorial (Paleo-Indian), near Brownsville.
    Fort Ancient State Memorial (Hopewell Indian), near Lebanon.
    Fort Hill State Memorial (Hopewell Indian), near Hillsboro.
    Inscription Rock (petroglyphs), near Sandusky.
    Knob Prairie Mound, Enon.
    Leo Petroglyph, near Jackson.
    Miamisburg Mound State Memorial, Miamisburg.
    Mound City Group National Monument, near Chillicothe.
    Newark Earthworks, Newark.
    Seip Mound, near Bainbridge.
    Serpent Mound State Memorial, near Peeples.
    Steubenville Site (Middle to Late Archaic Indian), Steubenville.
    Story Mound, Chillicothe.
    Tarlton Cross Mound, Tarlton.

Recent fieldwork opportunities offered by:
    Department of Archaeology, Ohio Historical Society (address above).

Regional Archaeological Preservation Office, Department of Anthropology, College of Social and Behavioral Sciences, Ohio State University (address above).

Department of Anthropology, Loyola University of Chicago (6525 North Sheridan Road, Chicago, IL 60657); survey and excavation work on Little Miami River in southwest Ohio.

Department of Anthropology, University of Pittsburgh (234 Atwood Street, Pittsburgh, PA 15260) in cooperation with the College of Steubenville.

Department of History, the Defiance College (Defiance, OH 43512).

Relevant legislation:

The Ohio Historical Society (address above) is granted the authority to acquire and administer archaeological sites.

OKLAHOMA

Contact:

State Archaeologist
Oklahoma Archaeological Survey
Department of Anthropology
The University of Oklahoma
1335 South Asp Avenue
Norman, OK 73019

Oklahoma Anthropological Society
c/o Harvey E. King
1000 Horn Street
Muskogee, OK 74401

Chapters:

Kay County (522 North Pine Street, Ponca City, OK 74601).

Tulsa Archaeological Society (915 East Elgin Avenue, Broken Arrow, OK 74012).

Muskogee Archaeological Society (1000 Horn Street, Muskogee, OK 74401).

Oklahoma City (2217 Arlington Drive, Oklahoma City, OK 73108).

Lawton (2101 Oak Street, Duncan, OK 73533).
East Texas (Box 374, Jacksboro, TX 75056).

Site to visit:
Fort Towson Historic Site (1824–65), Fort Towson.

Source material:
Various publications of Oklahoma Anthropological Society (address above); write for free publications list, enclosing self-addressed, stamped envelope.

Recent fieldwork opportunities offered by:
Oklahoma Anthropological Society in cooperation with Oklahoma Archaeological Survey (address above); annual dig for amateurs interested in learning and applying proper archaeological techniques under professional supervision.

Oklahoma Archaeological Survey (address above); investigation and excavation at late-prehistoric mound and village site, Sequoyah County; survey and testing of Salt Creek Watershed, Osage County; excavation and stabilization of Fort Towson.

Relevant legislation:
Anyone making any investigation, exploration, or excavation of any archaeological site, whether it be on private, state, or federal land, must first obtain a license from the chairman, Department of Anthropology, University of Oklahoma (address above). The license fee is $50. There is an annual renewal fee of $25. In obtaining the license, the licensee agrees to donate 50 per cent of all recovered articles to the Museum of Science and History of the University of Oklahoma. Violating any provisions of the law is a misdemeanor, punishable by a fine of $200, thirty days imprisonment in the county jail, or both.

OREGON

Contact:
Oregon Archaeological Society
Department of Anthropology
University of Oregon
Eugene, OR 97403

Department of Anthropology
Oregon State University
Corvallis, OR 97330

Site to visit:
Fort Rock Cave Historical Site (petroglyphs), near Silver Lake.

Source material:
Various anthropological papers of the University of Oregon
(address above).

Recent fieldwork opportunities offered by:
Summer Field Director, Department of Anthropology, University of Oregon, Eugene, OR 97403.
Department of Anthropology, University of Washington, Seattle, WA 98195.

Relevant legislation:
Permits to excavate on and remove artifacts from land owned or controlled by the state must be obtained from the president, University of Oregon (address above). Such permits are granted only to reputable educational and scientific organizations or institutions.

PENNSYLVANIA

Contact:
State Archaeologist
Commonwealth of Pennsylvania

Pennsylvania Historical and Museum Commission
William Penn Memorial Museum
Box 1026
Harrisburg, PA 17120

Dr. Roger Moeller
Society for Pennsylvania Archaeology
Box 260
Washington, CT 06793

Department of Anthropology
Pennsylvania State University
University Park, PA 16802

Department of Anthropology
University of Pennsylvania
University Museum
Philadelphia, PA 19104

Site to visit:
Sommerheim Site (Late Archaic Indian), Erie.

Source material:
Pennsylvania Archaeologist, official publication of the Society
for Pennsylvania Archaeology (address above), issued three times
a year.

Recent fieldwork opportunities offered by:
State Archaeologist, Commonwealth of Pennsylvania (address
above), salvage work at various sites.

Department of Anthropology, University of Pittsburgh (Pittsburgh, PA 15260); field school at Ashton Farm, Archaic through
Late Woodland periods.

Anthropology Program, Gannon College (Erie, PA 16501).

Archaeological Laboratory, Clarion State College (Clarion, PA
16214); annual summer field school involving excavation work
and individual research at a site near a ford in the Clarion River;
archaeological sequence ranges from Historic period to Pleistocene.

Anthropology Section, West Chester State College (West
Chester, PA 19380); excavation at Taylor burying-ground site,

one of country's only "controlled excavations" involving Colonial America; also testing at Hunters' Hill and other Indian sites.

Relevant legislation:
   Minimal; the Pennsylvania Historical and Museum Commission (address above) is responsible for conducting excavation of all prehistoric sites, but there is no provision for the issuing of licenses or permits.

RHODE ISLAND

Contact:
   The Narragansett Archaeological Society of Rhode Island
   c/o Elizabeth G. Weeks
   277 Brook Street
   Providence, RI 02906

Source material:
   Archaic Discoveries at Flat Rock, Sweet Meadow Brook; A Pottery Site in Rhode Island, Stone Pipe-Making, and other bulletins published by the Narragansett Archaeological Society (address above), available at $1.50 each. Write for free publications list, enclosing self-addressed, stamped envelope.

Relevant legislation:
   Minimal.

SOUTH CAROLINA

Contact:
   State Archaeologist
   Institute of Archaeology and Anthropology
   University of South Carolina
   Columbia, SC 29208

   South Carolina Archaeological Society
   1601 St. Anthony Drive
   Florence, SC 29501

Site to visit:
  Sewee Mound Archaeological Area, Francis Marion National Forest, near Charleston.

Source material:
  Publications available from the office of the State Archaeologist (address above). These include the *Anthropological Studies Sites;* also the *Notebook,* which carries reports of archaeological investigations and is mailed free to those requesting they be placed on the mailing list.

Recent fieldwork opportunities offered by:
  Department of Anthropology, Coastal Carolina College, University of South Carolina (Conway, SC 29526); research involving Paleo-Indian to Woodland sites.

Relevant legislation:
  Minimal, except as it refers to "underwater lands." Permits are required to search such lands.

SOUTH DAKOTA

Contact:
  State Archaeologist
  Archaeological Research Center
  P.O. Box 152
  Fort Meade, SD 57741

  South Dakota State Archaeological Commission
  State Historical Society
  Pierre, SD 57501

  University of South Dakota
  W. H. Over Dakota Museum
  Vermillion, SD 57069

Site to visit:
  Sherman Park Indian Burial Mounds, Sioux Falls.

Source material:

Introduction to Middle Missouri Archaeology, Donald L. Lehmer Anthropological Papers 1, National Park Service, U. S. Department of the Interior, Washington, D.C., 1971.

Prehistoric Man on the Great Plains, Waldo R. Wedel, University of Oklahoma Press, Norman.

Recent fieldwork opportunities offered by:

Mitchell Archaeological Site, Mitchell, SD 57301.

South Dakota Archaeological Research Center (address above).

Division of Natural Sciences, Augustana College (Sioux Falls, SD 57102).

Relevant legislation:

Permits are required to dig on any public land in the state. Such permits are issued by the State Historical Society (address above), and their issuance depends upon the "scientific fitness" of the applicant. There is a filing fee of $5.00 for the first site, and a fee of $2.50 for each additional site. A one-year renewal is $2.00. Permit-holders must agree to deliver one half of all material recovered to the state. Violation of the law is a misdemeanor, punishable by a fine of $100 or a maximum of thirty days' imprisonment in the county jail.

TENNESSEE

Contact:

Division of Archaeology
Tennessee Department of Conservation
5103 Edmondson Pike
Nashville, TN 37211

Tennessee Archaeological Society
Frank H. McClung Museum
The University of Tennessee
Knoxville, TN 37916

Sites to visit:

Chucalissa Indian Town and Museum (Early Woodland to Historic), near Memphis.

Shiloh Mounds, Shiloh National Military Park, near Savannah.

Source material:

Various publications of the Tennessee Archaeological Society, including *Tennessee Archaeologist*, Vol. 32, Nos. 1–2, 1976, $4.25, containing articles, illustrations, tables, charts, and references concerning Tennessee archaeology. Available from Tennessee Archaeological Society (Kenneth W. Steverson, Route 3, Ridgeview Estates, Columbia, TN 38401).

Relevant legislation:

Permits to excavate on state land are issued by the Division of Archaeology, Department of Conservation (address above). Artifacts recovered remain the property of the state.

TEXAS

Contact:

Director
Archaeological Surveys and Research
Texas Historical Commission
P.O. Box 12276
Austin, TX 78711

Center for Archaeological Research
The University of Texas at San Antonio
San Antonio, TX 78285

Texas Archaeological Society
P.O. Box 161
Southern Methodist University
Dallas, TX 75275

Chapters:

Panhandle (Amarillo), South Plains (Lubbock), Nacogdoches, Houston, Midland, El Paso, Iraan, Coastal Bend (Corpus Christi), Central Texas (Waco), Tarrant County

(Fort Worth), Dallas, Travis County (Austin), Fort Hood and Young County (Graham).

Southern Texas Archaeological Association
c/o Shirley Van der Veer
123 East Crestline
San Antonio, TX 68201

Sites to visit:
Alibates Flint Quarries (Paleo-Indian), near Amarillo.
Hop Hill (Archaic Indian), Gillespie.
Lubbock Lake Site (Clovis to Historic Indian), Lubbock.
Mitchell Ridge (Paleo-Indian and Historic Indian), Galveston Island.
San Gabriel River Area (Paleo-Indian to Historic Indian), Georgetown.

Source material:
Various publications of the Center for Archaeological Research (address above), including *A Guide to the Identification of Burins in Prehistoric Chipped Stone Assemblages,* Jean M. Pitzer, $2.00; *Hunters and Gatherers of the Rio Grande Plain and Lower Coast of Texas,* T. R. Hester, $1.00; and *Early Human Occupation in South Central and Southwestern Texas,* T. R. Hester, $2.00. Write for free publications list, enclosing self-addressed, stamped envelope.

Bulletin of Texas archaeology and newsletter, *Texas Archaeology,* publications of the Texas Archaeological Society (address above).

Quarterly *Journal* and occasional newsletters published by the Southern Texas Archaeological Association (address above).

Recent fieldwork opportunities offered by:
Center for Archaeological Research (address above); the center has conducted more than 130 projects, involving prehistoric and historic archaeology, ethnohistorical research, and historical studies (see map). Volunteers are welcomed on many Center excavation projects.

Texas Archaeological Society (address above); survey and field school at Mitchell Ridge, prehistoric and historic site on Galveston Island for members of the Texas Archaeological Society.

The Museum, Texas Tech University (Lubbock, TX 79409); research at Lubbock Lake site, Clovis to Historic period.

Division of Social Sciences, University of Texas (San Antonio, TX 78285); field school at Hop Hill site, Archaic period.

Institute of Applied Sciences (P.O. Box 5057, Denton, TX 73603); research, survey, and salvage work at Paleo-Indian through Historic sites near San Gabriel River.

Relevant legislation:

A seven-member Antiquities Commission issues permits to private institutions, companies, and individuals for salvage, excavation, or scientific or educational study involving state landmarks, when, in the opinion of the commission, "the permit is in the best interest of the State of Texas." The permit-holder may, depending on the terms of the permit contract, retain a portion of the artifacts recovered. Violation of any provisions of the law is a misdemeanor, punishable by a fine of from $50 to $1,000, imprisonment for thirty days, or both.

UTAH

Contact:
Utah Archaeological Society
Department of Anthropology
University of Utah
Salt Lake City, UT 84122

State Park Board
Boulder, UT 84716

Sites to visit:
Alkali Ridge (Anasazi Indians), near Monticello.
Anasazi Indian Village State Historical Monument, Boulder.
Butler Wash Archaeological Project (Anasazi Indians), near Blanding.
Canyonlands National Park (Anasazi Indians), north of Moab.
Grand Gulch Archaeological Primitive Area (Anasazi Indians), Grand Gulch.

Natural Bridges National Monument (Anasazi Indians), near Blanding.

Parowan Gap Indian Drawings, Parowan.

Zion National Park (Anasazi Indians), near Kanab.

Source material:
Utah Archaeology, quarterly publication of the Utah Archaeological Society (address above).

Recent fieldwork opportunities offered by:
Department of Anthropology, University of Denver (Denver, CO 80208); research and field school at Butler Wash site near Blanding.

Relevant legislation:
Archaeological investigation or excavation on state or federal land is prohibited without a permit from the State Park Board (address above).

VERMONT

Contact:
Vermont Archaeological Society
Box 663
Burlington, VT 05402

Department of Sociology and Anthropology
University of Vermont
Burlington, VT 05401

Source material:
Archaeology in Vermont; Some Reviews Supplemented by Materials from New England and New York, John C. Huden; available from University of Vermont (address above).

Various monographs and quarterly newsletter of the Vermont Archaeological Society (address above).

Relevant legislation:
Minimal.

VIRGINIA

Contact:
  State Archaeologist
  Virginia State Library
  1101 Capital Square
  Richmond, VA 23219

  Archaeological Society of Virginia
  (address above)

  Virginia Historic Landmarks
  Ninth Street Office Building
  Richmond, VA 25219

Site to visit:
  Flint Run Complex (Paleo-Indian, Archaic, Woodland), Lime-
  ton.

Source material:
  Quarterly Bulletin of the Archaeological Society of Virginia
  (address above).

Recent fieldwork opportunities offered by:
  Director, Summer Field School, College of William and Mary
  (Williamsburg, VA 23185); research and field school at Flower-
  dew Hundred, involving prehistoric and early Colonial periods.
  Anthropology Department, The Catholic University of America
  (Washington, D.C. 20064); research and field school at Flint Run
  complex, involving Paleo-Indian through Woodland periods.
  Department of Sociology, Anthropology, and Social Work,
  James Madison University (Harrisonburg, VA 22801); research,
  salvage, and survey work involving prehistoric sites in Bath
  County.
  Department of Anthropology, the American University (Wash-
  ington, D.C. 20016); research and field school at Jeffrey-Harris
  Rockshelter, involving Early Archaic to Late Woodland periods.
  Virginia Research Center for Archaeology, College of William
  and Mary (Williamsburg, VA 23186); research at Drummond

site (Governor's Land Archaeological District), involving period from 1650 to 1780.

Department of Sociology/Anthropology, Washington and Lee University (Lexington, VA 24450); research and field school at Liberty Hall Academy, involving period from 1780 to 1803.

Thunderbird Research Corporation (Route 1, P.O. Box 212-D, Front Royal, VA 22630); excavation work at Thunderbird and Fifty sites, two different types of Paleo-Indian habitations.

Relevant legislation:

A nine-member Landmarks Committee is responsible for surveying the state for archaeological sites. There is no provision for the issuance of permits or licenses for archaeological investigation or excavation.

WASHINGTON

Contact:
Washington Archaeological Society
Department of Anthropology
University of Washington
Seattle, WA 98195

Department of Anthropology
Washington State University
Pullman, WA 99163

Sites to visit:
Indian Painted Rocks (pictographs), near Spokane.
Lake Lenore Caves (prehistoric), near Coulee City.
Roosevelt Petroglyphs, near Roosevelt.

Source material:
The Washington Archaeologist, official publication of the Washington Archaeological Society (address above).

Recent fieldwork opportunities offered by:
Department of Anthropology, Eastern Washington University, Cheney, WA 99004.

Relevant legislation:

Minimal; prohibits the destruction or removal of any cairns, graves, or painted records except as provided for the president of the University of Washington or Washington State University.

WEST VIRGINIA

Contact:

Archaeology Administrator
Geological and Economic Survey
State of West Virginia
P.O. Box 879
Morgantown, WV 26505

West Virginia Archaeological Society
Morgantown, WV 26505

Site to visit:

Grace Creek Mound State Park, Moundsville.

Source material:

West Virginia Archaeologist, journal of the West Virginia Archaeological Society (address above).

Introduction to West Virginia Archaeology, Edward V. McMichael, 1968, $1.75; available from Geological and Economic Survey (address above).

Relevant legislation:

The nine-member West Virginia Antiquities Commission directs all archaeological research. Archaeological sites on state and private land, once investigative rights have been acquired by the state, cannot be disturbed without the approval of the commission.

WISCONSIN

Contact:

State Archaeologist
The State Historical Society of Wisconsin

816 State Street
Madison, WI 53706

Wisconsin Archaeological Society
Box 1292
Milwaukee, WI 53201

Sites to visit:
  Aztalan State Park, National Historic Landmark (mound build-
  ers), Aztalan.
  Devils Lake State Park (mound builders), near Baraboo.
  Gullickson's Glen (petroglyphs), near Black River Falls.
  High Cliff State Park (mound builders), near Menasha.
  Lizard Mound State Park, near West Bend.
  Man Mound, near Baraboo.
  Menasha Mounds, Menasha.
  Muscoda Mounds, near Muscoda.
  Wyalusing State Park (mound builders), near Prairie du
  Chien.

Source material:
  Wisconsin Archaeologist, quarterly publication of the Wisconsin Archaeological Society (address above).

Recent fieldwork opportunities offered by:
  University of Wisconsin—Madison (Madison, WI 53706);
  summer field school.
  University of Wisconsin—Milwaukee (Milwaukee, WI 53201);
  summer field school.
  University of Wisconsin—Stevens Point (Stevens Point, WI
  54481); summer field school.

Relevant legislation:
  Only the state archaeologist or individuals or institutions
  granted permits by the Historical Society of Wisconsin (address
  above) may excavate on state land. In the case of private land,
  written permission of the landowner must be obtained.

WYOMING

Contact:
  State Archaeologist
  Department of Anthropology
  University of Wyoming
  Laramie, WY 82071

  Wyoming Archaeological Society
  (address above)

Source material:
  The Wyoming Archaeologist, publication of the Wyoming Archaeological Society (address above).
  Prehistoric Hunters of the High Plains, George C. Frison, New York, 1978.

Relevant legislation:
  A permit must be obtained from the State Board of Land Commissioners to conduct archaeological investigation or excavation on federal or state land.

APPENDIX

ABSOLUTE DATING A type of dating that expresses a specific period of time, either in terms of years old or years ago. The date on a coin is an absolute date, so are A.D. 1492 or 794 B.C.

ADZ A cutting tool in which the plane of the blade is set at right angles to the handle.

ANASAZI An Indian civilization of canyon dwellers that existed between A.D. 100 and the 1700s in northeastern Arizona, northwestern New Mexico, southeastern Utah, and southwestern Colorado.

ARCHAEOLOGY The systematic recovery by scientific methods of material evidence remaining from man's life and culture in past ages, and the detailed study of that evidence.

ARCHAIC PERIOD A period of Indian history and culture that began some ten thousand years ago when big game began to die out. People of the Archaic period have been described as hunter-gatherers.

ARGILLITE A metamorphic rock, immediately between shale and slate.

ARTIFACT Any object made or modified by human workmanship; a simple tool, weapon, or ornament. The most common artifacts are pieces of broken pottery, stone chips, projectile points, and tools.

ATLATL   A primitive spear throwing depicted in early North American rock art.

B.P.   The abbreviation for Before Present, a term sometimes used in connection with carbon 14 dating. In order for carbon 14 dates to have uniformity, the "Present" in Before Present has been established as A.D. 1950.

BALK   The stand of earth between two excavated units, usually squares.

BRONZE AGE   The period of archaeology following the Stone Age, characterized by the use of bronze weapons and implements.

CAIRN   A mound of stones.

CARBON 14 DATING   A method of dating once-living objects based on the principle that all plants and animals, while they are alive, take in small amounts of a radioactive form of carbon—carbon 14. When they die, this intake ends. By measuring the loss rate of the carbon 14, the age of the object can be established.

CELT   An ungrooved ax of the Archaic period, often shaped like a chisel.

CHALCEDONY   A milky or grayish quartz that is marked with distinctive parallel bands of contrasting color.

CHERT   Any of the various crystalline mineral varieties of silica.

CONTACT PERIOD   A period in the history and culture of the American Indian wherein the first impact of European explorers or settlers was made manifest.

DATUM POINT   The reference point used for all measurement at a site.

DENDROCHRONOLOGY   The study of the growth rate of rings in trees to determine and date past events.

DIG   An archaeological excavation. (The term is shunned by most professionals.)

DIORITE   A dark, granite-textured, crystalline rock.

EXCAVATION Digging or related types of salvage work, scientifically controlled so as to yield the maximum amount of data.

FEATURE An area in or on the ground where evidence of past human activity can be perceived. The features most common to archaeological sites include fire pits, storage pits, burial pits, postholes, and hard-packed house floors.

FLINT An opaque, fine-grained quartz.

FLOTATION A method of screening in which minute pieces of food evidence are separated from the soil by agitation with water.

FOLSOM CULTURE A Paleo-Indian culture believed to be ten thousand to thirteen thousand years old, and named for Folsom, New Mexico, where important artifacts representing the culture have been found.

HIEROGLYPH A picture or symbol that represents a word or a sound.

HISTORIC ARCHAEOLOGY A branch of archaeological study and interpretation that begins with the introduction of writing in an area; the sixteenth and/or seventeenth centuries in most parts of the United States.

HOHOKAM An Indian civilization that existed from approximately 300 B.C. to A.D. 1400 in sections of Arizona and northern Mexico.

IN SITU In its original place.

INTAGLIO A prehistoric incised carving.

IRON AGE The period of archaeology following the Bronze Age, characterized by the introduction of iron metallurgy; in Europe, beginning around the eighth century B.C.

LITHIC Pertaining to stone.

MALACOLOGY The study of mollusks.

MANO A stone used to grind seeds and nuts by crushing or rubbing them against a stone base; dates to the Archaic Indian period.

MAUL A heavy, long-handled hammer dating to the Archaic Indian period.

MENHIR A prehistoric structure consisting of a tall, upright megalith.

MESOLITHIC A period of archaeology between the Paleolithic and Neolithic ages, characterized by the appearance of bow and cutting tools.

MIDDEN A deposit of cultural debris.

MOGOLLON An Indian civilization that existed from before 500 B.C. to approximately A.D. 1400 in southeastern Arizona and southwestern New Mexico.

NATIONAL REGISTER A federally maintained list of archaeological, architectural, historical, and cultural sites of local, state, or national significance.

NEOLITHIC A period of archaeology beginning around 10,000 B.C. in the Middle East, and later elsewhere, and characterized by the invention of farming and the making of technically advanced stone implements.

NEW WORLD The Western Hemisphere; North and South America.

OBSIDIAN A lustrous volcanic glass, usually black or banded.

OGHAM, OGAM An alphabet used for writing Irish from the fourth or fifth century to the early seventh century.

OLD WORLD The Eastern Hemisphere, with special reference to Europe.

PALEO-INDIAN A period of archaeology beginning with the earliest stone tools, about 750,000 years ago.

PALEOBOTANY The study of ancient plant life.

PALEOLITHIC The Stone Age; the earliest stage in the cultural history of man.

PALEONTOLOGY The study of past geological periods.

PALYNOLOGY The study of spores and pollen.

PETROGLYPH A prehistoric carving on a rock.

PICTOGRAPH A prehistoric painting on a rock.

PLANE TABLE A portable surveying instrument that consists of a drawing board and a ruler mounted on a tripod and used to sight and map topographic details.

PLEISTOCENE A geological period that began about two million years ago and ended approximately ten thousand years ago; the Ice Age.

POTHUNTER One who seeks historically or archaeologically important artifacts merely for their intrinsic value, usually to sell or collect.

POTSHERD A fragment of broken pottery.

PREHISTORIC ARCHAEOLOGY The branch of archaeological study and interpretation that pertains to that time before recorded history.

PROJECTILE POINT An arrowhead or spearhead, used in hunting or warfare.

PROVENIENCE The source or origin of something.

RANGING POLE A graduated pole used for measuring vertical distances and frequently included in photographs of an excavated site.

RECONNAISSANCE Surface examination and sometimes testing of an area to assess the number and extent of archaeological resources.

RELATIVE DATING A type of dating in which one body of material is placed in a time period relative to another body of material, that is, before or after it.

RUNE One of the letters of the alphabet used by ancient Germanic groups, especially by Scandinavians and Anglo-Saxons.

SERIATION Classification of artifacts of one particular type in a chronological sequence of styles.

SHARD A pottery fragment.

SITE Any location utilized by humans for a sufficient period of time to develop features or become a deposit ground for artifacts.

STONE AGE The oldest known period of human culture, characterized by the use of stone tools.

STRATIGRAPHY The study and interpretation of natural or cultural deposits with the idea of establishing a relative dating sequence for them.

STRATIFICATION The arrangement in a sequence of layers or strata of natural or cultural deposits.

SYENITE An igneous rock composed mostly of feldspar together with other minerals.

TELL A mound resulting from the accumulation of debris of a long-lived settlement.

THERMOLUMINESCENCE A method of dating ceramic materials by measuring the stored energy created when they were first fired.

WOODLAND PERIOD A period of Indian history and culture that began about 1000 B.C. when big game began to die out. People of the Archaic period have been described as hunter-gatherers.

National Organizations

American Anthropological Association
1703 New Hampshire Avenue, N.W.
Washington, D.C. 20009

Anthropologists, educators, students, and others interested in the biological and cultural origins of mankind make up this professional organization. It has approximately ten thousand members.

The Association publishes *The American Anthropologist*, a quarterly journal that features scholarly articles concerning the various subdisciplines of anthropology. A newsletter, published monthly, except in July and August, contains information of important developments in the field, events and meetings, and grants and support. Research reports are also reprinted. These publications, plus the organization's annual report, are distributed free to members. The organization also has available a wide variety of other publications, including bulletins on career opportunities. Annual membership: $30; student membership: $20.

American Association for State and Local History
1400 Eighth Avenue, South
Nashville, TN 37203

While this organization is meant more for individuals responsible for administering a small historical society or museum, it does provide some services of interest to the archaeologist. These include the publication of how-to-do-it guides on such subjects as *Cataloguing Photographs*, *Preparing Exhibits*, *Genealogical Research*, and *Securing Grant Support*. The organization also publishes a *Directory of Historical Societies in the United States and Canada*. Write for a publications list. Annual membership fee: $16.

American Association of Physical Anthropologists
1703 New Hampshire Avenue, N.W.
Washington, D.C. 20009

A professional society of approximately fifteen hundred physical anthropologists and scientists in closely related fields, this organization seeks to advance the science of physical anthropology through teaching and research. It publishes the *American Journal of Physical Anthropology*, a bimonthly publication containing articles on human evolution, primate morphology, genetics, adaptation, growth development, and behavior. Membership dues: $35; student membership: $25.

American Ethnological Society
1703 New Hampshire Avenue, N.W.
Washington, D.C. 20009

Founded in 1842, this is the oldest scholarly anthropological society in the United States. It calls its specialty "living cultures, their description and historical background." Membership includes a subscription to the organization newsletter, and members also receive two book-length monographs and a volume of essays compiled from those presented at the society's annual meeting. Migration, Economic Anthropology, and Spanish-speaking People in the United States are typical essay topics. Annual dues: $16; students: $12.

American Geological Institute
5205 Leesburg Pike
Falls Church, VA 22041

The pre-eminent organization for the lay person in the field of geological sciences, the American Geological Institute is composed of eighteen scientific and technical societies, all of which are involved with the earth sciences, including geology, geophysics, and chemistry. The institute publishes a monthly magazine, translations of foreign-language papers, dictionaries, guidebooks, and technical books, and also operates Geo Ref, a computer-based reference file of worldwide geological literature.

American Indian Archaeological Institute
Box 260
Washington, CT 06793

Since the opening of its research and visitors center in 1975, the AIAI has offered a wide range of activities for individuals of all ages and educational backgrounds. There are instruction programs in native crafts and culture history; in anthropology and field archaeology. The laboratory is a center of activity for sorting, identification, and the cataloguing of artifacts. There are demonstrations in the use of Indian tools and implements. Qualified members and volunteers are invited to participate in excavations and field surveys. Scholars may use the AIAI library. The institute's quarterly publication, *Artifacts*, is distributed free to members.

The institute has available a free book list, describing more than sixty titles, and a museum shop mail-order catalogue, offering modern handcrafted American Indian jewelry, sculptures, and other items.

American Institute for the Conservation of Historic and Artistic Works
1522 K Street, N.W.
Suite 804
Washington, D.C. 20005

Made up of professional practitioners, educators, and scientists in art conservation, this organization seeks to encourage education, study, and research in the protection and preservation of rare and historically significant objects and structures. With close to a thousand members, the institute publishes a quarterly newsletter and a semiannual journal.

American Institute of Nautical Archaeology
P.O. Drawer AU
College Station, TX 77840

Founded in 1973 as a nonprofit scientific and educational organization, AINA gathers and disseminates information of man's past through the physical remains of what the organization calls "his nautical activities." AINA's investigative work is conducted entirely by professional archaeologists and advanced students. Amateur archaeologists can benefit from AINA publications, including the organization's newsletters, formal reports concerning research projects, and books on the subject of nautical archaeology.

Since its founding, AINA has become active on four continents, studying ship remains that cover a range of more than three thousand years. Projects have included the excavation of the brig *Defence*, an American-built vessel sunk in 1779. Maine's Penobscot Bay is the site. Surveys of other vessels lost in the same engagement are being undertaken.

The first scientific ship excavation in East Africa is being conducted by AINA in cooperation with the Fort Jesus Museum of Mombassa, Kenya, with divers investigating the wreck of the *Santo Antonio de Tanna*, an armed merchant ship built in Portuguese Goa, and sunk while attempting to aid a besieged garrison at Fort Jesus in 1697.

Since 1976, the institute has had close ties with Texas A&M University and has established its headquarters at College Station, Texas, where the university is located. Several AINA staff members hold faculty positions at Texas A&M. Annual dues: $15.

American Society of Conservation Archaeology
c/o Department of Anthropology
Oregon State University
Corvallis, OR 97331

This is a three hundred-member professional organization, the objective of which is the "preservation and protection of historic and prehistoric archaeological values." While that definition may be a bit nebulous, the society does provide a useful forum for those with a special interest in archaeological conservation.

Members receive a bimonthly newsletter which contains articles concerning policies and practices in conservation, and copies of federal legislation and excerpts from the Federal Register which are pertinent. The newsletter also publishes papers presented at the organization's annual symposium. Annual dues: $10.

Anthropological Society of Washington
1703 New Hampshire Avenue, N.W.
Washington, D.C. 20009

The parent organization of the American Anthropological Association, the society offers an annual program of monthly lectures beginning in October and continuing through May. The lectures are organized around a central theme, which, in recent years, has included such themes as Urban Anthropology, Language in Society, and Anthropological Archaeology in the Americas. Annual dues: $7.50.

Archaeological Institute of America
53 Park Place
New York, NY 10007

Since its founding in 1879, the AIA has had two goals: to facilitate
archaeological research throughout the world and to disseminate the
results of that research to the American public. The organization has
a staff of eight based in New York City, more than eighty local groups
throughout the United States, and close to seven thousand members.
You don't have to be a professional archaeologist to join the AIA;
anyone interested in archaeological research and study can become a
member.

How much value you derive from membership in the AIA depends
to a large extent on how well your local group seeks to serve your interests. Local branches often publish newsletters listing events of archaeological interest in the area, including courses in archaeology
being offered and citing excavations being conducted by professionals.
They also sponsor trips and tours to local archaeological sites, museums, and special private collections. Professional lecturers often ac-
company tour groups. Foreign tours are also arranged.

Local members also form study groups and organize film festivals.
They sponsor lectures, too, with lecturers often furnished by the parent organization.

As a member of the AIA, you receive *Archaeology* magazine, the
pre-eminent archaeology magazine for the layman. A handsome publication, issued six times a year, *Archaeology* contains articles by professional archaeologists concerning excavations and discoveries around
the world. Recent articles have included a discussion of Von Däni-
ken's theories, a history of California's Chumash Indians and their
rock paintings, and a survey of the newly discovered Hellenistic tomb,
said to contain the remains of Philip of Macedon.

Each issue of the publication presents a list of museums offering archaeological exhibitions. Twice a year, *Archaeology* lists archaeological
sites where visitors are welcome to observe archaeologists at work. If
you don't wish to become a member of the AIA, but do want to receive *Archaeology*, be advised a one-year subscription is $15.

The AIA also publishes the *American Journal of Archaeology*, a
more scholarly publication than *Archaeology*. If you pay a membership fee of $32.50 (instead of $25), you'll receive the *Journal*, as well
as *Archaeology*.

The AIA also distributes information concerning careers in archaeology, awards annual fellowships for travel and study, and sponsors
awards for distinguished archaeological achievement. The organization's valuable *Fieldwork Opportunities Bulletin* is discussed in
Chapter 5. Annual membership: $25.

Archaeological Survey Association
P.O. Box 516
La Verne, CA 91750

Devoted to conservation, preservation, and scientific study, this
thirty-year-old, California-based organization numbers both amateurs
and professionals among its membership. The ASA sponsors weekend
field trips to survey possible archaeological sites and conducts salvage
or excavations at sites in danger of being destroyed. Such trips are also
scheduled for the purpose of viewing and photographing petroglyphs
and pictographs.

The organization maintains a reference collection of bones, minerals, plants, and shells; an exhibit room; a gallery of petroglyph and
pictograph reproductions; a laboratory for processing artifacts; a photographic laboratory; and a publications office. It enjoys an affiliation
with La Verne College in La Verne, California, about thirty miles
east of Los Angeles.

General meetings are held four times a year. Several times a year
the ASA publishes a bulletin concerning organization activities, and
twice a year a journal is issued. Site reports are also distributed to
members. There are several categories of membership: regular, $10;
student, $5.00; junior, $1.00; and contributing, $25.

Association for Preservation Technology
Box 2487
Station D
Ottawa, ON
Canada K 1P 5W6

This organization's thirteen hundred museum curators, conser-
vationists, restoration architects, archaeologists, and other individuals
involved in preservation activities, seek to improve the quality of professional practice in the field, promoting the publication of technical
information and encouraging the training of craftsmen in traditional
techniques. The association publishes a bimonthly newsletter and
quarterly bulletin.

CEDAM International
436 Monssen Drive
Dallas, TX 75224

Archaeology is but one of the concerns of this three hundred-
member organization, as the acronym that is formed from its name
suggests—Conservation, Education, Diving, Archaeology, Museums.
The purpose of the organization is to explore, study, and help con-

serve underwater historical sites. CEDAM's headquarters are located at Akumal, near Cancun on Mexico's Yucatan peninsula.

Members receive CEDAM's quarterly bulletin, containing articles on underwater archaeology and marine sciences, and are offered training courses in diving technique, including a course in the basis of underwater archaeology.

Members are eligible to participate in underwater archaeological tours sponsored by the organization. The 1978 tour—eleven days, $450—concerned itself with "archaeological renaissance" at Chinchorro Bank Reef, a remote and primitive site just off Mexico's southernmost point. Annual dues are $15, with an initiation fee of $20.

Central States Archaeological Societies, Inc.
c/o Ben W. Thompson
1228 West Essex
Kirkwood, MO 63122

This organization seeks to develop a better understanding of regional archaeology among students, professional and nonprofessional archaeologists, and museums and educational institutions. The chief means of accomplishing this goal is by means of a handsome and informative journal, which has been published quarterly since 1953. Each member of the society receives the journal.

The journal accepts articles from both professionals and nonprofessionals. Recent articles have included these titles: "The Mueller Site; Evidence of Paleo-Indian Occupation in St. Clair County, Illinois," "Deer Jaw Tools," and "Early Amerind Wood Dugout Discoveries in North America." Articles are illustrated with drawings and photographs, sometimes color photographs. For anyone interested in archaeology in the central states, the journal is an important information source. Annual dues: $7.50.

Nine archaeological societies have joined together to form the Central States Archaeological Societies. They represent the states of Illinois, Indiana, Arkansas, Kentucky, Tennessee, Iowa, Wisconsin, Georgia, and the city of St. Louis.

Committee on Public Archaeology
Society for American Archaeology
Dena F. Dincauze, Chairman
Department of Anthropology
University of Massachusetts
Amherst, MA 01003

With representatives in each state, this organization seeks to protect and preserve archaeological sites and resources by working to increase the public's awareness and understanding of their importance. Committee representatives provide information about state archaeological activities and educational programs.

Council for British Archaeology
112 Kennington Road
London SE11 6RE, England

Archaeological societies, museums, universities, and local authorities have united to form the Council for British Archaeology, the aim of which is to promote all aspects of British archaeology. This mission includes the safeguarding of ancient monuments and historic buildings, coordination of archaeological research, and providing advisory information and counsel.

The organization conducts conferences and seminars, bestows grants for archaeological publications, and maintains a broad range of information services. This includes the publication of a listing of fieldwork opportunities in Great Britain (see Chapter 5).

Council for Old World Archaeology
Anthropology Department
Boston University
755 Commonwealth Avenue
Boston, MA 02215

This is an information-disseminating organization, publishing area reports covering Old World archaeology from the Paleolithic up to and including the Late Historic period. Each report surveys current archaeological activity in an area and presents an annotated bibliography of recent books and articles.

Eastern States Archaeological Federation
Box 260
Washington, CT 06793

An organization of individuals and institutions interested in supporting and participating in regional archaeological activities and events. Its annual publication, *Archaeology of Eastern North America*, analyzes and interprets current excavations in the eastern United States and Canada. ESAF members receive the current yearbook, a triannual newsletter, and publication lists referring to each of the member states of the Federation.

The Epigraphic Society
6 Woodland Street
Arlington, MA 02174

With a membership of over five hundred, representing every state and twenty-eight foreign countries, the Epigraphic Society "exists solely to publish information on inscriptions and related matters," according to Barry Fell, the organization's prime mover. The published information is contained in an annual volume of reports the society issues, with the reports often taking the form of decipherments, e.g., "Celtic Iberian Inscriptions of New England," "An Ancient Judaean Inscription from Tennessee," and "Ancient Iberian Compass Dials from Spain and Tennessee." Annual dues: $12.

Friends of Cast Iron Architecture
44 West 9th Street
New York, NY 10011

Cast-iron construction for commercial buildings began in the 1850s in New York and Philadelphia, and spread quickly to the rapidly growing cities of America. This organization identifies the cast-iron buildings that remain, seeks to draw attention to them, encourages their appreciation, and campaigns for their preservation. Annual membership: $3.00.

Indo-Pacific Prehistory Association
Department of Anthropology
University of Hawaii
Honolulu, HI 96822

Individuals active in research involving the prehistory of the Far East and Oceania (an area extending from northeast Asia to Australia and New Zealand, Easter Island to India and Pakistan, plus Madagascar) have formed this information-gathering and distributing organization. Made up of archaeologists, anthropologists, professionals in related fields, students, and others interested in the area, the organization arranges symposiums and international meetings and publishes a newsletter.

International Institute for the Conservation
of Historical and Artistic Works
6 Buckingham Street
London, WC 2N 6BA, England

Restorers, conservators, curators, and directors of museums and galleries make up this organization, the aim of which is to coordinate and improve the knowledge and techniques involved in protecting and preserving precious objects and materials of all kinds. The institute publishes a bimonthly bulletin and other publications that discuss advances in preservation and conservation.

National Geographic Society
17th and M Streets, N.W.
Washington, D.C. 20036

Well known for its monthly magazine, *National Geographic*, this organization sponsors expeditions in geography, archaeology, natural history, astronomy, ethnology, and oceanography. It publishes, besides the magazine, maps, books, and monographs, and maintains a library of more than fifty thousand volumes. It currently has a membership of 9.5 million; a staff of two thousand.

National Society for the Preservation of Covered Bridges
44 Cleveland Avenue
Worcester, MA 01603

Historic covered bridges are a vanishing breed. This organization seeks to save and preserve these structures, contacting public officials on their behalf and distributing bulletins and guidebooks concerning them. The organization has approximately five hundred members.

National Trust for Historic Preservation
748 Jackson Place, N.W.
Washington, D.C. 20006

A private organization chartered by Congress, the National Trust seeks to facilitate the public's participation in the preservation of those structures, objects, sites, and districts deemed significant in American history and culture. Its membership exceeds 100,000. The organization acts as a clearinghouse for information on state and federal preservation programs, advises community leaders on how to organize preservation groups, and distributes information concerning restoration and preservation. It publishes a monthly newsletter and quarterly magazine.

New England Antiquities Research Association
4 Smith Street
Milford, NH 03055

Founded in 1964, NEARA focuses its activities upon the unexplained stone structures of New England, with particular emphasis on Mystery Hill, New Hampshire. NEARA publishes a quarterly journal that features articles concerning its discoveries and theories. The organization has approximately 250 members.

Members take an active role in NEARA projects—locating, measuring, and mapping stone structures (more than two hundred of which are described in the organization's records); researching and recording local traditions and legends for information bearing on the organization's archaeological projects; researching archaeological books and articles for the same purpose; and assisting in the organization's administrative and clerical work. Annual membership: $10.

"While NEARA encourages active fieldwork in the way of locating and recording sites," says an organization spokesman, "it does not encourage unsupervised excavation." Two field trips a year are scheduled for members.

Prehistoric Society
Department of Prehistoric and Romano-British Antiquities
British Museum
London WC 1B 3DG, England

Founded in 1908, and now having about two thousand members, this organization seeks to encourage prehistoric study and archaeological excavation. Anyone with a scholarly interest in prehistory is eligible for membership. The organization's only publication, *Proceedings of the Prehistoric Society*, is issued annually.

SEARCH Foundation
P.O. Box 43388
Birmingham, AL 35243

SEARCH is an acronym for Scientific Exploratory Archaeological Research. The objective of the organization is, through research and field expeditions, to locate and identify the biblical ark of Noah. SEARCH maintains a library of documents, articles, and photographs pertaining to the ark.

Society for American Archaeology
c/o Alfred E. Johnson, Secretary
Director, Museum of Anthropology
University of Kansas
Lawrence, KS 66045

The principal organization devoted to the study of New World archaeology, the society seeks to stimulate research in this sphere by creating closer professional relationships among archaeologists, and by establishing a bridge between the professional and others interested in the field. Its various publications and its annual meeting are two means by which the organization hopes to achieve these goals.

The society's most noted publication is *American Antiquity,* a quarterly journal that contains articles about New World archaeology, current research, and book reviews. The publication is distributed free to members. Others of the society's many publications include: *Your Career in Archaeology,* by G. E. Stuart, 1976, $1.00; and *Archaeology and Archaeological Resources: A Guide for Those Planning to Use, Affect, or Alter the Land's Surface,* by Charles R. McGimsey, III, 1974, 40¢. Members are permitted to present papers to the membership concerning their research efforts, participate in the annual meeting, and vote in SAA elections.

Anyone can become a member of the society. The chief requirement, aside from the payment of dues, is the signing of an application form in which you agree to support the society's objectives and ideals. The SAA's Constitution states, "The Society shall not approve of applications for membership from persons who habitually misuse archaeological materials or sites for commercial purposes or who violate accepted standards of professional ethics." Annual membership: $20; for students: $12.

Society for Applied Anthropology
1701 New Hampshire Avenue, N.W.
Washington, D.C. 20009

A professional society of approximately four thousand anthropologists, sociologists, psychologists, psychiatrists, industrial researchers, and educators, this organization seeks "to promote the scientific investigation of the principles controlling the relation of human beings to one another, and the encouragement of the wide application of these principles to practical problems." The society was founded in 1941. It publishes *Human Organization,* a quarterly, and occasional monographs. Annual membership: $17.

Society for Historical Archaeology
1703 New Hampshire Avenue, N.W.
Washington, D.C. 20009

Founded in 1967, this twelve-hundred-member organization of archaeologists, historians, anthropologists, ethnohistorians, and others interested in historical archaeology, focuses upon "the era since the beginning of the exploration of the non-European world by Europeans." The Western Hemisphere is the geographical area of prime concern. The organization publishes *Historical Archaeology*, an annual, and a quarterly newsletter. Subscription to these publications is by membership in the society. Annual dues: $10.

Other publications available from the society include a career pamphlet, *Opportunities in Historical Archaeology*, 25¢; and *Historical Archaeology and the Importance of Material Things*, edited by Leland Ferguson, 1977, $5.00.

Society for the Preservation of New England Antiquities
141 Cambridge Street
Boston, MA 02114

"Antiquities," in this instance, refers to historic buildings and furnishings, which the society, composed of forty-five hundred members, seeks to preserve and restore. The organization publishes a quarterly newsletter and maintains a library of books, town histories, photographs, broadsides, and newspaper clippings that concern the old and historic buildings of New England.

Society for the Preservation of Old Mills
P.O. Box 435
Wiscasset, ME 04578

With approximately one thousand members, this organization strives to help in preserving or rebuilding old grinding mills. The society publishes *Old Mill News* four times a year and issues lists of mills that are still standing.

Society of Architectural Historians
1700 Walnut Street
Room 716
Philadelphia, PA 19103

Obviously, this organization is of greater interest to architects than archaeologists, but it has value to the last named in that it serves as an international forum for those interested in the preservation of and scholarly research concerning all structures of historical and aesthetic importance. Founded in 1940, the society publishes a bimonthly newsletter and, four times a year, *The Journal of the Society of Architectural Historians,* a much respected publication.

Chapters are active in Washington, D.C., and these states: Arizona, California, Illinois, Iowa, Louisiana, Mississippi, Michigan, Minnesota, Missouri, New Jersey, New York, Ohio, Oregon, Pennsylvania, Texas, Virginia, Washington, and Wisconsin. Annual dues: $25.

Society of Professional Archaeologists
c/o Stanley South, Secretary-Treasurer
Institute of Archaeology and Anthropology
University of South Carolina
Columbia, SC 29208

Archaeology's leading professional organization.

Tuscan-American Institute for Mediterranean Archaeology
Northern Kentucky University
Highland Heights, KY 41076

Tuscany, an archaeologically rich region of northwest Italy—its capital is Florence—is this organization's chief interest. Institute officials organize summer excavations there and provide for an exchange of scholars with the University of Siena. Northern Kentucky University offers a degree program in classical art and architecture, with the activities of the institute as a focal point.

United States National Committee for the International Council
of Monuments and Sites
1522 K Street, N.W.
Washington, D.C. 20005

As its name suggests, this organization promotes the study and conservation of historic monuments, buildings, and also districts. Members participate in a wide range of preservation activities, including seminars, symposiums, study trips, and other specialized activities. Individual membership: $25.

Additional Reading

BOOKS

The Amateur Archaeologist's Handbook
Maurice Robbins and Mary B. Irving, T. Y. Crowell, New York, 1965.
An all-embracing guide to the techniques and methods of surveying, excavation, mapping, photography, dating artifacts, and restoring finds.

America's Ancient Treasures
Franklin Folsom, Rand McNally & Co., Chicago, 1974.
A comprehensive travel guide to prehistoric archaeological sites and museums.

Archaeological Bibliography of Eastern North America
Roger Moeller, editor, Eastern States Archaeological Federation/ American Indian Archaeological Institute, 1974.
With more than 8,000 references to books, journal articles, and films, divided among such categories as culture history, artifacts, ecology, physical anthropology, and techniques, this is a necessary reference book for any serious student of prehistoric archaeology.

Beginner's Guide to Archaeology
Louis A. Brennan, Stackpole Books, Harrisburg, Penna., 1973.
Directed to what is termed the "citizen archaeologist," this is a comprehensive examination of archaeological techniques—surveying, excavation, reporting, and cataloguing, with an emphasis throughout on prehistoric man in the Western Hemisphere.

A Dictionary of Archaeology
Warwick Bray and David Trump, Penguin Books, New York, 1976.
The terms, techniques, and personalities of archaeology; more than 1,600 entries.

A Field Guide to Conservation Archaeology in North America
George McHargue and Michael Roberts, J. B. Lippincott, Philadelphia, 1977.
A complete and easy-to-read handbook.

Field Methods in Archaeology
Thomas R. Hester, Robert F. Heizer, and John A. Graham, Mayfield Publishing Co., Palo Alto, California, 1975.
The definitive book on excavation procedures, frequently used as a teaching text. Amply illustrated with photographs, recording forms, map reproductions, and diagrams.

A Guide to Artifacts of Colonial America
Ivor Noël Hume, Alfred A. Knopf, New York, 1970.
A thorough and detailed examination of about every type of artifact likely to be recovered at a seventeenth- or eighteenth-century historical site.

A Guide to Salvage Archaeology
Fred Wendorf, Museum of New Mexico Press, 1966.

Historical Archaeology
Ivor Noël Hume, Alfred A. Knopf, New York, 1969.
Complete and authoritative advice on every phase of digging a site. Highly recommended. The author is the director of the Department of Archaeology at Colonial Williamsburg.

History Under the Sea
Mendel Peterson, Smithsonian Institution, Washington, D.C., 1965.
A discussion of techniques used in underwater investigation; also, an examination of a laboratory procedure.

In Small Things Forgotten
James Deetz, Anchor Books, Garden City, New York, 1977.
Subtitled *The Archaeology of Early American Life*, this is one of the

more readable books on the subject, with the author, a professor of anthropology at the University of California, explaining how the artifacts left behind by early Americans have revealed how they thought and lived.

Industrial Archaeology
Theodore Sande, The Stephen Green Press, Brattleboro, Vermont, 1976.
Subtitled A *New Look at Our Industrial Heritage*, this book examines different types of industrial artifacts and presents a roster of sites deemed significant in the field of industrial archaeology. Almost two hundred illustrations are included.

Introduction to Archaeology
Shirley Gorenstein, Basic Books, New York, 1965.
A lively and anecdotal survey of archaeological investigation and interpretation.

An Introduction to Prehistoric Archaeology
Frank Hole and Robert F. Heizer, Holt, Rinehart and Winston, New York, 1969.
The best book of its type on the subject.

Invitation to Archaeology
James Deetz, Natural History Press, Garden City, New York, 1967.
A personal and thoughtfully written introduction in which the author examines the methods and problems of present-day archaeologists, and also explains the field in broad terms.

Man in Prehistory
Chester Chard, McGraw-Hill, New York, 1974.
A splendid summary of Old World archaeological knowledge, from the first man more than three million years ago in Africa, through the Neanderthal period in Europe, the Bronze and Iron ages, and into the Far East.

The New Archaeology
David Wilson, Alfred A. Knopf, New York, 1975.
A review of how modern-day scientific techniques have affected archaeological research and interpretation.

Prehistory of North America
Jesse Jennings, McGraw-Hill, New York, 1974.
Excellent summary of archaeologically defined prehistoric cultures, from man's first entry into the New World, through Paleo-Indian and Woodland ages in the United States, Mexico, and southern Canada.

Public Archaeology
Charles R. McGimsey III, Seminar Press, New York, 1972.
A detailed survey of state and federal legislation affecting archaeology, along with recommendations for a model state archaeological program.

PERIODICALS

American Antiquity, quarterly journal of the Society for American Archaeology, 1703 New Hampshire Avenue, N.W., Washington, D.C. 20009.

Archaeology, bimonthly publication of the Archaeological Institute of America, 53 Park Place, New York, New York 10007.

Art and Archaeology Newsletter, quarterly, O. F. Reiss Co., 242 East Thirty-ninth Street, New York, New York 10016.

The Biblical Archaeological Review, quarterly, 1737 H Street, N.W., Washington, D.C. 20006.

Popular Archaeology, bimonthly, P.O. Box 4211, Arlington, Virginia 22204.

INDEX